Re^married with Children

ALSO BY BARBARA LeBEY

FAMILY ESTRANGEMENTS

Remarried with Children

Ten Secrets for Successfully

Blending and Extending

Your Family

BARBARA LeBEY

BANTAM BOOKS

New York   Toronto   London   Sydney   Auckland

REMARRIED WITH CHILDREN
A Bantam Book

PUBLISHING HISTORY
Bantam hardcover edition published October 2004
Bantam trade paperback edition / November 2005

Published by
Bantam Dell
A Division of Random House, Inc.
New York, New York

Library of Congress Catalog Card Number: 2004049726

Bantam Books and the rooster colophon are registered trademarks of Random House, Inc.

ISBN-13: 978-0-553-38200-6
ISBN-10: 0-553-38200-4

Printed in the United States of America
Published simultaneously in Canada

www.bantamdell.com

10 9 8

For Nicholas and David

Author's Acknowledgments

First, to those who took the time and courage to contribute their most intimate family relationship stories. They cannot be acknowledged by name. I can only hope that I have done them justice, and that their experiences can provide real value to the readers.

To Toni Burbank, my editor on this book, I thank her for her insights, her organizational skills, her wise suggestions and the gentle way she offered them. She is an icon in her field, and now I know why. From her, I've learned a lot. And to Toni's assistant, Melanie Milgram, who has been there for me whenever I needed her. And to the expert staff at Bantam Dell who gave life to this project.

And my thanks go also to Ann Fisher, my initial editor who pushed and pulled me to do more and to do it better.

I am deeply grateful to Ellen Geiger, my literary agent, who, from the beginning, has been enthusiastic and supportive. Ellen is a woman of fine personal and professional qualities, and I am lucky to know her and to be represented by her.

I owe a primary debt to Robert Petix, a wills and trust attorney who exemplifies the best *our* profession has to offer. My appreciation to Gwen Bate, Ph.D., a psychologist and family relations expert, who generously took the time to give me the benefit of her experience and analysis. And to the many family counselors, teachers, and clergy, who offered a broad range of views and good anecdotal illustrations.

And to my blended and extended family, who, wittingly and unwittingly, became the source of my inspiration to write this book.

And a special hug for my husband, my rousing champion who can only cheer me on because he's blind to my faults.

Contents

        Secret Five: The extended family is always with you.

six   **The Pleasure of Your Company . . .**   150
        Secret Six: Holidays and celebrations call for
        flexibility and creativity.

seven   **Dollars and Sense**   171
        Secret Seven: Get money issues out in the open
        as soon as possible.

eight   **Sensitive Issues and Bad Influences**   203
        Secret Eight: You have the right to set the rules
        for the way people live in your home.

nine   **A Death in the (Blended) Family**   232
        Secret Nine: A child who loses a parent needs
        special attention and understanding.

ten   **Can We Talk?**   253
        Secret Ten: Make civility, respect, and compassion
        the touchstones of your communication.

        Appendix   275

        Author's Note   289

        Bibliography   295

        Resources   299

Re∧married with Children

Introduction: The Ten Secrets

First marriages are, in the beginning, all about *us*. The children come along one by one, and we get to know and love one another in a natural, evolving way. Second marriages begin all about *them*—the children, the ex-spouses, the former in-laws, and the new in-laws. The relationships joined together by a remarriage become a *blended-extended family*. This term, now often used interchangeably with "stepfamily," refers to a family unit in which one parent is not the biological parent of at least one child.

Even in the best of families, remarriage with children is no walk in the park. It is, however, a walk well worth taking if two people love each other and can prepare for the range of problems they're likely to encounter. One woman interviewed for this book said, "If the joining of two people in marriage is comparable to joining two different cultures, then the joining of two people who have been married, divorced, and have children would be more like merging two different galaxies." She was one of the success stories.

In most families, day-to-day life presents many challenges, but after extensive research and observation, I have discovered that blended families are made up of well-intentioned people who have to work through more problems than nuclear families do, for the obvious reasons: they have more kith and kin to deal with and a whole range of emotions to confront during the early years of the newly blended family. What's more, our society—churches, schools, and communities—are not according these families the respect they deserve, and, most importantly, our legal system is not accommodating their needs.

Most people just stumble their way into remarriages, making it up as they go along. So it should come as no surprise that 60 percent of these remarriages will end in divorce. But more than 51 percent of nuclear marriages also end in divorce, and more than 85 percent of these divorcés will remarry. And second marriages *with* children are twice as likely to end in divorce as those without. More than half of Americans today have been, are now, or will be in one or more blended families during their lives. To avoid becoming one of the unfortunate statistical failures, people need to educate themselves about blended-family dynamics before jumping into remarriage. The willingness to risk and the courage to change are admirable, but they can still lead down a blind alley—for lack of foresight. It's not simply a challenge; it's a perilous journey for the uninformed. As Samuel Johnson, the notable eighteenth-century English writer, once said, "Remarriage is the triumph of hope over experience."

Unfortunately, most couples impose a familiar fantasy on their union. They think it will be a joyous and loving new bonding of their respective families. When it doesn't turn out the way they expected it to, they are already playing catch-up. They need to learn beforehand all they can about the problems they are likely to face, how to prevent them, and how to solve them if they do arise. They need to read about the subject of blending families, talk to their clergy, and talk to their friends who have already been through a remarriage. And, when the going gets really rough, seek professional help with a good marriage and family counselor.

Of her own remarriage, Carrie Taylor, a California communications skills trainer, said, "Our relationship became one of strategizing, educating ourselves, and herculean efforts to understand and save the relationships with our children. This has been a continuing process. I didn't have a clue about the depth of pain children suffer in divorce and remarriage."

Before Carrie and her new husband had a chance to get comfortable with each other, there was a ready-made family to deal with. They came into the marriage with a set of losses and with preexisting relationships that needed stabilizing and nurturing. Despite the fact that Carrie's husband, Gordon, is a family therapist, they both acknowledge how hard they had to work to find time for each other, but after fifteen years and many war stories and victories, they are finally satisfied that they have blended their families successfully. The point of the Taylors' experience is the years it took them, even with their specialized training.

According to *American Demographics* magazine, as of the year 2000, blended-extended families became the norm—that is, the dominant family structure—with more than 50 percent of U.S. families falling within this definition. The high failure rate of these reconstituted families often has a devastating effect on the children of these remarriages. And yet children often conspire to sabotage a remarriage for reasons of their own—to bring their parents back together or because they are put up to it by angry ex-spouses or by ex-spouses in denial. When these second marriages fail, the children are the sad losers again. They have already had to experience either the death of a parent or the divorce of their parents and the adjustment (usually of enormous scope) to the new blended-extended family, and now they must face another disconnect, another dislocation, another trauma to their young lives. This risk of failure and damage to children is the primary reason couples need to prepare themselves to cope with the problems they will inevitably face. Not once in all my interviewing did I meet a couple who had had a completely smooth ride blending their families.

Divorce ends a marriage, but not a family. The couple divorces; the children don't, so they remain the constant link between their divorced parents. When one or both parents remarry, the children continue to be the link to the former spouse. And for that reason, remarriages jolt the entire family dynamic, affecting ex-spouses, in-laws, and all the children. Everyone wonders how things are going to change. Their guard is up. The stepparent is usually blamed for any negatives that occur. The wife's family will blame the new husband, his ex-wife, and his children. The husband's family will blame the new wife, her ex-husband, and her children. There's so much blame to go around, it's hard to imagine how anyone can get beyond it. But they can, and will, if they enter the uncharted waters with a loving heart, an open mind, and a willingness to allow for vast differences.

My passionate interest in this subject grew out of my own experience, not only from my years as a judge dealing with conflict resolution but also from the research done for my first book, *Family Estrangements,* and from my own remarriage of more than twenty-nine years. Both my husband and I were previously married and had children from these marriages. Everything that could have gone wrong went wrong for us and for several of the six children that made up our new family. There were relentless problems with angry ex-spouses, complicated by alcoholism, abuse, and bitter resentment. The children became pawns, torn between their parents and even between parents and grandparents. Some of the children were resentful of their stepparents and some weren't; some were filled with feelings of abandonment, insecurity, jealousy, and divided loyalties. Some were just plain angry. And sometimes they had a right to be. Their natural parents and their stepparents made mistakes.

Over the course of our marriage, many of the problems have been resolved, but not all of them. One of my husband's children is estranged, not only from us but also from her siblings. My husband adopted my children after their own father faded from their lives. Five of the six children were educated, have rewarding careers, and now have families of their own. My husband's oldest child has serious learning problems and other impairments, so she could not continue her education. There are eleven grandchildren, but we don't have contact with all of them, though we wish we did. We were confronted with situations that could have been avoided or more easily defused had we known the pitfalls that were ahead of us. But we were like so many other couples who enter these complicated relationships with the belief that love conquers all. I can only say we were lucky that our marriage survived. Our determination to stay together, and our enduring love and respect for each other, helped us avoid becoming one of those dismal statistics of failure. But it was a long struggle and still has some more speed bumps along the way.

For those of you who remember *The Brady Bunch,* a long-running '70s TV show about the adventures of a happily blended family, it was the ideal, but only because it was fiction. Blending a family is the real thing. And yes, that is the way to view these reconstructed families, because *blending families* implies that this is an ongoing process. As one young wife told me, "We're a stepfamily—and we have lots of steps to take together."

Blending families creates a strange kind of magnification: Every little issue that surfaces can seem like a threat. You begin to believe everything's a big *test* on which rides the success or failure of your remarriage. In fact, situations can be so complicated, it becomes difficult to know whether there's *been* a success or a failure. It's not the sort of endeavor that gets a gold star for a job well done, nor does it get a demerit, or a time-out for bad behavior. Rather, blending a family is a continuous process with good periods and bad periods.

In professional journals and books on the subject, experts have not offered a clear definition of success. But such a definition of success is so critical that I offer my own: If the couple has been able to stay married for all the right reasons, and the children turn out relatively well-adjusted and are able to create productive lives of their own, then the couple can know they have succeeded.

My goal in this book is to help your family to succeed. Each chapter focuses on one of the ten essential secrets I arrived at after sifting through the research and the stories offered by the people who were successful in blending their families, using the definition of success set forth above. The ten secrets are the common denominators that run through the remarriages that really worked. They can be your blueprint, too. These secrets are not always easy to follow, but they're not impossible ideals, either. When the going gets rough and things are spinning out of control, the secrets will help you focus your attention on your goals. Learn these secrets. Apply them. They work.

I am grateful for the wisdom and experiences of the many people who spoke to me at a heartfelt, gut-wrenching level—they are the ones who became the real authorities behind this book. As I reviewed notes and relistened to tapes from the interviews, I began to realize how innovative and resourceful people are, and what lengths they will go to in order to achieve a happy, healthy family. My story, along with the many included in this book, are testaments to the strength and goodness of the human spirit and the desire of parents and stepparents to nurture and love even the most resistant of offspring.

Because of the highly personal nature of their disclosures, these people who generously revealed their stories were given anonymity— different names are used, and sometimes their professions and locales are altered.

Behind the anecdotal evidence, *Remarried with Children* rests on a bedrock of research from professional journals, as well as the expertise of specialists—marriage counselors, teachers, sympathetic clergy, and other professionals—who have worked with me so that I could offer sound advice.

This combination of the personal and the professional has given me a new and different take on this subject of remarriage with children. I want to challenge the conventional wisdom, and it is a key reason for writing this book. Too many experts in this field tend to put the interests of the children above those of the couple. *I think it should be just the other way around.* As the first secret states: *Put the marriage first.*

This is not about being selfish or in any way ignoring or diminishing the interests of the children, but rather the opposite. From my own personal experience and observation, and the extensive interviews I did for this book, I sincerely believe that the remarriage itself should head the list of priorities. Couples should be advised that when they enter into a blended-family marriage, they must first succeed as husband and wife before they will be able to offer the secure home environment that the children need. The strength of the newly married couple's relationship is essential in deflecting outside interference from ex-spouses, in-laws and former in-laws, and extended-family members. You can't build a two-story house until there's a firm foundation and a well-constructed first story. When the marriage is built on love, mutual understanding, and real commitment, the couple will realize that long-term happiness and fulfillment depends on a comfortable blending of their respective families, especially the children from prior marriages. These children are usually traumatized by their parents' divorce and must be spared a reenactment of that trauma and upheaval. What they need most is a happily married couple who will provide them with a calm, caring, and enduring family.

Most of the pitfalls of the blended-extended family can be avoided if people will just take the time to learn how to handle this new and different—and difficult—family. They will experience a ripple effect in which knowledge brings better choices and greater satisfaction for everyone—the couple courageous enough to take another chance with marriage and the children who are once again living in a two-parent home. Reading this book is a very good start.

The following people are those who will benefit most from this book:

- Those planning to remarry

- Stepparents of children who visit

- Stepparents of children who live with them full-time

- Remarried people with biological or adopted children from prior marriages

- Those who still have conflict with ex-spouses

- Grandparents who are cast aside because of divorce and/or remarriage

- Former in-laws and extended families dealing with the challenges of blending families

- Adult children who have parent and stepparent problems due to divorce and remarriage

While a blended family is usually born of loss, through either divorce or death, it also holds the potential for discovering the deepest joys and satisfaction of family—a lifelong commitment to caring for one another. Others have successfully traveled this road before. So can you.

o n e

The Obstacle Course

S e c r e t   O n e :

Put the marriage first.

As a more mature person, you can do it right this time. You are entitled to another chance at happiness, but this time the love that you start your marriage with has to be big enough and wise enough to embrace a ready-made family. Divided loyalties, guilt, unreasonable expectations, unscrupulous people, and manipulative children, even your own, can be obstacles in your way to a successful remarriage. Anticipating them and understanding them will help you to achieve your goals.

While it's true that all families have a past, blended families have a more complex one—the ghosts of marriages past. These ghosts of prior marriages and divorces can haunt your house and everyone in it, even ruin your present marriage.

"After we returned from our honeymoon, my husband's two children from his first marriage came to visit for the weekend," says one distraught second wife. "I had no idea what I was getting into. I was so emotionally drained after their visit, I almost packed my bag and left, except that it was *my* house, and I certainly didn't intend to leave my own house. Had I been living in my husband's home, I probably would've left, and that would've been the end of a very short marriage."

Today, when we talk about the blended family, we mean parents and the children and stepchildren from the various marriages. But the distressing fact is that former in-laws, present in-laws, your ex, and your spouse's ex are as much a part of your new family as the cantankerous old uncle or boozy cousin who used to disrupt every family gathering. This may not be the news you want to hear, but it's a reality that cannot be ignored. They are and will remain the extended family.

The emotions generated from this archive will invariably spill over into your new family. How much should couples allow this history to penetrate their new lives together? As little as possible. But there's the rub, because sometimes the new family is virtually held hostage by ex-spouses and ex-grandparents and the damage they can cause, not only to the adults of the remarriage but to the children. Sadly, the children themselves are often enlisted to play the role of saboteurs. It's true. That kid you love can be out to destroy your new happiness.

Wittingly or unwittingly, ex-spouses, natural children, stepchildren, former in-laws, as well as present in-laws, can trigger unlovely emotions in you, too. Jealousy, unreasonable expectations, divided loyalties, and guilt are common even in the most well-adjusted adults. Those are the obstacles we put in our own way. Typically, these emotions lead to defensive or manipulative behavior as one attempts to eliminate these new intruders from one's life or, at the very least, to minimize the damage they can cause.

Human relationships work like the law of physics—matter cannot be created or destroyed. It's the same way with a previous marriage. It cannot become a marriage that never existed; the ex-spouses never disappear, and the kids are never unborn. Maybe your husband's ex-wife is still pining away or showing up at odd hours to peek in your windows or calling at the last minute to change visitation dates.

In the stories that follow, heightened emotions of family members are vividly illustrated by the events of the blending process. *You will see that when you put the marriage first, you benefit the blended family far more than if you as a newly married couple had focused only on the children's adjustment to your new relationships.*

SACRED VOWS

Ancient words of wisdom from the Bible advise newlyweds to place their loyalties to their spouse—"leave your father and mother and cleave to your [spouse.]" (Gen. 2:24) If it were written today, I believe the adage would certainly encompass second marriages, where the stakes are even higher and where many more people have claims on the time, attention, and emotions of the married couple.

With first-married couples trying to form an independent family, they must renegotiate relationships with parents and extended family. And since those bonds took years to form, the process of breaking away to create a new unit isn't automatic. It's an ongoing task. But we don't break away from children, so the challenge of forming a solid and loving marriage must include the connections to children from prior marriages as well as to the people who are related to those children.

A successful remarriage is a gift to everyone concerned, and particularly to children who have already suffered through the death of a parent or through a failed marriage. They don't need another loss or failure. Experts who advocate that the children must come first are losing sight of the effect another divorce would have on the children. Nevertheless, it's not unusual for children of divorce to view the new marriage as a threat to achieving their fantasy—getting their natural parents back together, restoring what they have sadly lost, and maintaining the close and loving relationship they had with a parent who is now in the throes of love and passion with a new partner. This means that putting the marriage first is, in every sense, the ultimate challenge of most remarriages with children.

The first remarriage I'll discuss began with an adulterous affair. This is not the best way to begin blending a family, but it happens more often than most of us would care to admit. It is a particularly interesting story because so many of the people involved agreed to be interviewed— the remarried couple as well as a child from each of their prior marriages. It is also a microcosm of the multiple problems that can plague a blended family.

THE "SPOOKABOOS" OF
PREVIOUS MARRIAGES

At the time of our interview, Cynthia, a vivacious fifty-year-old woman, had been married to her second husband, Ted, for over twenty years. Cynthia and Ted have two children each from their first marriages.

"My dream all through childhood was to have a family of my own," Cynthia told me. "I was the third child in my own family, the youngest by eleven years, so I always felt like an only child, with much older parents who had little time or patience for me. What I saw in other families was warmth and a sense of belonging that I never felt.

"As soon as I graduated from college, I rushed into my first marriage, because that was what my friends were doing, but I really didn't know my first husband very well. I married for all the wrong reasons, not the least of which was to get away from home and because, as I said, it was the thing to do at the time.

"We turned out to be totally mismatched—different values, interests, and different goals for the future—only I didn't know that when we got married. After five years and two children, I knew that I wanted a divorce, but I didn't have the financial means to go it alone. Besides, if we divorced, my husband's alimony and child support payments would be very limited. That's when I decided to become a real estate agent. For the next five years, I worked hard and built a good career. My husband and I tried to get along, but we just couldn't."

To understand the problems that developed in Cynthia's second marriage, it's important to know the circumstances of their lives when she and Ted first met.

"Ted was married but wasn't living with his wife. We both got our divorces and married about a year later. During the early years of our relationship, his first marriage was always a 'presence' in our home. It was as if his first wife, Valerie, was literally haunting us."

What Cynthia wasn't prepared for was the shock and difficulty of dealing with some very troubled people. When she got to know Ted's children, she understood what the late Ann Landers had to say on the subject: "The biggest cause of the breakup of a second marriage is the children."

"Ted's two children were the same ages as my children, which could have been an advantage, but it wasn't. It only aggravated the problem. Ted's twelve-year-old daughter, Rose, was hell-bent on destroying me, destroying our marriage, and getting her father to go back to her mother. With her mother's prompting, Rose told terrible lies to her grandmother—Ted's mother. She made up a story about my husband and me having sex in front of her and the other children. She accused me of using foul language and inflicting cruel punishments. At first I laughed at the absurdity of the accusations—until I realized how damaging they were, mainly because my husband's mother wanted to believe they were true. In fact she did. That way she could convince herself that her son had married a depraved woman with monstrous kids who were having a destructive influence on her precious grandchildren. By playing into Valerie's strategy and collaborating with her, my new mother-in-law could insure that her regular weekend visits with her grandchildren continued, instead of their coming to visit us.

"Having children of my own, I should've realized when divorced people marry each other, they're getting involved with all the people from both former marriages. But when Valerie managed to drag *my* ex-husband into this test of wills, I thought I would lose my mind. She persuaded him to participate in her plan to destroy us as a couple.

"Despite the fact that my ex-husband knew me well enough to know there wasn't any truth to these stories, he was so angry about my leaving him, and about his financial obligations to the children, that he was willing to collaborate with Valerie, even if it hurt our children.

"So, when my two children were with him for weekends or other visits, he vilified me. My daughter began to resent him. She refused to go with him when he came to pick her up. My son was too young to understand what was happening, so he continued his visits, and had to listen to all the vitriolic lies about me. When my daughter told me what her father was saying, I should've tried to stop it. But I'm not sure what I could've done, short of going back to court and having my daughter testify as to what was going on. And that was also true for Ted, because Valerie and his mother were doing the same thing—poisoning his daughters against us. There were times when I wanted to call it quits, but I loved Ted and knew that he loved me. We felt we deserved a chance to have a good life together. We hoped that our love for each other and for the children would save the day."

My interview with Ted filled in the picture of his first marriage. "My wife came from a broken home. She was raised by an aunt and uncle, both staunch fundamentalists who believed spare the rod and spoil the child. I believe it had a very damaging effect on her. The first few years of our marriage were fine; then Valerie developed a serious drinking problem. When she was drunk, she became physically abusive to me and to our two daughters. We fought all the time, though it was usually Valerie screaming at me, and me taking it. I usually didn't respond. That only made her angrier until she became physically violent. I should've left her years before I actually did, but I was afraid to leave the kids in her custody, and I certainly couldn't work and take care of them."

Nonetheless, when Ted divorced Valerie, he made no attempt to gain custody of his two daughters, then nine and twelve years old. He wanted to avoid a jury trial and the ugly revelations of Valerie's alcoholism, the abuse, and *her* repeated infidelity. Instead, he agreed to a generous property settlement, alimony, and child support.

Though Ted was no longer living with Valerie when he met Cynthia, Valerie believed Cynthia was the cause of her marriage breakup. In the months before Ted and Cynthia's marriage, Valerie began her campaign of vengeance. She placed an "anonymous" call to the Family and Children's Service accusing Cynthia of abusing her own children. Cynthia hired a lawyer, who obtained a copy of the taped call. Valerie's voice was unmistakable. Nevertheless, it triggered a full and humiliating investigation of Cynthia's home life, which ultimately came to nothing.

To avoid an escalation of the problem, Cynthia and Ted chose not to retaliate against their former spouses. All four children were being used as pawns in this dangerous game, particularly Ted's older daughter, who had nothing but contempt for Cynthia.

The vicious intrusion from their prior marriages into their newly reconstituted family created an anguished environment for Cynthia and Ted. They would have been better off if they could have relocated to another city, but their careers and the visitation agreements precluded such a move. After three years of enforced visitation, Ted's two children stopped seeing him.

"There was no point making them do something they didn't want to do," he said. "And their visits just caused havoc for all of us, so I decided to let it go."

Both Cynthia and Ted say if they had it to do over again, they would still marry each other even if it meant going through the torment of those first few years. But they both admitted how naïve they had been. "What we needed," Cynthia said, "and didn't have was someone to tell us what we could expect. We were both blindsided."

Once Ted's children stopped visiting, Valerie became less of a problem, though she still made drunken calls in the middle of the night. Although Cynthia and Ted finally settled into a comfortable and relatively happy marriage, the fallout for the children had left indelible scars. Cynthia's older child, Amanda, remains close to both of them. One of Ted's daughters remains distant to him and to her mother and sister. Cynthia's son is not close, but Amanda believes it is due to the "years of awful lies my father told about my mother." Amanda was old enough to see through them, but her younger brother was "easily brainwashed."

When Amanda stood up for her mother, her father cut her out of his life forever. "I'm just glad I have my mother and Ted," Amanda told me. "He's been a wonderful stepfather. Both of them have done everything for me."

"In families like ours," Cynthia said, "bitterness, revenge, and anger are constantly threatening to undermine the new family. Even destroy it. I'm just so grateful that the children have thrived and that Ted and I have had so many wonderful years together."

MANY PERSPECTIVES

What could Ted and Cynthia have done to prevent these painful and enduring family rifts? Were they truly helpless in face of the damage that was being inflicted by their former spouses and even Ted's mother during the early years of their marriage?

One answer lies in Ted's handling of his relationship with Rose, his older daughter, who had worked so tenaciously to break up her father's marriage to Cynthia. She tried to turn into reality what many children fantasize about—that their parents will get back together again and reestablish the home that was broken. Right at the beginning, Ted should have sat down with Rose and explained to her that many times a married couple find that they are unable to live together anymore but that it doesn't mean they love their children any less. This is particularly important for the parent who has moved out, since the children will inevitably experience a sense of rejection, abandonment, and jealousy of the new spouse. Rose's world had fallen apart, so she tried to manipulate the situation in order to get her family back—the only family she ever wanted. And this was the time when Cynthia needed to show her new stepdaughter some real understanding and greater affection, though it was the hardest time to do both.

Ted's younger daughter, Paula, shed additional light on the situation. In our interview, Paula blamed her mother for most of the problems but said she resented that her father had given up so easily when she and her sister had stopped their visits with him. She felt that he should have tried to gain custody of her.

"My father knew how destructive my mother was when she was drinking, and that was most of the time. But he did nothing. He was too passive. Rose was the one who told all those lies, but it was at my mother's instigation. Rose became a very mean-spirited person, a lot like our mother." Paula also felt that Cynthia didn't seem to want anyone in her life except Ted and her own children.

Paula admitted that Cynthia had tried hard to make the new family work, "but I could tell how angry she was at my sister—she had good reason to be angry, and I know Cynthia was relieved when we stopped coming to the house for visitation. I don't blame her. She had it pretty rough with all that my mother did to her."

When asked if she wanted to build a closer relationship with her father, Paula said yes. "He did a lot of harm by never letting me know that I meant something to him, but I love him and know he loves me."

Both Ted and Cynthia should have been more realistic about the potential fallout from their quick remarriage. According to one Episcopal priest I consulted, Ted and Cynthia should have put their relationship on hold, properly divorced their spouses, and then allowed themselves more time to heal their first families before marrying. "The stigma of Cynthia being viewed as the home wrecker might have been avoided. The fury of both ex-spouses might have been lessened had they waited an appropriate amount of time before beginning their courtship."

In response to this advice, Cynthia said, "We loved each other and didn't want to wait. For too long, we'd both been through hell. We felt we deserved some peace. Granted, we were foolish to not get ourselves better prepared to deal with all these heightened emotions, but I suppose because we were in love, we expected too much. And Ted couldn't handle the guilt he felt about leaving his kids, but he thought fighting for custody was out of the question. We just wanted to be happy."

A different perspective comes from Jean Rosenbaum, M.D., a psychiatrist and author of *Stepparenting*. "Those marriages that are broken over love affairs were probably not very satisfactory to begin with. It is rare for happily married people to risk spoiling a marriage by having affairs." However, even if the divorce was inevitable, the ex-spouse is likely to perceive the current spouse as a home wrecker, triggering "the wrath of the [spouse] scorned." And, as in Ted and Cynthia's case, the children are frequently brought into the crossfire.

Dr. Rosenbaum urges that the spouse labeled the seducer or home wrecker not become overly defensive, because "people's gossip will quickly fade. They will become bored with the first mate's endless idealizing of the old, long-dead marriage. Time will reveal to all that you and your mate are actually happy." It's still important, however, to empathize with the abandoned ex-spouse, who may be glorifying a failed marriage to shore up sagging self-esteem.

Yet another opinion was voiced by a marriage counselor who heard the taped interviews. She concluded that both Ted and Cynthia were so damaged by the unhappiness of their first marriages that they were really incapable of handling this reconstituted family without the help of an experienced therapist. There were too many issues—divided loyalties, guilt, and power plays—in this situation. Also, Ted's passive nature was a major contributing factor in perpetuating the damage to himself, first in his long-term endurance of his first wife's abuse and then in allowing his children to walk out of his life rather than maintaining contact with them, even if it meant less frequent visits that wouldn't have included Cynthia. By not seeking to enforce visitation, he conveyed the wrong message to his children—that is, they didn't matter to him enough to fight for them. Unfortunately, Ted saw adversity as inevitable while, at the same time, he retreated from it.

"When people are being edged off their territory, battles begin," Ted said. "There's nothing much to be done about it."

Despite the problems with two of the four children, Cynthia and Ted's remarriage can be called "successful" by the definition offered in the introduction—the marriage endured happily and the children grew up to lead productive lives. Some people might not agree with these criteria for success, but what other measurement could there be? Even in nuclear families there are estrangements, unhappiness, and sibling rivalries that continue through adulthood. The fact that Ted and Cynthia loved each other and made their marriage a priority ultimately worked toward the good of the children.

MISSTEPS

In her book *Family Politics: Love and Power on an Intimate Frontier,* Letty Cottin Pogrebin says of children in stepfamilies: "Beyond the complex interactions is one stunning surprise: The stepfamily configuration seems to increase the power of the child. That is to say, compared with other parents, remarried parents seem more desirous of their children's approval, more alert to the children's emotional state, and more sensitive in their parent-child relations. Perhaps this is the result of heightened empathy for the children's suffering, perhaps it is a guilt reaction; in either case, it gives children a potent weapon—the power to disrupt the new household and come between the parent and the new spouse."

Jealous children can do unscrupulous things, even when they are motivated primarily by a need to protect themselves from the wrenching dislocations taking place in their lives. You do your children no favor to allow them to engage in destructive behavior. Certainly you can try in positive ways to make up to them for the hurt you may have caused.

But that doesn't mean buying them off, nor does it mean ruining your new marriage to satisfy their need to get back at you. You can teach them to treat you and your new spouse differently. Let them know that whatever they're doing to hurt you is destructive not only to you, but also to them. Most children don't enjoy being hateful. What they really want is the feeling that they are loved and secure, with clear parameters and structure. This was a lesson that Joyce and Leonard learned the hard way.

THE TAMING OF A STEP-BRAT

Leonard married Joyce after a long and loving courtship. He felt close to Joyce and looked forward to being a good stepfather to her thirteen-year-old daughter, Elise. He wanted to give them all the things they could not afford on Joyce's small salary and the inadequate child support she received from her first husband. Leonard had never been married before, though he'd been engaged to a young woman who had died of cancer before their marriage. Leonard fantasized that Elise would be happy to have a stepfather who was eager to look after her and provide some of the luxuries she had never had. Elise was polite but aloof during the two years of her mother's courtship with Leonard.

Just before Joyce married Leonard, Elise begged her not to go forward with the marriage. Joyce was shocked to discover that Elise didn't want anything to do with Leonard as a stepfather, that what she really wanted was to have her mother all to herself. And that Leonard's presence made Elise feel disloyal to her own father, who couldn't give her all the "nice things" Leonard could give her. "Once," Joyce said, "Elise told me she felt that Leonard was trying to buy her away from her father."

Joyce knew that Leonard was a kind and gentle man and felt confident that Elise would eventually learn to love him. Certainly Elise was old enough to understand and respect the marriage. Wisely, Joyce refused to allow her daughter to stand in the way of her happiness. But she underestimated Elise's desperation and determination.

After the wedding, Elise's politeness vanished, and what emerged was a pattern of rejection of Leonard's attempts to be a good stepparent. She ignored him and spoke only to her mother. At mealtimes, she treated him as if he weren't there, or she was hostile and rude to him. She typically acknowledged his presence only with the phrase "Oh, *he's* here." Every time Leonard entered a room where Elise was, he received her hateful stare. He ignored Elise's bad behavior. Eventually, she began to bait him into disciplining her by attacking her own mother with angry outbursts in Leonard's presence.

Leonard's hopes of becoming a wonderful new father figure were quickly diminished. Joyce, not knowing what to do to keep everything from falling apart, wondered if she'd made a big mistake by marrying Leonard while Elise was still going through adolescence. But because Leonard was a mature and patient man, he continued to be affable while ignoring the spiteful behavior of his stepdaughter. Joyce was increasingly saddened and anxious in her own home.

One morning after Leonard had gone to work, Joyce finally confronted her daughter. "Elise, you're behaving like an ungrateful, spoiled brat. No matter how badly you treat Leonard, he is always kind and giving, which only makes me love him more. I'm not going to subject Leonard to your rudeness at the dinner table. Frankly, I'm embarrassed by your behavior. You can have your dinner before we do and then go to your room."

Joyce's clear boundary setting resonated with Elise—it jarred the girl's fear that she might lose her mother's devotion.

Elise didn't suddenly love Leonard, but she did stop treating him like the enemy. Joyce regained control of her own home, and her marriage to Leonard thrived. After a couple of years, Elise not only accepted Leonard, but actually grew fond of him. He harbored no resentment toward her, understanding that she was an adolescent who had had her mother's undivided attention until he'd come into their lives, and a feeling of disloyalty to her biological father. Stepparents should expect that the children will be jealous of the relationship between their parent and the new stepparent. This jealousy abates as the children begin to accept the presence of the stepparent as routine, and actually begin to receive some emotional benefit from the relationship. Leonard was mature enough to understand that. Everyone learned something valuable—that it takes a family time and patience to blend, and if the new marriage is successful, ultimately everyone benefits.

WHAT ABOUT THE KIDS?

Do we actually know whether the children of divorce are better or worse off if their parents remarry? Without consulting the data, we can easily construct an argument for how children benefit when their parents enter a new marriage. First, the presence of a new parent helps relieve the stresses and demands of single parenthood. Someone else is around to share the household responsibilities and help raise the children. Second, the remarriage can bring another earner into the family. A stepfather's income can reverse the economic slide that afflicts many divorced mothers and their children. According to Greg Duncan and Saul Hoffman, the authors of *Economic Consequences of Marital Instability,* children in remarriages are almost as well off economically as children in first marriages.

But a counterargument can be made: Adjusting to so many new relationships and having the natural parent's attentions diverted may add a layer of problems over and above that of divorce.

Though there are comprehensive studies of families after divorce, there have not been comparable studies of blended families done in the United States over the extended period of time needed to evaluate children growing to adulthood. We can extrapolate from a landmark divorce study done in this country by researcher E. Mavis Hetherington (now an emeritus professor of psychology at the University of Virginia), because she includes children who have been raised in stepfamilies after divorce. And there are two studies of stepfamilies, one by James Bray, Ph.D., a psychologist at Baylor College of Medicine in Houston, and the second, an extensive research project done in Great Britain.

As reported in *For Better or for Worse,* Hetherington's research study followed 1,400 families, including adult children from stepfamilies. Hetherington's most notable findings challenged earlier warnings about the negative long-term effect of divorce on children. These, she asserted, have been "exaggerated to the point where we now have created a self-fulfilling prophecy." Her conclusion: "Most of the young men and women from my divorced families looked a lot like their contemporaries from non-divorced homes." However, some of her most disquieting interviews revealed the pain and confusion felt by those living in stepfamilies. Fifty percent of the remarriages she studied failed. Nonetheless, 75 percent of the youngsters in her study ultimately did as well as children from intact families.

Outcomes, Hetherington says, depend on many factors: the reasons for the divorce; parenting skills; the level of support both adults and children receive from family and friends; the individuals' willingness to change and grow in the face of new challenges. "Although [children] looked back on their parents' breakup as a painful experience," Hetherington writes, "most were successfully going about the chief task of young adulthood: establishing careers, creating intimate relationships, building meaningful lives for themselves."

James Bray's study, which was funded by the National Institutes of Health, followed one hundred white, middle-class stepfamilies and one hundred comparable non-divorced families over a nine-year period. His book *Stepfamilies* focuses primarily on stepfamilies consisting of a natural mother and stepfather. He concludes that stepfamilies are happiest when the husband and wife view their relationship as a "partnership" rather than as a "matriarchal" family. Like Hetherington, he also found that though children in stepfamilies tended to have behavior and emotional problems, 75 percent of stepchildren did well, compared with 85 to 90 percent of kids in non-divorced families.

The largest study involving stepchildren is the British National Child Development Study, which was based on a long-term survey of seventeen thousand children born in 1958 who were followed through adulthood. The authors of this study (two family therapists, a research professor, and a child psychiatrist) identified fifty subjects who had become stepchildren by the age of sixteen. When these children reached age twenty-three, the researchers conducted "lifestory interviews," which took two to six hours.

The goal of the study was to gain an understanding of the long-term effects of children's growing up in nuclear families that transitioned to stepfamilies. What is remarkable, especially given the real hardships faced by the people interviewed, is how well they fared, in both love (all but seven had married, with three-fourths of the ever-married still in a first marriage) and work. Almost all of these young people were thriving in their careers and had risen above their own parents' level of achievement.

Overall, the study presents a positive picture of a stepchild's ability to adapt to the remarriage of one or both of their parents. The authors concluded that children in blended families are generally doing well and that the most important factor in determining the impact of stepfamily experience for children was the quality of their relationship with their remaining natural parent.

The findings also demonstrate how important it is to communicate with children about the transitions taking place in their lives during divorce, death, and remarriage. Talking openly and supportively lessens the confusion and fear that usually accompanies these profound alterations in a child's life.

Researchers consistently tell us that family structure itself—nuclear, single-parent, or blended family—does not determine how happy, how socially well-adjusted, or how academically successful children will be. From the available research, it would be safe to say *that children from nuclear families do not fare that much better overall than those from second-marriage families*. What experts in the field continue to report is that exposure to prolonged conflict is harmful to children and that it is the *quality* of relationships, not the *type* of family, that makes a difference to children's psychological well-being. Where a stepfamily is loving and nurturing, and where the children are able to continue good relationships with their natural parents, they will thrive almost as well as children from intact families.

DIVIDED LOYALTIES

Divided loyalties are almost inevitable in blended families:

- Parents may feel torn between loyalty to their own children and loyalty to their new partners.

- Parents struggle to balance loyalties between their stepchildren and their natural children.

- Children may feel compelled to take sides between their divorced natural parents, and they often feel that liking a stepparent is disloyal to the natural parent.

- Children experience divided loyalties between whole siblings, step-siblings, and half siblings.

When children feel pressed to take sides, they may boycott a remarried mother or father, refusing to visit or to accept gifts from that parent. In extreme cases, adolescent and young adult children may refuse to even talk to the remarried parent or refuse to invite that parent who "betrayed" them to weddings, graduations, and so on.

Divided loyalties often appear where one of the parents has not remarried but is living alone. One fourteen-year-old girl refused to respond to her stepfather's good-natured parenting, believing, "We're a family, but my real father is alone. He has no one to care about him but me." That was her misperception, because actually her natural father was leading a relatively happy bachelor's life. But it's another example of how divided loyalties can manifest in a child's mind.

Steve, now thirty, was thirteen when his parents divorced. His father remarried and had another son with his second wife. When Steve got married, he refused to allow his father to bring his wife and their son to the wedding. When his father said he wouldn't come to the wedding under those conditions, Steve argued that the presence of his stepmother and half brother would ruin his mother's happy day. As a result, the father did not attend his son's wedding. Steve's loyalty to his mother precluded a positive relationship with his father and his father's second family. Steve's mother had certainly engendered these feelings, though Steve couldn't recall any particular words or actions that had led to his loyalty conflicts.

DIVIDED LOYALTIES WITH
A LAYER OF GUILT

Frequently, stepfathers remain uninvolved with stepchildren because they feel guilt for having left their own children. As one stepfather put it, "I have to keep my distance to avoid the feeling that I give my wife's children more attention than I give my own kids. They already feel I abandoned them."

A mother often feels pulled between her current spouse and her children from a previous marriage. Maureen divorced her first husband when their daughter was thirteen years old. A year later, she married her current husband and had another daughter with him. He had never been married before.

She says, "I feel a tug-of-war between my husband and my daughter from my first marriage. She sees me as the parent in charge, the one responsible for her. When my husband disciplines her or tries to influence, for instance, her choice of colleges, I feel torn. No matter what, I'm 'betraying' one of them. There's even a conflict on what to spend for each child. When my older daughter wanted a car, my husband refused, saying it was an unnecessary expense, though I felt she deserved to have a car. It seemed only fair, since I have my own money, plus the fact that her natural father has offered to help pay for it. She's a good student and a responsible person, but I don't know what I can do to please both of them. My husband gets jealous if I take her side, and then tries to control the situation by having his way. He's punishing me for loving my own daughter and wanting her to have nice things."

Remarriage after the death of a first spouse brings its own forms of disloyalty and guilt. Remarried widows and widowers often have difficulty sharing activities, rituals, and experiences they used to enjoy with their deceased spouse. Sometimes they won't even talk to the new spouse about the first spouse, because they feel it's disloyal to reveal personal information.

But even a divorced spouse may feel protective of an ex. Janet becomes defensive whenever her current husband criticizes her ex-husband for making late child support payments or for failing to pay for the health care of the children from the first marriage. Janet feels her first husband was a basically good man who never had much education, but he had been her childhood sweetheart. "I feel as if my husband's criticism of my ex is directed at me for being stupid enough to marry a man who couldn't make a good living."

These are just some of the land mines that can strew the ground on which newly blended families tread. However, when you understand your partner's feelings about his or her past, his or her kids—and yours—you're better prepared to navigate the terrain. Leftover emotional baggage almost always resurfaces in a blended family, and it's likely that everyone involved is carrying at least one suitcase. Awareness that these problems are going to arise is a big step in the right direction. Making the assumption that they won't arise for you—and then being blindsided by these conflicts—is a sure route to failure. *Having reasonable expectations can go a long way to defuse loyalty conflicts and guilt.*

HOME IS WHERE THE TOYS ARE

There are those people who negotiate relationships on unconditional terms, hold all the trump cards, and seem to control everyone around them. One couple I interviewed had been previously married but did not have custody of their respective children. For many happy years, they seem to have escaped all the usual problems of divided loyalties, unreasonable expectations, guilt, and other burdens of the past. But wait!—circumstances have a way of changing.

Gerald is a frantically busy man, a senior vice president of a publicly held corporation. Like many men, he was reluctant at first to talk candidly about his personal life. He agreed to an interview, however, because he wanted to get some problems off his chest. As a corporate executive, he was accustomed to problem solving, and he had never before faced a situation in which he felt virtually powerless. His domestic life was in shambles. And he was distraught.

Gerald was in the midst of a department overhaul when we spoke. "There's not enough of me to go around," he began. "The calls from colleagues are just a minor part of my day. The interruptions from my wife, my ex-wife, and all the kids are about to drive me up the wall."

Gerald admitted to being at a loss in his role as stepfather to two teenage boys who had never wanted him in their mother's life. "Frankly, I can't wait until they both go off to college so I can have my wife back. The boys were supposed to live with their father, but these kids have a much more luxurious life at our house, so when they were old enough to choose who they wanted to live with, they chose us. They've got fancy cars, a big house, money in their pockets, and a mother who feels so guilty about breaking up their home that she virtually lets them get away with anything. If I try to discipline them, they just smirk, wait till I leave the house, then resume whatever they've been doing. And I've got my own kids to contend with as well. It's 'gimme, gimme, gimme' with all four of them, her two boys and my two girls. If it weren't for the kids, Arlene and I would be fine."

Gerald described his divorce from his first wife and mother of his daughters as a case of "uneven growth." She was totally dependent on him. "I gave her enough to keep her happy and moved out. Now she won't leave me alone—can't make a decision about *anything* without calling me. No wonder my daughters want out, too."

Arlene, Gerald's second wife, also wanted to explain why she divorced her first husband, the father of her two sons. When Arlene met Joe, she was working as an account executive with a high-powered Madison Avenue advertising agency. Joe was a psychiatric social worker. Within the next three years, their two sons were born, and Arlene decided to become a stay-at-home mom. The absence of Arlene's salary meant that they had to drastically reduce their expenses. They needed a bigger place but had to move to a smaller one. As soon as the boys were old enough to go to preschool, Arlene returned to work. Before long, she found herself dreading the end of the workday, when she had to pick up the children and go home. The boys became the focus of intense competition between her and Joe. He wanted athletes. She wanted academic wunderkinds.

"There's nothing more sanctimonious than a man who's been jogging for ten years," Arlene said. "His idea of success is to get the whole family running around all hours of the day and night, being chased by vicious dogs."

Joe did less and less at home and never seemed to advance in his career. He spent his time coaching Little League, working out with the boys at the gym, and jogging. When the boys were ten and eleven, Arlene and Joe divorced. Joe wanted custody of his sons. Reluctantly, Arlene agreed as long as she had liberal visitation and the right to have the boys on all holidays. She even agreed to pay substantial child support so that Joe could hire domestic help.

"My divorce was like a weight lifted from my shoulders," she said. "I resumed my relationships with old girlfriends who were also divorced. I began to really enjoy my sons, instead of having a continuous battle with them. Joe had a love/hate thing going for me. I think he alternated between wanting to murder me and wanting to get me back. But I had no intention of ever going back to him. I started taking courses in business and finance. And that's how I met Gerald. He was one of the guest lecturers. One year after my swan dive into the world of independence, I fell in love and married Gerald."

Arlene believed Gerald's assurances that they would never have to deal with the problems of their former families, since their former spouses had custody of the children. And it worked for a time, but soon all the kids arrived, bag and baggage, at the large Westchester estate Gerald had bought. Arlene's boys loved having their own swimming pool and tennis court, a membership at the country club, bedrooms of their own, and Gerald's pretty daughters as constant visitors. The house became a gathering place for teens with too much money and too little supervision and responsibility.

"Gerald's first wife began to intrude in our lives," Arlene said, "accusing us of running a free-for-all at our house. I should've learned— you never outgrow your need to be paranoid."

When Arlene and Gerald realized they had lost control, they began to quarrel about who should be handling the day-to-day problems. Gerald complained that he had to work to pay for all their lifestyle expenses. Over protest, Arlene quit her job to stay home and bring some discipline into their children's lives. At that time, all four children were between thirteen and sixteen. With the boys, she had some leverage, because they were her own children, but Gerald's daughters rebelled.

"My whole personality changed," Arlene said. "I became a nervous wreck just trying to keep the kids from doing the wrong things, like staying out all night, drinking and driving, getting bad grades at school. This wasn't what we bargained for. As long as Gerald and I were living alone with just occasional visits with the kids, we were great together—happy and relaxed. We love each other, our lifestyle, and our work. We were determined to preserve our marriage."

Arlene told me she begged Gerald to have his girls stay with their mother and not spend so much time with them. Gerald balked at this request, arguing that Arlene's sons weren't supposed to be living with them either. Four teenagers were too much, she said, plus the fact that one of her sons and one of Gerald's daughters seemed to be getting too chummy. Arlene declined to expand on that issue.

Gerald's position was that the kids would all leave for college soon anyway, so why couldn't Arlene just manage things for a couple more years? Gerald justified his daughters' long stays by saying *he* hadn't been able to live with their mother, so why should *they* have to?

During the interview, Arlene's ex came to pick up their sons. The boys hugged Arlene, then reluctantly marched out the door. "The boys hate going there," she explained. "They have to sleep on air mattresses on the floor, and they miss their friends."

The ambivalence of wanting what is best for her sons, but not wanting to deal with the everyday conflict of providing discipline, plagues Arlene. She believes they need the strong presence of a father. Their own father, though, has never been a strong presence, and Gerald carries no weight with them, because he is their stepfather, and one who is rarely there when conflicts arise. The resentment that Arlene feels from Gerald's daughters is another source of constant friction. They know she doesn't want them spending so much time there, so they misbehave just to rile her.

Arlene is unsure about where to begin to resolve the problems of her blended family. At one point, she sought professional help, but that proved to be of little value, "because the advice I got was unworkable with children who were, for the most part, raised by their other parents."

When asked how she would advise others on building and managing a blended family, Arlene shrugs. "I could say get the terms in writing and stick with them, but that would be impossible. You can't forbid your children from living with you or forbid your spouse's children from visiting. I think if we could've had real communication with my ex-husband and Gerald's ex-wife, the children would have been better off. We were all being played off against each other by these four teenagers, to their detriment and ours. I don't know what could have possessed me to expect that this marriage could have gone on without a hitch. I never *expected* the kids would come to live with us."

One family therapist marveled at the disconnect between Arlene's astute perception of this family dynamic, and her actions. Gerald, who had a strong personality, should have played an important role in the household, but he deferred to Arlene, who was not able to handle four determined and rebellious teenagers by herself. A four-parent powwow would have been a good way to arrive at a consistent pattern of discipline and structure for this family, but the tensions among the adults prevented a useful discussion of the problems. In Arlene and Gerald's case, because they didn't have custody when the children were young they had never had to develop a well-thought-out plan to deal with behavior problems. Once the teenagers arrived in full force, his guilt and her unrealistic expectations made it impossible for them to support each other in effective parenting. The result was an undisciplined, overindulgent environment where the teenagers were for all practical purposes holding the adults hostage.

It's not too late for Gerald to step in and set boundaries for this reconstituted family. He holds the trump cards at home, just as he does at work. What the four children want, to their detriment, are the luxuries Gerald provides and the freedom they enjoy thanks to having a nonfunctioning adult in the house. Gerald needs to spend more time at home and use the leverage he has to help Arlene manage these teenagers. Otherwise, the conflicts will not only leave permanent scars on the kids but may well destroy the marriage itself.

BEYOND MANIPULATION

Manipulative people, including children, continue to engage in manipulative behavior because it works for them. The best way to get somebody to stop doing something is to make it less enjoyable or profitable for them to continue. Essentially, this means not challenging their threats directly, but defusing them dispassionately.

A child who threatens to sabotage your marriage as a means of getting his/her parents back together needs reassurance and clear boundaries. Here is the essence of the message you might want to convey:

"I'm sorry you're having trouble accepting that your mother/father and I are divorced. It wasn't your fault. It was our doing. We're not getting back together. I'm remarried, and that's the way it's going to be. If you continue to create problems for us, then we're all going to suffer, you included. I love you, but I don't love your mother/father anymore. I want to see you, not her/him. If you don't want to spend time with me, I'll be deeply hurt, but I'm not going to risk losing my wife/husband because of all of the chaos you're causing, and I hope you understand that. I have room to love you both, and I want us to remain close for the rest of our lives. To do that, we need to be together. If you're here for the weekend, we'll take some time to be together—just us. I want you to understand that we want to be a family, and you're part of that family."

It is a hallmark of the manipulator to keep trying different strategies until he/she finds one that works. Guilt works best between children and parents—in either direction. It's effective because in both roles there is a lingering feeling that we could and should have done more for the other person. Parents may feel resentful of the attempt to manipulate them, but still go along with the program, baffled as to why the tactic is so successful. Somebody who is very good at influencing people to do things they don't want to do or shouldn't do has a highly developed sensitivity to vulnerability in others.

Parents know their kids, and kids know their parents. Parents usually use this sensitivity to get kids to do what they should do. Kids use it to get what they want.

Guilt preys on all the unfinished business of life, wherever you still feel the need to correct past mistakes. To shield yourself against attempts by others to *guilt* you into doing things you do not want to do, you must first accept your own fallibility.

In the case of Gerald, whose daughters wanted to be where the toys are, he knows he's not a perfect parent. He divorced his daughters' mother because she no longer interested or excited him. This had the effect of breaking up their home. His chief struggle during the years of his second marriage has been coming to terms with some of his selfishness and the impact it has had on his daughters. A similar situation existed in Ted and Cynthia's story. Ted knows the divorce broke up his daughter's home even though he had an intolerable situation and was perfectly reasonable in seeking the divorce.

Once divorced/remarried parents acknowledge that they are not perfect or superhuman, they will be far less vulnerable to manipulation. Of course, parents do make mistakes. Had they known then what they know now, they might have been able to do things differently. If they can accept that *they did the best they could with what they knew at the time,* then and only then will they be able to resist emotional blackmail. They will be far less likely to ruin their remarriages in a mistaken attempt to buy their children's love.

THE GREEN-EYED MONSTER

When Diane and Carter married, neither of them expected that Carter's thirteen-year-old daughter, Penny, would want to live with them in Connecticut. Carter had been divorced from Penny's mother for many years, during which time Penny lived in Colorado with her mother, her mother's live-in boyfriend, and her fourteen-year-old brother, Gary. After the divorce, Penny and Gary saw their father during summers and alternate holidays. When Diane came on the scene, Penny seemed loving and friendly and thrilled that her dad was getting married. This meant a "family" again. And for Penny, that meant everything. It meant her dad no longer had too many girlfriends and parties, and no longer lived the playboy lifestyle that had left him with little time for Penny.

Diane said, "Dealing with Carter's children was easy, especially with his son, Gary, who always had an upbeat attitude, and at first even with Penny. Penny would tell me how much she preferred me to any other woman in Carter's life. When Carter and I married, I was pregnant, and Penny looked forward to having a new brother or sister. I miscarried, and Penny was extra sweet toward me. I think it was genuine.

"But within a year, Penny's attitude changed. Whenever she came to visit during spring break, at Christmas, or for a few weeks during summer vacation, it was a painful, depressing experience. She started treating me terribly. I was now in the way of her relationship with Dad. I was barely tolerated. She glared, said mean and hurtful things, never showed respect, let alone kindness. She wanted only to be with her father and have his undivided attention. What added insult to injury was having to hear Carter excusing her rude behavior—'She only spends a couple of months of the year with us,' he would say pleadingly.

"At dinner, she would speak only to her father unless she had something to complain about. She never liked any of the meals I prepared. 'Chicken again, Diane. And it's so overdone. Yuk!' " Diane said, imitating a sarcastic fourteen-year-old.

One night, after finding a letter Penny had written and tossed into the wastebasket, Diane could no longer restrain herself. Holding up the crinkled page, she said, "Penny, what about this?"

Angrily, Penny said, "Why are you snooping around my room and reading my letters?"

"If you didn't want me to see it, why didn't you destroy it?" Diane retorted. "It's pretty obvious you meant for me to find it. You said you never loved me and wished I was dead or some such silliness. And I'm supposed to cook and clean and do everything for you when you're here. How do you think it makes me feel to know you wish I was dead?"

"I'm sorry," Penny said, and for the moment seemed to be sincerely apologetic.

Penny then made a startling about-face that was even more destabilizing.

"Penny began to beg to come and live with us. At that point in our lives, Carter and I knew that we wanted to be kid-free. We wanted to make our marriage work, because it, too, was on shaky ground."

Diane sensed trouble in her relationships not only with Carter but also with her stepdaughter. "I could see how Penny, a typically self-absorbed teenager, was orchestrating a plan for herself to be the center of her father's life."

The visits became more and more difficult. Penny would try to plan a day trip with her father that excluded Diane. She'd beg Carter to talk to her mother about changing custody. Diane and Carter knew that Penny's mother would never give up custody, plus the fact that Penny did well in school and had lots of friends and a better lifestyle than she would have living with her father. But she would not stop begging. Crying tantrums started days before she was to go back home.

Penny would say, "I love my father and he loves me, but he can't have me here, because you don't want me here, and that's why he won't fight for custody."

"It was pitiful," Diane said. "I was fed up and took her to the airport to go home a week earlier than planned."

Carter worked on convincing his daughter that he'd never win a custody battle, but she kept on blaming Diane for obstructing her relationship with him. Over the next few years, Penny's visits were less frequent but always tense and filled with resentment. After the initial hug upon arrival, a cold shoulder would prevail for the rest of the time. On a daily basis, she worked hard to get her father away from Diane so that she could be alone with him.

When Diane realized how disruptive Penny was to their marriage, she decided to lay down ground rules, starting with a promise from Carter that he would put their marriage first. They both interpreted this to mean that Penny could no longer spend weeks on end staying with them and turning their lives upside down. Without Diane, Carter went to Colorado and had a weekend visit with Penny. He let Penny know that until she could be kind and respectful to Diane, he wasn't going to have her visit with them but would travel to Colorado to see her a couple of times a year. Diane, in return, stopped complaining to Carter about his daughter, and worked extra hard to be hospitable to Gary, who continued to visit. This went on for another year, until Penny finally called her father to say that she wanted another chance. When she arrived at the airport, she greeted Diane with an apology, then took Diane's hand as they walked to the car.

"I won't say there weren't some glaring looks from time to time," Diane said, "but for the most part Penny behaved herself, helping me with small chores around the house. Never again did she suggest an outing that excluded me."

Diane acknowledged Penny's efforts by taking her out shopping and buying her some new clothes and other small gifts that Diane knew a teenager would love. She went with Penny to a hairstylist and even took the time to work with her on her college applications. After college, Penny found a job in New York City, a train ride away from where her father and Diane lived. With a coworker, she rented a small apartment. As is typical of young single women, she saw her father and Diane only for an occasional dinner and during holidays.

Diane took a real chance standing firm against Penny's jealousy. She realized that Carter might question his decision to marry her, but she believed strongly that the marriage would not have survived the presence of a teenage daughter who wanted desperately to be first in her father's eyes. She was fortunate in that Carter really hadn't wanted full custody of his daughter, nor had his ex-wife wanted to relinquish custody.

Was Diane right to put the marriage first and risk alienating both her husband and his daughter? To answer that question, we must look at the outcome. The marriage has lasted, and Penny's relationship with her stepmother has remained cordial to this day. *Perhaps the most significant factor was Carter's continued, though curtailed, contact with his daughter. This kept their relationship alive and served to give his daughter the confidence of knowing that her father continued to love her, even if he couldn't tolerate her mistreatment of his wife.* Penny soon understood that to spend more time with her father, she would have to treat Diane with respect, and that's when she asked for another chance. Her response ratified the wisdom of Carter and Diane in putting their marriage first.

Your mate is the only family member you can actually choose, but your mate's family comes as part of the deal. Living in peace with your stepchildren and your in-laws is a serious commitment, and can actually contribute toward a better and more fulfilling marriage—as long as you make a priority of the marriage itself. Whenever possible, protect the intimacy of your new marriage. Set boundaries, make clear your allegiance to your spouse, and minimize contact with troublesome relatives. Your success as a couple will ultimately benefit the children and the entire family.

Helpful Guidelines

- **Love does not conquer all.** Though optimism and a good sense of humor will go a long way toward reducing the stress of everyday life, be realistic about the challenges of blending two families, each with its own history, rituals, and problems. Remember that marriage changes passion: suddenly, you're in bed with a relative.

- **Be prepared for hidden agendas.** In-laws, former in-laws, ex-spouses, children, and stepchildren can, and often do, play the role of saboteurs. Try to understand that you and your spouse chose each other, but others related to you might not have made the same choice. Now these related others are being asked to fully accept this reconstituted family that has been thrust on them. They, like you, are forced to play a challenging role. Give them the benefit of the doubt and the time to adjust to this new family structure.

- **Don't let yourself be blindsided.** Lack of background information on other family members can hinder effective communication. The courtship provides necessary information about the new spouse but offers little about the children or the in-laws or the former spouse. Make sure you extract this knowledge from your spouse, and get to know the children as soon as possible. It can make all the difference in your handling of problems as they arise—which they surely will.

- **Don't get stuck in the past.** Expect the past to intrude on your new lives together, but don't dwell on the past. Face it, examine it, and learn from it. Above all, work hard not to repeat the mistakes of the past. One of the consequences of divorce and remarriage is separation from the former family and not seeing them as often as you would like. However, you have a new life and a new marriage, and your former family also has a new life without your constant presence.

- **Be aware of the legacy of adultery.** If an adulterous affair is at the foundation of your new marriage, be prepared to encounter many more difficult problems than you would otherwise have to face. Even if your marriage was a sham, or hell on earth or for convenience or solely for the kids' sake, adultery is still a betrayal and likely to produce intense feelings of anger and revenge. If possible, wait at least a year from the time of the divorce to give all of the related others a chance to acclimate, regroup, and move forward. *But don't be surprised if the problems continue to be severe, so be absolutely certain this new person is worth the risk.*

- **Acknowledge and empathize with your spouse's emotional turmoil.** Whether the emotions are guilt, conflicting loyalties, anger, fear, or resentment, express your understanding of what he or she is going through and offer to help. Give of yourself to this hurting person you love. Be aware that a noncustodial parent may overindulge visiting children out of a sense of guilt. Try to be sympathetic in your approach and reasonable in your demands.

- **Don't allow your children to manipulate you by playing on your guilt.** Do everything you can to be a good parent. Do it because you love your child and because what you're doing is for the child's benefit, and not because you've been emotionally blackmailed into doing what your child wants.

- **Understand what children want.** Children want love and security. Setting reasonable boundaries and structure are necessary to convey that love and sense of security.

- **Don't get into personal denigration of your spouse's former family.** Even if you're being abused by your spouse's ex and/or his or her children, stick to a discussion of issues without resorting to name-calling or "street fighting." If you have to get the rage out of your system, find a good friend to talk to, preferably one who's been through a similar experience. Whatever else is happening, remember the spouse you love was once married to this other person, who is also the parent of his or her children.

- **Be the best person you can be even in difficult situations.** Express yourself warmly. Show love, compassion, interest, and respect to everyone, unless they become openly destructive. If that happens, don't retaliate, but minimize contact. Civility is essential. Whether the conflict is with children, relatives, or your new spouse, show approval of the person even if you don't always approve of their actions. You can offer criticism as long as you can convey that the actions are unacceptable but your love is constant.

- **Establish new ground rules.** You and your partner must establish firm ground rules in your home, irrespective of how your stepchildren have been allowed to behave in their own homes. When the children are on your territory, you have authority over and responsibility for their behavior. Explain that everybody has different rules and that everybody has to abide by the rules of the house they are visiting exactly as they have to abide by certain rules in school.

- **Make it clear that your new spouse is number one in your life.** Try not to convey that your children are more important than your spouse, even if they are often more in need of your time. Always set aside a time when your spouse has your undivided attention. When other adults in your family make unkind remarks or do unkind things to your new spouse, set the record straight immediately. Let them know where your priorities lie. Point out that they would expect the same thing of their spouses.

- **Don't allow your children or stepchildren to play one parent off against the other.** Children want their biological parents to stay together, and when a new stepparent comes into the picture, children can do some diabolical things to create a wedge between the new couple. It doesn't mean they're diabolical children. They're just doing what divorce-traumatized children often do. Time and expressions of love and understanding will usually work to overcome these problems.

- **Don't force your spouse to choose between you and his children.** If a serious psychological problem or criminal actions are affecting you or your children, you can call a halt to contact with the destructive person—particularly if it's an adult—but don't force an estrangement between your spouse and his or her children.

- **Don't be afraid to defend your own children if you genuinely believe that they are being treated unfairly.** Be sure to do so in a tone of conciliation, not hostility.

- **Find support groups.** Check the local paper to find support groups for stepfamilies, and don't be too proud to attend. You may learn a whole lot more than you thought you would. Most cities have organizations set up to help blended families (stepfamilies). Your church or synagogue can usually be of assistance, too, in dealing with family problems.

- **Make time for yourselves.** Set aside special time each week for your partner and yourself. You both need time to be yourselves and to show each other just why you chose to be together.

t w o

The Ex Factor

S e c r e t   T w o :

Respect and support the child's relationship with the other parent.

Horror stories abound about those crazy, vindictive, destructive ex-spouses. Perhaps *you're* someone who's been on the receiving end (surely not the opposite end!) of some totally unprovoked and even bizarre retaliation by an ex.

In Karen Karbo's memoir, *Generation Ex,* she describes how her boyfriend's ex-wife broke into his house and cut the crotch out of Karbo's underpants with a pair of cuticle scissors. Karbo noted that she wasn't wearing her underpants at the time, but she certainly learned what she was up against.

Before the advent of cell phones, answering machines, voice-messaging systems, call-waiting, call forwarding, fax machines, pagers, and e-mail, ex-spouses had more difficulty achieving their ends. Now access is immediate, and exes always have a reason to call—to convey information or ask a question about the warranty on the car battery or to see if the alimony check is in the mail—and then, after they reel you in, it turns ugly. No doubt about it; these exes believe they are the real lords of the rings, entitled by virtue of the children and the wedding rings once placed on their fingers to make their ex-spouses suffer forever.

How Do You Know If You're Dealing with a Lunatic Ex-Spouse?

- After you packed a few bags and moved out, did you find the rest of your clothes on the front porch, shredded like confetti? Or Clorox bleached? Or your best cashmere sweaters covered with grease?

- When you left the office and went to your car, did you find the tires slashed, the body spray-painted with obscenities or, even worse, beaten with a sledgehammer?

- Did your joint bank account suddenly have a zero balance, while every charge card was maxed out?

- Have you been arrested and dragged into the local police precinct for breaking and entering when you returned home to get the rest of your things?

- Has the UPS man been making daily deliveries of merchandise you never ordered?

- Has your phone been ringing, at all hours of the day and night, and you pick up, only to find heavy breathing on the other end, and the caller ID window says "pay phone"?

- After a period of being shunned by friends, have you found out your ex has told them you've come "out" of the closet, when in fact you've never been "in" the closet?

- In the evening when you're out, have you noticed that you're being tailed by a car that belongs to your ex-spouse's best friend?

- Are your children suddenly afraid of you? Is the social worker from the children's services agency arriving regularly to check on your child's condition after receiving anonymous tips that you're an abuser or a molester?

• Has your boss suddenly been acting funny, as if he wants to have a talk with you but doesn't know quite how to begin? And when you finally do sit down to chat with him, does he ask you if you think you're capable of dealing with the stress of the job in your condition? And you're almost afraid to ask him what he means?

If you've answered yes to one of these, you've probably answered yes to more than one. Ex-husbands can be pushed to the brink and may even threaten to cut all the utility wires to the house—despite its being jointly owned and the residence of the ex-wife—especially if he's still paying the bills. But typically it's an ex-wife who behaves childishly and vindictively toward the ex-husband and his new wife. Sometimes divorce and the remarriage of a former spouse can even trigger pathological behavior that cannot be ignored. Sadly, the sense of betrayal produces such rage that some people lose all their ability to reason and will use children as levers to avenge the wrong they believe was done to them. This chapter explores the many ways children are caught in the crossfire.

EX MANIA

One woman described it this way: "My husband's alcoholic ex-wife is terrorizing my children. While I was at work, she called our house and told my children I won't be coming home anymore, because she killed me!"

Unfortunately, this extreme degree of acting out cannot be defused by normal means. Anyone doing to children what this ex-wife has done requires the heavy hand of the law, because committing acts of terror against children is a crime. In addition to notifying the local police department, you need a lawyer so you can obtain a restraining order. If this ex-wife has custody of her children, serious questions about her drinking and her fitness to raise children should be explored. Fortunately, few people resort to this degree of psychotic behavior and potential emotional harm to children. But what can be done when the acts are not of such magnitude yet must be stopped?

Take some advice from our leading military strategists in the war against terrorism—build homeland security. This may be easier said than done, but it works. So hunker down. Play a defensive game. Get a burglar alarm system. Stay out of his or her scope of vision as much as possible. Get caller ID, and don't pick up the phone when the lunatic fringe is calling, unless you absolutely have to. It's best to say, "He's not here right now. I'll give him your message." Click. If you and your spouse train yourselves not to react, the ex will eventually stop calling, or damaging property. Games are fun only if everyone is participating.

If it gets intolerable, don't resort to an eye for an eye, or everyone will wind up blind. When there are legal or criminal issues, let the lawyers deal with them. Keep the children in mind, and realize that you can't defeat this enemy and walk away, because the children are going to keep you connected for a long time.

So there is a legitimate reason to try, in every way possible, to be civil to this person, the mother or father of your child or your spouse's child, even though this is the very same person who has been systematically trying to destroy your happiness. In effect, what you're doing is *tolerating* this person for the sake of your remarriage and the well-being of the children—assuming, of course, that no direct acts of harm are being done to the children.

To keep the level of animosity down and the civility up, it's best not to talk about this ex any more than is necessary. Even when we don't think we're obsessing about our ex or our spouse's ex, if we're discussing him or her most days out of the week, then it's time to honestly evaluate the situation. The new husband/wife doesn't need to know everything there is to know about your ex. That only causes more preoccupation. Bear in mind that most people lie about the cause of their divorce. Even if your spouse doesn't mean to lie, withhold, or distort the stories about his or her ex, what he or she says won't always be the entire truth. Both were probably, to a greater or lesser degree, at fault for the split. Besides, that shouldn't matter. What matters is the *new family*.

Even the most well-intentioned divorced parent, living under a stress few happily married people can comprehend, sometimes succumbs to the urge to use the children to zing the ex. He/she may slip and say "Your mother's crazy" or "Your father's a no-good bastard." If you've lost it and spoken disparagingly about the child's other parent, tell the child that sometimes you lose your temper and say things you don't mean. (Even if you do mean it, tell the child that you don't.)

Both men and women are capable of turning the children into weapons. What most men do with difficult ex-wives is try to get back in their good graces, or they cower, fearing that she'll launch a major offensive to poison the children against them. That isn't to say there aren't plenty of divorced men who actively work to alienate the children from their mother by speaking of her in a demeaning or hateful way. Vengeful women, on the other hand, will put more obstacles in the way of visitation than a road full of broken glass. Their need to hurt their ex-husbands clouds their judgment and causes them to forget the children's need for their father.

FATHERS ARE PARENTS, TOO

Children need both parents equally. 50/50 parenting is on a mounted banner that overhangs the Massachusetts Turnpike. The banner gets honks of support by motorists whizzing by, but many divorced men nevertheless have ex-wives who are thwarting their efforts to see their children—even when they have clear visitation rights. Mothers, too, may face this problem now that more fathers are seeking and winning custody of the children.

In June 2001, as part of a nationwide protest, Elizabeth Schnee of College Point, New York, organized a march across the Brooklyn Bridge. Having lost custody of her four children, she fully understood what divorced fathers go through in dealing with intractable ex-wives. The aim of the protest was to draw attention to the plight of fathers who get short shrift when it comes to spending time with their children. They call themselves "deadbolted dads," complaining that courts typically give mothers custody of kids, and then fail to act when ex-wives lock fathers out of their children's lives by ignoring visitation schedules.

Whether you are the ex-spouse or the current spouse, unless there is serious harm to a child, interfering with the noncustodial parent's visitation is indefensible, because of the harm it does to the children.

Ira Daniel Turkat, Ph.D., a psychologist who teaches at the Florida Institute of Psychology and the University of Florida College of Medicine, has written extensively on the subject of child visitation. He maintains that divorce-related child visitation interference is a national problem affecting more than six million children. According to Dr. Turkat, "the majority of custodial parents are female, and these ex-wives are the major source of interference." He cites J. A. Arditti's two surveys in support of his findings, as reported in the *Journal of Divorce and Remarriage*. Arditti found that 50 percent of divorced fathers related that their ex-wives interfered with their visitation. Similarly, more than 40 percent of custodial mothers admitted denying their ex-husbands visitation in order to punish them.

An angry ex-wife can find many ways of subverting visits. "This is the weekend Johnny is going on an overnight with his friend. Why don't you get him next weekend?" Or "Johnny has a chance to go to Six Flags with my parents." Or "He doesn't feel well this weekend." Visitation with the noncustodial parent is vital to the well-being of the child. What these interfering parents are doing is what they least want to do—they're hurting the children they love. Divorced parents should try hard to encourage visitation and to conceal their anger when they are in the presence of the children.

Visitation problems have a dramatic impact on blended families. Being denied access to your children results in frustration, anger, and depression. This is a problem not only for the noncustodial parent but also for the new spouse, who has to deal with these painful emotions. It is a likely source of strife in the new family at a time when the best is needed from everyone to make the blending work.

THE DEMON OF ALIENATION

"Parental alienation," a term commonly used by family therapists, is often triggered by remarriage, according to Richard A. Warshak, Ph.D., a leading expert on the subject. "Parental alienation syndrome" is another term, one coined by psychiatrist Richard Gardner, M.D. The terms are not interchangeable. "Parental alienation" is defined by Dr. Warshak as witting or unwitting behavior that causes serious problems in the relationship between the child and the other parent. Clearly the first term, "parental alienation," refers to the person, usually the custodial parent, who is engaging in destructive behavior to alienate the children from the noncustodial parent, but it may be the other way around. The term "parental alienation syndrome" encompasses the children themselves, who have adopted the views of the alienating parent and are now enlisted in "unjustified and/or exaggerated" denigration of the other parent. In a real sense, the kids are brainwashed against one parent.

Is Your Ex-Spouse Turning Your Children against You?

Does your ex-spouse:

- Refuse to allow you to speak to your child on the telephone?

- Plan other activities for the children during your visitation times?

- Try to influence the children to see his or her new spouse as their real parent?

- Belittle you or start petty arguments in front of the children?

- Trash the mail and gifts you send the children?

- Disobey court orders by refusing visitation with your children?

- Speak negatively about your current spouse?

- Neglect to inform you about your child's medical, dental, psychological, or other important appointments?

- Enlist the help of his or her family to help brainwash your children against you?

- Attempt to change the children's last names?

- Refuse access to the children's school or medical records?

- Go away for a vacation and leave the children in someone else's care without telling you where they are?

- Threaten to punish the children if they contact you by telephone, mail, or e-mail?

- Blame you for the children's problems?

- Influence the children to denigrate or criticize you more than once in a while?

If you answered yes to several of these questions, you have a problem with "parental alienation" and/or "parental alienation syndrome."

DADDY DEAREST

Annabelle, a law school professor, was married to Ross, a clinical psychologist, for fifteen years, and they had two children, Patty and Mark. At the time of their divorce, Patty was twelve and Mark was nine. Because Annabelle had become involved prior to her divorce with the man she later married, Ross was a man on a mission to get back at Annabelle in any way he could. Under the terms of their divorce agreement, Annabelle had custody of the two children and Ross had alternate weekend visitation, alternating holidays, and two weeks in the summer.

At first, Annabelle was glad that the children would continue a good relationship with their father. Though she and Ross had a miserably unhappy marriage, he had been a good father. Seven months after her divorce was final, she married Paul. At the same time, Ross began living with a woman half his age, who had been his mistress during his marriage: a fact he had managed to keep secret from Annabelle, while castigating her for her relationship with Paul. Ross knew that Annabelle was a devoted and nurturing mother to both children. In truth, she and Ross had stayed married as long as they had only out of the fear that a divorce would devastate the children they cherished.

Ross was an experienced therapist who counseled children, especially adolescents, so it is fair to say he was an expert when it came to influencing children. That is why it is all the more despicable that he chose to influence his own children against their mother.

Within months after visitation started, Annabelle began to notice that the children returned home in an agitated state. Patty was clinging to her more than usual, while Mark was pulling away—becoming sullen and distant from the family, not even allowing Annabelle to embrace him. It would take days after the visit with their father for Mark to return to normal.

Annabelle knew she was not doing anything to alienate Mark, nor was her husband, who was always a kind and loving stepfather to both children. She finally talked to her daughter and found out that her ex-husband and his live-in girlfriend were trashing her every chance they had.

Patty didn't want to talk about it, but as time went on, Annabelle pushed her to open up so that she could find out exactly what was happening during the visits. Patty told her that most of the time when she was supposed to be with her father, she was at an indoor roller-skating rink where there were older teenagers. Patty admitted they were "pretty wild." On the other hand, Mark was the one who spent time with his father, and was also the one hearing a steady stream of defamatory comments about his mother.

Patty revealed that she had told her father she didn't want to hear the things he said about her mother. That was when he had started depositing Patty at the skating rink at noon and leaving her there until late at night, both days of the weekend. When Annabelle confronted her ex-husband about the situation, he denied that he was doing what Patty accused him of. Patty called him a liar, which ultimately led to a serious rift between father and daughter. Though Annabelle wanted to shield Mark from the trashing, she didn't know what to do. Because of Ross's continuous threats to seek full custody of Mark, Annabelle allowed his visits to continue until Ross unilaterally stopped picking up either child.

Eventually, Ross remarried another woman, one who could not have children, and they moved out of state. Today neither of the children sees their father. He cut off all contact with Patty when she graduated from high school, and a couple of years later he completely stopped seeing Mark, then eighteen and a freshman in college. Ross never offered an explanation for this complete rupture in the relationship with his children.

Patty remains close to her mother and stepfather, but Mark is estranged from everyone. Annabelle is convinced that losing Mark is directly related to her ex-husband's parental alienation campaign. As a child, he was powerless against that kind of expert negative influence.

MAKE-BELIEVE MOTIVES FOR ALIENATION

Even in friendly postdivorce relations, the jealousy triggered when one of the divorced parents finds love again can lead to mishandling of the children as pawns to hurt the ex-spouse. A common tactic is for the parent doing the denigrating to claim that it's due to concern over the children's being upset by the remarriage. Dr. Warshak calls this a "pretended motive," and recognizes it as rationalization when a parent says, "It doesn't matter to me what she wants to do with her life, but my children are being harmed by all of this." Too often this is said when the children have demonstrated no signs of distress over the remarriage. When the parent says he's not upset about the remarriage itself, but by the SOB his ex-wife married and his bad influence on the children, it's usually another rationalization.

Of course, pretended motives for parental alienation exist the other way around. The remarried spouse and the new partner may believe they have the perfect family setting and wish the ex would disappear from their lives. By driving a wedge between the children and their other parent, they attempt to fulfill this fantasy.

With remarried families who engage in parental alienation, in addition to the obvious one of revenge, there are three key inducements:

1. The desire to make the stepparent more important by expelling the ex-spouse from the children's lives

2. Rivalry between the ex-spouse and the stepparent

3. The new couple's effort to unite around a common enemy

MOM VERSUS STEPMOM

Stepparents, particularly those who have no children of their own, often feel a sense of rivalry with their spouse's ex. In its mildest form, these feelings pose no problem, and may even benefit the children by motivating the stepparent to do a better job of nurturing the children. When it becomes a strong rivalry, the stepparent may resent sharing the children's love with the other parent, and so he/she begins a pattern of trashing the other parent.

Joey was willing to discuss a very private and painful part of his life. He married Connie a few years after his divorce from Lucy. He and Lucy had two sons, then ages eight and eleven. Connie had never been married before and was looking forward to having a child of her own, but soon learned that she could not conceive. After several years of unsuccessfully trying in vitro fertilization, Connie gave up. Gradually she began a campaign to alienate her stepchildren from their mother in hopes that they would become more her children. When that failed, she set out to persuade her husband to take a better job in another state. Though Joey caved in to her pressure and agreed to the move, he was unhappy at losing contact with his children. Because they lived very far from the nearest airport, the logistics of visitation became almost impossible except on long holidays. Connie felt threatened by Joey's obvious resentment. She then set out to alienate Joey from his children. Again she failed. Connie and Joey ultimately divorced, and Joey relocated close to where his sons were living with their mother and revitalized the relationship with his children.

Joey said, "There was no way I was going to lose my children. When I realized what Connie was doing, I could no longer love her."

Even though Connie was not sending out poisoned messages about

Joey, he understood that not seeing his sons for long periods of time was causing them to withdraw from him. Dr. Warshak cautions that absence of contact with children creates a fertile environment for "poisoned messages to take root and crowd out loving memories of the parent-child relationship."

Stepparents need to understand that they can carve out a place for themselves without having to undermine the child's attachment to the natural parent. Doing what's best for the child also means the custodial parent should support the child's relationship with the non-custodial parent and that parent's spouse. When the remarriage is safe and sound, the need to destructively compete for a child's love is greatly diminished.

The rivalry can also work in reverse: When the ex-spouse is still single, he or she may worry that the child will prefer the two-parent household, because it more closely resembles the intact family that was lost with the divorce. Driven by these worries, the single ex-spouse may try to undermine the child's sense of love and security in the remarried household. In most cases, the child will manifest discomfort and/or anxiety in the presence of the reconstituted family.

THE COMMON ENEMY

When Joan and Frank married, each had children from a first marriage. Joan's children lived with them and visited their father. Frank's children lived with his ex-wife, but Frank had liberal visitation. Frank's ex-wife was independently wealthy, but Frank had to pay generous child support as part of his divorce decree. Joan resented all the money Frank had to pay his ex-wife for child support, although she'd been well aware of Frank's financial obligations when she married him. They quarreled about finances as many families do, particularly remarried families.

One way to strengthen family unity is to find a common goal. Unfortunately, in some families one or even both of the former spouses become the enemies in common. Perversely, constructing an enemy camp becomes a substitute, a deflection, for other problems in their household. Sometimes, this protects the couple from the worry generated by the prospect of another divorce.

Joan did most of the bad-mouthing of Frank's ex. Even though Frank didn't want to participate, he allowed it to go on rather than risk losing his wife's affections. When he began to see the adverse effect it was having on his children, he begged Joan to stop. She took that as a sign that Frank was rejecting her. Hostilities between them escalated until they went to see a family therapist. Through the therapist's efforts, Frank was able to assure Joan of his love. The therapist also helped Joan understand how important it was to Frank's sense of self-worth to be able to support his children even though his ex-wife had ample funds. Usually, when the common enemy is vanquished, the conflicts reappear, but that did not happen with Frank and Joan. Thanks to the intervention of the family therapist, they were able to repair their relationship because of their love for each other and their desire to make the marriage work. In time, Frank and Joan were able to blend their families successfully, primarily because they were wise enough to seek help when it was desperately needed.

Remember this: There is no reason that children should be subjected to adult misbehavior, nor should children have to choose between parents. They are capable of having close ties to both their father/mother and stepfather/stepmother. Divorce is traumatic enough. Don't add to the trauma by setting up opposing factions. The more adults who are nurturing to the children, the better it is for the children and, ultimately, for the successfully blended family.

HOW TO COMBAT ALIENATION

It is essential to recognize the problem of alienation as soon as it rears its ugly head, because early intervention is critical in maintaining access between the "target" parent and his or her children. As previously explained, remarriage is often the event that sets off a parent to begin a campaign of alienation. Don't hesitate to ask your ex to put himself/herself in your place and imagine how he/she would like you to react with the children in the event of remarriage.

Counseling is a good beginning, but often the alienating parent is unwilling to see a therapist—plus the fact that it rarely works fast enough to halt the destructive behavior. It doesn't take a vindictive parent long to turn a young child against the other parent. Bear in mind that alienation can occur with either the custodial or the noncustodial parent. The parent who relies on visitation may be denied access, or the child can be brainwashed to such an extent that the child doesn't want the visits. But the visiting parent can also be destructive in turning the child against the custodial parent by a campaign of bad-mouthing that parent. Whatever form the alienation takes, it's a serious problem that needs decisive action.

Joy Browne, Ph.D., a California psychologist, acknowledges that there are occasions when a parent should intrude on the children's visitation with the other parent: ". . . when you feel something is terribly wrong in the relationship, and I do mean terribly." Dr. Browne's definition of this extreme situation: the child seems genuinely fearful of the visit, in which case the custodial parent needs to investigate the basis for the child's fear. The same is true if the child is visiting and doesn't want to return home.

Of course, any serious psychological or physical abuse is reason enough to intrude in the relationship. Dr. Browne cautions, however, that mere reluctance to see the noncustodial parent is not enough to interfere with visitation. Nor would a custodial parent want to interfere if he or she knows the child doesn't want to come home simply because it's not as much fun as visiting with the noncustodial parent who is spending the weekend entertaining the child.

DIVORCE-RELATED MALICIOUS MOTHER SYNDROME

Some cases of chronic visitation interference go beyond attempts at alienating a child from a parent. Ira Daniel Turkat, Ph.D., is a Florida psychologist and expert in the area of child visitation interference. He coined the phrase "divorce-related malicious mother syndrome" in a 1999 article in the *Journal of Family Violence*. He has reported on cases where divorcing wives have attempted to get their ex-husbands fired from work, have had them investigated for (falsely alleged) sexual abuse, have publicly ridiculed them, or have physically harmed them. The disorder is characterized by the mother's (1) attempting to unjustifiably punish her ex-husband; (2) interfering with the father's visitation and access to the child; and (3) engaging in a variety of malicious acts toward the husband, including lying and violating the law. Such individuals rarely see themselves as having a problem, are adept at manipulating others in the campaign against the father and his new family, and are skilled fabricators.

CORRECTIVE STEPS

These corrective steps are intended to apply not just to malicious mother syndrome, but to all aspects of parental alienation and child visitation. Before the situation reaches critical mass—that is, before severely harmful and/or illegal behavior takes place—there are degrees of remedial action that can be taken before the big guns of legal action are brought out. The obvious first step is talking to your ex about the negativity the child is displaying. This needs to be done in a calm and conciliatory tone.

You might say, "I'm beginning to see signs of resentment toward me whenever Johnny comes home after visiting with you. It may be that he's enjoying his time with you, and doesn't want to come home, but if it's a result of things he's hearing that you're saying about me, then I want it to stop. I make a point of not saying negative things about you, and hope you will do the same. Johnny loves both of us, and I want it to stay that way. That would be best for Johnny and for both of us."

If warnings don't work, family therapy is the next best step. If you can get your ex to agree to participate in therapy, that would be all the better, but if that's not possible, then it's worthwhile to proceed with just you and your child. Often good therapists can enlist the cooperation of the resistant parent by explaining that the child is being harmed. If the problem continues to grow and the damage is evident, then the only way to get a resistant parent into therapy may be through legal action. If you're the visiting parent and visitation is being interfered with or denied completely, court intervention may be necessary before serious damage to the relationship occurs.

To fully understand what it means to enlist the court, it's best to understand judicial limitations. First, bear in mind that the adversarial tone is likely to worsen once legal action commences. That's why it's wise to use legal action only as a last resort. Second, from a practical perspective, there is little the courts can do to prevent alienation. The legal system has a variety of characteristics (such as the length of time and expense of getting a decision) that unfortunately perpetuate interference with visitation by a parent dedicated toward that end.

The *time factor* is always a major hurdle. For one thing, it can often take months to get a court appearance. Also, most judges will bend over backward to allow each side to adequately present the case at its own pace. Giving everyone his or her day in court slows the process. And attorneys are prone to procrastinate either by design or by laxity.

Expense is another complicating factor. Attorneys' fees are especially high for court hearings. The family whose income supports two households is in an especially poor position to raise the money for these legal fees.

And the *matter of proof* is another complicating factor. The court system can be powerfully manipulated by a good liar. For example, a father who accuses the mother of interfering with visitation may find that the mother not only denies the accusation but charges that the father doesn't keep to the visitation schedule. Typically, there are no witnesses, so the court is faced with a swearing contest. That's exactly when courts are prone to sidestep the issue and order both sides to cooperate. And that means the father is thrown right back to square one. Rarely will a court impose jail time or heavy fines on the custodial parent, so these savvy and malicious parents learn to take full advantage of the court's ineffectiveness. It should be noted the judicial system is well aware of its own shortcomings when there is an absence of proof.

Family court is the best venue for such cases, but not every state has courts devoted exclusively to family issues. (Family court works best when the child can be brought in to testify, particularly when there is serious abuse.) These are the courts that employ mediators and family therapists, and can actually do some good.

The court that handled the divorce also has continued jurisdiction and can be asked to intervene. This court has the power to provide external motivation for the parties to do the right thing. By external motivation, I mean the court's power to impose fines or even incarcerate the violator.

No one likes to run to court to solve problems, but in this situation, where profound harm can be done so quickly, the court must be called upon to step in and impose its power to order evaluation and treatment as soon as possible. Separate treatment for the child and for the alienating parent is usually necessary. Therapy is particularly useful in allowing the alienating parent to release hostility and to better understand the damage inflicted on the children by his or her actions.

Failure to comply with the court's order means that sanctions can be imposed. When the perpetrating parent knows that the court has the ability to change the terms of custody and visitation, that parent usually becomes receptive to therapy and the alienating behavior is more likely to abate.

A word of caution: Establish proof before enlisting the court to assist you. It may even be necessary to employ a private investigator to help you gather evidence of the wrongdoing.

REPAIRING A RUPTURED RELATIONSHIP

If you have been the target of an alienation campaign, don't wait patiently for your child to want to see you. That time may not come until it's too late to repair the relationship. Enforce your right to see your child. Lost time with your children can never be recaptured. And at all times, let the alienating parent know that you have no intention of relinquishing your child—that it is not an option! Following are some suggestions for repairing the rift:

• Be calm and kind with the children. Don't prove your ex to be right about you. Don't engage in tit for tat—"If you don't want to see me,

I don't want to see you." Or as one parent said, "You need to re-member that this is a two-way street." It isn't! It's one way as long as the child is not an adult. The parent is the adult and must offer an open door and unconditional love.

- Make sure your spouse understands the importance of this relation-ship. Stepparents should do all they can to provide a warm and re-ceptive environment for the visiting children. They must also be supportive of the relationship by allowing the targeted parent to spend important remedial time alone with the child.

- When you are with the children, do things that are fun and free of conflict.

- Don't argue with them about the derogatory comments they are making. Realize that they are obviously repeating what they've heard from the alienating parent. Change the subject. Distract them from the negative attacks.

- Don't babble in a steady stream of self-glorification or look-what-I've-done-for-you lists. They won't sell.

- Don't retaliate by devaluing the parent who is doing the alienating. When the child says, "Mom says you're no good," you could try ig-noring it, but if the comments keep coming, you might try this ap-proach: "Your mom's been upset or working hard, and she's mad at me. People who are mad say things they don't really mean. She knows I love you."

- When your children insist they want to go home long before the visit has ended, try to plan something you know they enjoy, and re-mind them how much you want to be with them. Gentle persuasion is best. If that doesn't work, arrange to take them home. Forcing a child to be with you against their will can backfire.

- Don't make a habit of turning your visiting children over to the step-parent while you go to the office or to the golf course. It's okay to do so once in a while, but try to avoid it. Kids of divorced parents are

supersensitive and know when they're being pawned off on someone else.

• Make sure you're complying with your financial obligations according to the terms of your divorce decree. By staying in compliance,
  you will have the court's sympathetic ear.

EX-SPOUSES ARE PEOPLE, TOO

If your ex-husband has remarried, his wife has to deal with you, the
same way you are dealing with your new husband's ex-wife. Put in
terms of fair play, we should begin to understand ex-spouses are people, too. Sometimes exes are troublesome even if they're not awful
people. They, too, have pressures on them that affect the way they speak
and act. While that is not an excuse for bad behavior, we may want to
avoid overreacting and being petty about small matters.

Assume for a moment that you are remarried and have an ex-husband.
If you can see your ex-husband living in a furnished apartment because
that's all he can now afford, or getting ill, or spending holidays alone
and having no one to help him, then dealing with him will be easier.
Even if these images are sappy, it doesn't make them any less real. Or,
if you have an ex-wife, think of her suddenly having to manage her
job, the children, and the house all by herself. Remember when you
came home and gave the children a bath while she cooked dinner? Now
she's doing it all—cooking, serving, cleaning, checking on homework,
plus putting the children to bed. If she hasn't remarried, there's no one
to help. You can say it serves her right, and she can say the same thing,
but what does that achieve, not only for the two of you but for the
children?

Divorce can leave people in a miserably unhappy state even when
they agreed to the divorce or actually initiated it. Everyone needs time
to heal the wounds, and during that time of healing, people often do
things that are unkind, unfair, unjust—or downright mean. There is
bound to be a degree of hostility that grows out of this transitional period,
not only between former spouses but between the current spouse and
the husband or wife's ex.

This hostility is particularly evident between second wives and ex-wives, especially when there are children. If you are the second wife, remember the "ex-" before the word *wife* does not obviate the fact that the husband previously lived in a married state with a different woman, one he made vows to just as he made vows to you. He and this other woman had children together, so they are intrinsically bound to each other in a way that all the legal divorce language cannot totally negate. This connection doesn't mean he still loves his ex-spouse, the mother of his children. Although her relationship to her ex-husband has been legally reduced to alimony, child support, or both, the arrangement can still produce stress, frustration, and complex entanglement, and of course varying degrees of dependency. Furthermore, she has power and influence because of the children. As has been graphically shown, she can be your worst nightmare and make everyone crazy, or the two of you can work toward an amicable relationship for the benefit of all. Even when baited beyond reason, try not to say something so hurtful that it can never be forgotten. The worst of situations can improve, so it is best that hurtful language not be indelibly etched in the mind of the former spouse.

THE FURY OF FIRST WIVES

There is a boundless well of shared female fury among discarded first wives. It is directed at the imbalance of power that allows men to use up the best years of a woman's life, then trade her in for a newer and younger model. The fury righteously grows out of every aspect of that scenario—the obsession with youth and looks, the disparity of income, and the devaluation of the woman's contribution to the family and to the man's success. Is it any wonder the first wife goes through temporary insanity when replaced by an ingenue who can now partake in all the glory and luxury these men have achieved and when often their success is due to the support they received from their disposable first wives?

"We're talking about betrayal," said author Olivia Goldsmith, who wrote *The First Wives Club* and was herself a divorced and down-sized first wife. "These guys are stealing not only the present but also the past. And after they steal part of your life, then they steal your property." After Goldsmith wrote her best-selling book, her publisher sponsored a contest that produced 1,500 tragic stories of first wives. The winning story told of a husband who after twenty-three years of marriage ran off with his secretary, leaving the wife to cope with their child's cancer. That brings to mind former Speaker of the House of Representatives Newt Gingrich, who chose to ask his first wife for a divorce while she was recuperating in the hospital after a bout with breast cancer. In short order, he married his second wife, Marianne.

In a similar fashion, Marianne Gingrich was replaced by another ingenue, but not before she had her "pound of flesh" by going public with all the details of Newt's ongoing affair, which ultimately led to his resignation.

First wives often find themselves financial losers in the divorce. According to the Bureau of Labor Statistics, in 2001, divorced mothers earned salaries that were 50 percent lower than those of their ex-husbands. Women make up 46.5 percent of the workforce but earn 76 cents to a man's dollar. One out of every two marriages ends in divorce, with ex-wives' standard of living dipping significantly more than their husbands'. And court-ordered child support does not make up for the difference. According to a 1996 *Good Housekeeping* article, "Divorced Dads Fight Back," court-ordered payments for nearly five million fathers averaged a little more than $3,000 a year. This was about 7 percent of their incomes. Even at that, only about half of the divorced fathers managed to make their payments in full; another quarter paid none of it.

One woman—who for financial reasons had to relocate and move in with her mother—claims her ex-husband at first met his financial obligations, and then, for a period of three years, stopped paying her health insurance premiums, her alimony, and child support. And she couldn't afford to hire a lawyer to sue him for it. But when he saw the children during visitation, he bought them expensive toys, while she worked two part-time jobs to pay for braces for their teeth. "I was living paycheck to paycheck, while he had a fancy little sports car and a boat. I have to admit when he began to have back problems and a whole lot of pain even after two operations, I felt vindicated."

There is a strong temptation to categorize ex-wives as bitchy, cling-ing, demanding, nuts, and the like. Just as stepmothers get a bum rap, ex-wives do, too. It's important to the remarriage that the new spouse understand what gave rise to this rage. Empathy goes a long way. It can help the second wife tolerate some of the outrageous (not criminal) an-tics of a discarded, angry first wife.

THE STEPFATHER DIFFERENCE

Family counselors find that ex-husbands do not exhibit the same degree of animosity toward their former wives' husbands as ex-wives do toward their former husbands' current wives. When men become step-fathers, there's much less destructive rivalry with the natural father than there is between the stepmother and the natural mother. Many experts believe men are not as prone to engage in petty bickering, but maybe it's also because their identities are less under attack. Bickering is a tac-tic of defeat. Typically men are not as possessive and jealous as women are with their children. It isn't that men don't care about their children, but they aren't as viscerally attached, and beyond that, they are much more inclined to accept changes brought on by divorce.

A recent British study was reported in the book *Growing Up in Stepfamilies,* cowritten by G. G. Barnes. The study found that "step-fathers who were accepted and liked were those who remained at the margins of the household, bringing in additional income and com-panionship for the mother, doing small things for the child, but rarely becoming intimate, and leaving control of the household order and dis-cipline to the mother." The researchers concluded that there was an ab-sence of strong feelings, positive or negative, toward most stepfathers because they so often played a marginal role in the family.

"I wish things were different," says one father, "but there's not much I can do about the way it is. I have children living on the other side of the country with their mother and stepfather. I just hope he's do-ing for my children what I'm doing for my stepchildren."

Not all stepfathers escape negative campaigns, however. "My wife's family is ruining my role as a good stepfather by undermining me at every turn," says one unhappy new stepparent. There are certain pitfalls for stepfathers, particularly with former in-laws. Take the case of Rick and Ellen. This is Rick's first marriage, but Ellen is divorced and has custody of her two children.

"When I first married Ellen," Rick said, "her parents and her sister remarked on how well the kids behaved and thought I was doing a good job as stepfather. I was really flattered, and relieved. About a year later, the grandparents told Ellen I should back off, since I wasn't the children's real father. They resented the fact that the children and I had a good relationship and that they listened to me more than they did to the grandparents. They are forever buying things for the kids to win their love, and they let them get away with misbehaving. I tried explaining to Ellen that these kids need some discipline. It doesn't happen in a vacuum. Now Ellen's family refuse to visit when I'm home, and continue to say disparaging things about me to the kids—none of which are true, by the way."

The wife cannot make her parents change their attitude, but she can, in a kind and sensitive way, change their behavior by letting them know (1) that her marriage to Rick is very important, (2) that she wants them to overcome their resentment or she'll be very hurt by their actions, and (3) the children benefit most from a relaxed and friendly family atmosphere. When her parents realize what's at stake, they may start to play fair.

THREE ISN'T ALWAYS A CROWD

Though most stepmothers I interviewed found the ex-wife, particularly the still single ex-wife, to be extremely difficult to deal with, one stepmother, Charlotte, not only felt comfortable with her husband's ex-wife; she actually looked to her for advice and help with the children. Edward shared custody of the children and lived three miles away from his ex-wife, Elizabeth. Charlotte had never been married before, so when she married Edward, she entered a ready-made family and became an instant stepparent of two children, a boy and a girl, ages ten and six.

Charlotte and Edward started with a clean slate: the divorce between Edward and Elizabeth had been amicable, there was no infidelity in the picture, and they had agreed to joint custody of the children. Their divorce occurred because Elizabeth had a career that she loved and Edward, an old-fashioned chauvinist, resented the time that she had to spend at work. They were always at opposite ends of this important issue and could find no middle ground. They resolved that divorce was the only answer.

Charlotte was genuinely delighted at the idea of having stepchildren, because she had grown up in a family of six children and had looked forward to having a big family herself. She was now at an age when that was unlikely, but she did hope to have at least one child of her own. Before Charlotte and Edward married, they had Elizabeth over for dinner in the house they had just bought. Charlotte assured Elizabeth that she had no desire to replace her as the mother of the children, but hoped instead to be another loving adult in their lives. Because of her challenging career, Elizabeth welcomed the support of Charlotte in raising the children. In effect, Elizabeth sanctioned the remarriage of her ex-husband and made sure to convey her approval to the children. She spoke kindly of Charlotte and helped her children adjust to this new arrangement.

Three years later, when Charlotte had a baby, Elizabeth took the children to the hospital to visit their new half brother. Charlotte was able to accept Elizabeth's continued presence in their lives because, as a stepmother, she saw herself not as the mother's rival for the love of the two older children but rather as an older sister or aunt who was also loved, but in a different way. In fact, she encouraged the children to call her "Aunt" Charlotte so there would be no appearance of rivalry or displacement of Elizabeth. And Charlotte now looked to Elizabeth as a friend who would help her in her new role as mother of a newborn.

Without question, this is an exceptional story—all three adults had the right attitude that made this situation work. Charlotte particularly is a model for stepparents. *Making the effort to establish a compatible relationship with the ex-spouse of the person you intend to marry and assuring that person that you have no intention of usurping their parental role will go a long way in establishing a peaceful blended family.* As long as the stepmother concentrates on her own relationship with her husband, instead of trying to negate his relationship with his ex, she is moving forward to develop a healthy new family, one that includes the stepchildren and their mother's participation in a constructive way.

Helpful Guidelines

- **Don't be naïve.** Even in the best of circumstances, there are problems—and the likelihood is that they will always exist in one form or another. Address problems with a kind heart and a willingness to be flexible and forgiving.

- **Take the long view.** The presence of children from a prior marriage tethers that ex to your life, and not just when the children are small. It can easily continue to the time when the children are married adults with children of their own. Since there are so many years involved, it's best to never say or do anything that is unforgettable and unforgivable. Even if the ex is an incessant nuisance, say and do as little as possible that will create further antagonism. Remember that your attitudes and actions get recorded in the minds of the people you have to live with, including your children and stepchildren.

- **Don't obsess about the situation with his ex-wife.** The more you obsess about her, the more she gets to stay in your head and in your home without paying rent. If her presence is harmful to your marriage, stop thinking and talking about her. Don't enter the fray. It only exacerbates the situation.

- **Allow your husband to deal with his ex-wife regarding the children, especially on financial matters.** Even if you feel that your husband is being trampled and that he's turning into a wimp when it comes to his ex, you're not helping your marriage when you take over or nag him into doing things he doesn't want to do. If the situation is important enough to him, he'll do something about it himself.

He's a grown man and doesn't need you to do the job his mother should have done before she turned him out into the world. Staying out of his previous commitments takes practice and time. If you find it impossible to restrain yourself, get counseling to help you deal with feelings of loss of control over your marital life. *And be truthful with the counselor, because that's the only way to get help.*

- **Let your wife deal with her ex when it comes to finances.** The natural father's failure to pay child support on a timely basis, or pay it at all, is a common problem. Stepfathers should be supportive of their wives in dealing with this problem. Usually, these mothers are doing the best they can to collect child support. The last thing they need is an angry spouse telling them to get tougher. Even if it seems unfair for the new husband to have to support his wife's children from a previous marriage, it's better than destroying the marital relationship over the issue of money.

- **Don't buy the love of the children.** Whether you are the parents, the stepparents, or the grandparents, don't try to outshine one another by being a year-round Santa Claus. It doesn't help the children. It hurts them.

- **Harmony doesn't come from shared hatred.** Family unity and happiness cannot be based on sharing a common enemy—an ex-spouse. It may appear to work for a while, but it will ultimately backfire. If there is a contentious relationship between your spouse and his or her ex, don't jump into the fray. Instead, try to be a peacemaker and work toward defusing the hostility.

- **Try giving reasonable assurances to the mother/father of your stepchildren.** If your husband/wife's divorce from his or her former spouse was amicable, try offering reassurance that you have no intention of trying to replace his or her parental role with the children, but hope to be another loving and nurturing adult in the child's life.

- **Use court as the last resort.** If, after sincere and reasonable steps have been taken to placate a hateful and vindictive ex-spouse, that ex continues to be destructive—particularly by engaging in acts that are injurious to children, such as "parental alienation" or "malicious mother syndrome"—seek legal assistance to petition the court. The court has the power to order treatment or even change custodial arrangements. And remember, the courts work at a snail's pace, and not very well at all when there is a lack of proof.

three

The Fade-Out Father

Secret Three:

Remain a part of your children's lives. They need you.

Although you won't find the appellation "fade-out father" in Webster's dictionary, it is how I often referred to my first husband (over twenty-five years ago). More important, it *still* is a widespread and wrenching by-product of divorce, not just the acrimonious ones but, sadly, those divorces in which the parents parted amicably. In the most basic terms, a fade-out father is a divorced dad who has disengaged from his children and faded out of their lives. For a significant percentage of fathers, the disengagement becomes even more pronounced when he remarries and starts another family. Of course, not all divorced men relinquish their responsibility and connection to their children, but the vast numbers that do ("vast" because the divorce rate is so high) not only create an added painful break from their offspring but set up long-term resentments in their adult children. In addition, the children learn a bad lesson—how to use estrangement as a means of punishment. No one wins.

According to some studies, fathers who *remarry* are less likely to see their children, but other studies show the opposite—that remarriage can bring a father closer to his children from previous marriages. Why this discrepancy? These conflicting results arise out of varying circumstances, including the degree of closeness and interaction the father had with his children during the years he was married to their mother, the geographic proximity to these children after divorce and remarriage, whether he has had children with his new wife, the new wife's attitude toward her husband's previous family, and anger over financial obligations to the ex-wife and children. According to the Bureau of Census of the Department of Health and Human Services, nationwide there are ten million noncustodial nonpaying parents, the "deadbeat dads" who owe roughly $39 billion in child support. Most experts in the field of divorce see a high correlation between fade-out fathers and nonpayment of child support.

In her longitudal study of 1,400 families of divorce, E. Mavis Hetherington concluded that negative long-term effects of divorce have been exaggerated. Nonetheless, she also reported the disturbing finding that by the time the children in the study had reached fifteen, divorced fathers lived an average of four hundred miles away—and that seventy-five miles was the point at which men were less likely to visit. The emotional and physical disengagement of divorced fathers and children was clearly reflected in the interviews the researcher had with the adult children. Only one in three men from divorced families and one in four women reported feeling very close to their fathers, compared with seven out of ten adult children in intact families.

One factor not cranked into Hetherington's study or most other research studies is the changing role of men in today's young families. Many fathers pride themselves on their involvement with their children during the marriage, and are genuinely engaged and skilled parents. Unlike fathers of previous generations, they participate in day-to-day child rearing, and their involvement is often crucial when both parents work. In growing numbers, these men are up for night feedings, they diaper and bathe their toddlers, they tuck them in and read them stories. Whether or not these dads will fade out of their children's lives in the event of divorce is still an open question.

GOOD INTENTIONS GONE BAD

When Harold was divorced, he had the best of intentions to see his children regularly. His former wife, Sally, hoped he would. During the first year postdivorce, Harold showed up every Thursday evening and every other weekend. He would take his seven-year-old daughter and his four-year-old son out to a restaurant and try to catch up on the week's events. But little by little this arrangement began to crumble. Harold's questions to his kids would be met with silence. They told him they didn't remember what they did a few days before. And Harold began to realize that he, too, didn't have much to say to them. These weekday outings were filled with awkward silences and obligatory politeness. The weekend visits were slightly more satisfying, because Harold planned excursions, including visits to his parents' house, where his mother offered the warmth and love the children needed during this period of adjustment. Harold found that being a divorced father was not at all what fatherhood had been like when he and Sally were married. Back then he'd never had to deal with full-time child care—even for two days in a row. Suddenly, he realized how much of the responsibility had been carried by his ex-wife.

Two other major events in Harold's life now came into play. He became involved with Lorraine, a younger woman who had a daughter from her first marriage. And Sally began to ask for more money, claiming she couldn't get back into the workforce without some training and child care help. The road was no longer just bumpy—it was full of potholes. Not only did he and Sally begin to quarrel, but the children now started acting up when he was with them.

"I don't want to spend the whole day doing what you want to do," his daughter whined without a clue that Harold really didn't want to spend hours at the hot, smelly zoo or walk around the mall or sit impatiently in a movie for kids.

"I don't like fish and salads," his son complained loudly. "Why do we have to go to the same restaurant all the time? Why can't we just order pizza and watch TV?"

As Harold sighed with frustration, the milk would spill or the kids wouldn't stay seated or his son would crawl around under the table.

"I've had just about enough," Harold said. "If you can't behave, we won't go anywhere." His warnings went unheeded.

As the children seemed less and less interested in seeing him, Harold began to feel the way many fathers do—rejected and unappreciated. At the same time, Sally was urging him to spend more time with the kids so she could have extra hours to study and do things around the house that she couldn't get to because she was working part-time and taking some courses at the local community college. The more she asked of Harold, the less he wanted to be with the children. His emotions seesawed from anger to guilt about the anger.

Lorraine was the bright spot in Harold's life—they spent more and more time together. Her daughter was growing fond of him, an attachment that Lorraine encouraged. Only two and a half years after the divorce, Harold's visits with his own children were down to no more than once a month, and he wasn't sure his intestinal lining could stand any more McMeals, pizza, and disrespect.

Harold's fade-out is not an excusable reaction to a couple of misbehaving kids who have just had their world turned on its head. And it's that much harder to fathom because in Harold's case geography was not a problem. Nor was physical space for his children in his new apartment. Nor, even, was money. So what kept widening this familial gap? Where did Harold's self-imposed alienation come from?

Most fathers still base their sense of parental authority on their role as caretaker and protector. Once a father is out of the home, he quickly becomes marginalized, unless he makes a concerted effort to engage in the children's day-to-day activities. Visitation arrangements worked out in the lawyer's office or the judge's chambers have little to do with what actually happens. Fathers like Harold who stay in touch with their children in the first couple of years after divorce find it increasingly difficult to be a part-time parent in our culture, and most fathers cannot sustain this ambiguity very long. It didn't help that neither Harold nor his children were easy communicators. But despite the kids' unruly behavior, the ball was squarely in Harold's court.

The fact is Harold may be reaping what he sowed during the marriage. Many men, whether married or divorced, are not willing to give their time to their children, doing things that the children want to do but that the fathers don't want to do. They may be accustomed to claiming their weekends as their own, playing golf or tennis or going fishing with the "boys." After all, they work hard all week. They're entitled. And what are the wives doing all week? Whether they work outside the home or inside it, what about *their* weekends? Since this didn't matter a great deal to many fathers before the divorce, why should it matter now?

It matters for one good reason: fathers are vitally important to the emotional growth of children, particularly children of divorce who don't see their fathers all week. To allow the relationship to disappear is a form of abuse, and one that detrimentally affects the child's ability to form strong emotional ties as he or she reaches adulthood. Few things are as important as the father's presence. Dads often make lots of excuses, including the one Harold made—that the kids didn't seem to care one way or another. While the father pursues his new life without being bothered by the kids, his attitude is actually harming the children. All young children are self-absorbed, and that shouldn't be held against them or be used as a reason to spend less and less time with them. In twenty years, they'll all be wondering what happened to their relationship.

ANGRY ALL THE TIME

Sometimes a father's withdrawal has less to do with the children and more to do with resentment of the ex-wife. If it was her decision to end the marriage or if there is residual animosity between them, chances are he still feels bitter and betrayed. Some men succumb to what seems an easier out: they cut themselves off from any dealings with the ex-wife, to the extent of their not wanting to pick up and deliver the children because it means seeing *her*. Some fathers even admit to avoiding their children because they *remind* him (in looks and/or personality) of his ex-wife.

Bonnie and Dick had two children that they both loved; however, almost from the start, their fifteen-year marriage was miserably unhappy for many reasons. When they married, Dick was thirty years old and Bonnie was twenty. Dick was a clinical psychologist, and Bonnie, intelligent and ambitious, had already graduated from college with a high school teaching certificate. Dick expected Bonnie to *love, honor, and obey,* but she could never be the obedient and submissive wife he wanted. After eight years, two children, and Dick's numerous job changes and relocations, Bonnie's unhappiness was compounded by Dick's affair with one of his patients.

Bonnie knew that if she divorced Dick, he might renege on support. "His sports cars and golf always came before the kids' dental bills," Bonnie explains. When Bonnie went back to a university to get a law degree, Dick was at first agreeable but then resented the time he had to spend doing household chores and babysitting the children. It was the beginning of the end of their marriage. To Dick's chagrin, Bonnie graduated in the top 10 percent of her class and went to work for a law firm. And she met Dwayne, a man who was everything her husband was not: "kind, encouraging, and loving." Because of Bonnie's infatuation with Dwayne, Dick immediately filed for divorce and, in effect, won the race to the courthouse.

Dick's bitterness grew even deeper once Bonnie and Dwayne were married. He hated having to pick up his children, then ages twelve and nine, at the home of his now happily married ex-wife. Everything about Bonnie's new life angered him. And every time he pulled up the driveway of her home, his resentment and rage were evident. He "peeled rubber" as he drove away with the kids in the car. Once he was with the children, he spent a great deal of the time telling them what he thought of their mother.

After three years, Dick's visits with his children grew less frequent, and when he moved out of state, the visits became limited to alternate holidays and two weeks in the summer.

The children dreaded these visits with their father. They were in an unfamiliar place, far from friends, and didn't want to hear Dick's constantly disparaging remarks about Bonnie. They told him how they felt, and his reply was "This is a two-way street. If you don't want to come here, then we won't be seeing much of each other anymore."

And they didn't. There were only two more visits. One was to his oldest child's high school graduation—an awkward and unpleasant encounter—and two years later, he paid a visit to his youngest child's Ivy League university campus. He denigrated the prestigious school and showed no pride in the fact that his child was a student there. That was Dick's last contact with either of his children.

It's been almost twenty years since Dick has seen his children, and he's never seen his grandchildren. He doesn't even know he has any.

THE GRIEF RESPONSE

Surprisingly few researchers have focused on the convoluted relationships between fathers and their children postdivorce. In 1994 Edward Kruk, Ph.D., a professor of social work at the University of British Columbia, performed a survey of eighty noncustodial fathers. The most startling finding of Dr. Kruk's survey was that fathers who were highly involved and attached during the marriage were those most likely to become disengaged after divorce and remarriage. Some *completely faded* from their children's lives, explaining that they were unable to cope with the diminished contact that comes with being a noncustodial parent.

Dr. Kruk concluded that the father who must face less contact with his children because he is no longer living with them is so saddened by his diminished role that he finds it less stressful to walk away than to accept the new terms of his paternal relationship. Sixty-eight of the eighty fathers said that the absence of their children had serious negative effects on them. Depression, sense of loss, and constant worry or yearning for their children were the most commonly cited emotions. Fading out of their children's lives became their means of coping with the grief. Their egoism and their unwillingness to consider the long-term impact on their children is the real tragedy.

Gail Sheehy, in her book *Understanding Men's Passages,* found that one of the most prevalent emotional deprivations men experienced as adults was the feeling of "hunger" for the father who was missing from their lives as children. For most men, this need surfaced during middle age. She notes, "Father hunger is particularly sharp among men who have lost close contact with their children as the result of divorce."

Sheehy concludes that men who were harmed by lost contact with their own fathers are more prone to relive that feeling of loss when they lose a close relationship with their own children: "In one discussion after another, it was the men who described being intimately involved with their children who felt more manly, more indispensable, more emotionally grounded."

Logically, children who lose contact with their fathers will suffer the same harm, and experience the same "father hunger" as adults. The danger is that this entire fade-out-father phenomenon will be recycled over and over again from one generation to the next unless the cycle is broken. Children are the victims twice: first as children and then in adulthood.

Conversely, Dr. Kruk's survey found that fathers who during marriage took on the more peripheral role of breadwinner and occasional caregiver for their children were more likely to develop meaningful postdivorce father-child relationships. For these fathers, divorce and remarriage provided a new structure for more involvement in their children's lives.

THE REMARRIAGE FADE-OUT

When men invest in new family obligations and responsibilities, and particularly when they have additional children, the offspring from their first marriages often take a backseat to the new children. This attitude among some remarried fathers was tersely summarized based on one man's interview in a National Survey of Children conducted by Colby College Professor of Social Work Terry Arendell, Ph.D.: "I used to have them come visit me," the father said, "but I just have no room in my place for them now that I'm remarried. It's like the kids don't belong in my life anymore."

One father saw his new marriage as a fresh start: "I was moving on with my life; I wanted my kids to be as happy as I was." But his daughter viewed it as a disaster. "I saw it as the end of my relationship with my father as I had known it. And I *liked* my new stepmother!" Some fathers see remarriage as trading in old obligations for new ones. From

the father's point of view, he isn't callously disregarding his responsibilities but rather *redefining* his priorities. Everyone, including the father, should know that this is a selfish rationalization.

Happily, there is a significant percentage of fathers who actually
reengage after remarriage, because they can finally provide a happier,
more comfortable family environment for their children from previous
marriages. As one man I interviewed put it, "My bachelor apartment
didn't have enough room for both my kids. Besides, they hated my
cooking."

PRESENCE, NOT PRESENTS

The year after his parents' divorce, Joshua spent every other weekend
with his father, Martin, a man who thought the gift of love came in the
form of toys. Every time he came to get Joshua, he had a present. And
it was always a weekend of nonstop gift giving. Movies, the zoo, the
water park, the circus, or whatever was in town—his father was forever
trying to keep Joshua busy and amused. He gave Joshua anything the
boy asked for. But no matter how hard he tried, Joshua felt a constant
tension and anxiety. He wanted to just feel normal with his father, "like
we used to," he said. He missed quiet times and easy conversations with
his dad. Besides, he could tell his father was exhausted after the weekend and couldn't wait to take him home.

The second year after the divorce, Martin began dating a woman,
whom he included on these frenetic weekends. She turned out to be just
as stressed from them as Joshua and his father. Gradually, the visits ta-
pered off.

Joshua recognized that making an appointment to see a parent can
be so artificial that it's unpleasant even before they're in each other's
company: "Although I liked my father's girlfriend, it was easier to be
with him when she wasn't there. When she was, he talked to her, not
to me."

The following year, Martin married his girlfriend, and the visits
with Joshua became almost nonexistent. They had an occasional phone
conversation, but even then the level of discomfort continued. Joshua

admits that he has lost his dad, and he doesn't know what he could have done to prevent it from happening.

The sad truth is that there was probably nothing Joshua could have done to keep a close relationship with a father who was obviously losing the emotional tie to his son. *Parents can do so many things to maintain relationships with their children, but children can do very little to keep close to a parent who doesn't care about them anymore.*

NEW WIFE, NEW BABY

Common sense tells us that the new wife who encourages her husband to spend time with his children goes a long way toward preventing the chasm that develops between fathers and their children from previous marriages. This encouragement, however, is not likely to occur if the husband's ex-wife is on a campaign to discredit the new wife. Children naturally absorb the attitudes of their parents, particularly the parent with primary custody who is tending to all their daily needs. If their mother is feeding them a toxic brainwashing against the father's new wife, the children will naturally develop antipathy to her. Even if she understands the origin of the problem, no wife wants her husband to be in the company of stepchildren who are making disparaging remarks about her.

Thirty-year-old Joanne says of her own noncustodial stepmother, "I have always liked her. She's the main reason my father kept in touch with my sister and me, at least during the years immediately after my parents' divorce. Even when they were dating, she encouraged my father to pick us up on the weekends and do things with just my sister and me for part of the day; then we'd all do things together. A few years after she and my father were married, they had another child, my half sister, Roberta. That's when my stepmother stopped influencing my father to see us—and he rarely did after that. There aren't even any pictures of us in their house. Everywhere we look, there are pictures of Roberta. I honestly believe my relationship with my father would have continued to be close had it not been for Roberta."

In Dominique Browning's memoir, *Around the House and in the*

Garden, she tells of her teenage son's withdrawal into depression because of his father's marriage to another woman. The son's fears are poignantly expressed in his own words: "It isn't even the wedding. . . . I just know they'll have a new baby. I'll be going from your house part-time, to his house part-time. The baby will be living with him all the time. I'll be nobody's full-time baby."

These are the worries of children, even of teenagers, who are grappling with the prospect of being displaced from their parents' lives by the presence of a new family. For many children, it becomes even more intense when both parents have remarried and produced *two* new stepparents. The children's security is shaken. Ideally, the parents' remarriage should serve as a base for rebuilding that security, but it doesn't always work that way. These children are not living in Never Never Land. Their anxieties are not unreasonable, given the finite amount of time a parent has to give and the presence of others in that parent's life who are going to be making their own justifiable demands on that parent's time.

Especially hurtful to children is to see their fathers withdraw from them while being model dads to the offspring of a second marriage or to stepchildren. There's a powerful scene in Ron Howard's film *Parenthood* where a child asks his divorced father if he can come and live with him and he's told, "No, it wouldn't work out right now." The teenage son smashes everything in his father's office, including a framed portrait of his dad with his new wife and baby.

John Lennon was someone who devoted more time to his new son, Sean, than he had given to his older son, Julian. On the twentieth anniversary of his father's death, Julian posted a message on his Web site in which he attacked the ex-Beatle for having been a derelict father. "I had a great deal of anger toward Dad because of his negligence and his attitude. . . . Although he was definitely afraid of fatherhood, the combination of that and his life with [his second wife] Yoko Ono [and his son, Sean, by her] led to the real breakdown of our relationship." Because of his marriage to Yoko Ono, "Dad was sucked into a black hole and all of his strength was consumed."

Only at the end of his Web site message did Julian strike a more upbeat note, declaring his love for his half brother and saying, "Dad, wherever you are, may your light shine as long as we do!"

There are many variables that widen the chasm between the non-custodial father and his children. Experts agree that geographic distance is a major hurdle. Fathers who live a greater distance from their children, especially when resources are scarce, are less likely to maintain contact. Remarriage only adds to the problems of time and money, particularly when stepfathers are asked to assume the financial obligations for their new wives and stepchildren. That may not leave the father with money to pay for expensive airfare to transport his children for visitation. When the ex-wife has remarried as well, a father may feel that he has been replaced by the stepfather, and conclude that given the stepfather's daily access to the children, the father is not as needed or desired as he once was. There is also the father who lessens his contact with his own children in order to please his new wife. To forge good alliances with his stepchildren, he shows more concern for them than for his own children; after all, they're the ones now living under the same roof with him.

ARE YOU STILL MY DAD?

Jack's two children—Laney, age fourteen, and Tim, age eleven—lived with their mother after their parents divorced. During the marriage, Jack had been an active, nurturing parent. Jack has remarried, and his second wife, Carol, has custody of her ten-year-old son, Bobby. Carol's husband had visitation rights every other weekend, just as Jack did with his two children. It *seemed* like a good idea to have all the children one weekend and none the next. But this arrangement was an instant flop. Jack's two children would arrive to find inadequate space—they slept in sleeping bags, while Bobby continued to sleep in his bed in his own room. Laney was at the age when she wanted some privacy, not only from the adults but also from the two younger boys, her brother and stepbrother. She asked her father if she could have Bobby's room while she was visiting and the boys could sleep in the den in sleeping bags.

"This is Carol's house," Jack replied, "and I can't ask her to put Bobby out of his room."

Laney explained that she and Tim and Bobby had already talked it over and they were "okay with these sleeping arrangements," but Jack said the matter was not open for discussion. Laney, feeling hurt and rejected, said she didn't want to visit her new family anymore, and that included her father.

"Suit yourself," Jack said.

Laney began to cry. "Are you still my dad?" she asked.

CAST-OFFS BECOME FADE-OUT FATHERS

In original families, the mother performs many functions to validate the father's role in the family even if he's not spending that much time with the children—sometimes fewer hours than after divorce. Once the family comes apart, the mother is usually unwilling to encourage and sustain the father's connection to their children. This is especially true if the two are having fights about money or if the mother resents or is bitter about her ex-husband's remarriage.

The words of one divorced mother—"My ex-husband has visitation rights, but the kids don't want to be with him. Should I force them?"— are repeated by many women who have played a role in their children's diminished interest in seeing their fathers. Frequently, when a woman remarries after an embittered divorce, she will discourage the children from seeing their natural father and encourage them to bond more with their stepfather, particularly if the stepfather is kind and receptive to her children.

One now middle-aged woman recalled the subtle, and even unwitting, efforts made by her mother to turn her against her father: "My mother had the clear impression that whatever my father wanted to do was dangerous or inappropriate. But I remembered him as a fun-loving person, someone with whom I actually enjoyed skiing down a mountain on his shoulders and going to a piano bar at the local hotel and riding hell-for-leather around town in his old army jeep."

She recalled her mother's unwillingness to allow the relationship to develop naturally and her efforts to control every aspect of their interaction. "Not even once did she encourage me to send my father a birthday card, or do anything that might have allowed him to feel that it was a two-way relationship." Acknowledging that her father was a fade-out kind of man in the rest of his life and thinking aloud, she said, "None of those overtures might have done any good in preventing him from detaching himself from me, but I know he tried, and he was made to feel inadequate."

The damage isn't confined to younger children. Susan was a twenty-year-old college junior when her parents divorced. "My father simply disappeared out of our life for a year. While he was going through his midlife crisis, my mother was going through her own struggle—feelings of rejection and loss of confidence in herself as a woman."

It's now seven years later. Her parents rarely speak to each other except for their children's important events, such as graduations, or in the case of Susan, her wedding. When the parents are forced to be together, it's very awkward and unpleasant for everyone. Susan herself is considering divorce from her husband of five years. They have no children. "I feel as if I were cheated out of a father since my parents' divorce," Susan says. "My mother tried to transfer her bitterness toward him to us. When my dad walked away from all of us, I thought he had stopped loving me. I was angry at my mother because of having to deal with her rage toward my father. He didn't want to be married to my mother, but I have since learned that he still wanted to be my dad. The problem was that my mother made it almost impossible for him to see us without having to confront her wrath. You never really get over the loss, and it has backfired. I'm angry with my mother for cheating me out of a father. I keep thinking the scars of losing my father for so long have probably led to my own inability to make my marriage work."

Children strive to be loyal to the parent they're with, even if they've just threatened to move to the home of the other parent. Children of divorce are filled with contradictory feelings—mainly, divided loyalties and a fear of losing one or both parents. They want to please even though they don't fully understand what's going on between their parents. Add to that the manipulative quality of children and the result is that the child may balk when it's time to visit with Dad. They intuitively know the mother feels better when the child shows this preference for her. When the child is with the father and it's time to go home, using that same reasoning, that very same child might balk at going home to Mom. *For children, it's as difficult to leave a parent as it is for the parent to let them go.* They feel even less control and power over their lives than any adult does, less capable of doing what's necessary to make everyone happy.

One father described how on the drive home his daughter would have a sudden mood shift from happy to pouting. When he asked her why she was acting that way, she said, "If I walk in happy, Mom will be angry with me."

On a personal note, one day my youngest stepdaughter said she was glad her older sister couldn't come that weekend and visit her father and our family.

"Why?" I asked.

"Because I can have a good time, and she won't tell Mom."

"Why do you think your sister does that?'

"Mom hates for us to visit you and Dad. If Mom thinks we've had a good time, she takes it out on us. My sister's a tattletale anyway, and she plays up to everyone to get what she wants. Everyone but you."

A caveat to mothers: For the sake of the children you love, it's important to encourage a relationship with their father, to reassure them that they are going to have fun and that you will be there waiting for them when they return. In other words, it's necessary to validate the visit, to make it seem worthwhile, and to let the children know it's the best way to make their father feel good, because he truly misses them. Convince them that you are not upset by their decision to visit with their father, and dispel the notion in the child's mind that it's necessary to show a preference for you by hesitating to spend time with the father.

Ask yourself how you would feel if the roles were reversed. Children who are seemingly very close to the mother can reach adolescence and turn on her for good reason, for no *apparent* reason, and even for no reason. In most states, at fourteen, children can choose the parent they want to live with, so you might be faced with the very same problem you have created for your ex, and you might one day need his cooperation in order to visit with your children.

TIE BREAKERS

Here's a story of a mother who took the opposite tack: actively supporting the father-daughter relationship even when her child was ready to
cast it aside. Colleen lived with Madelyn, her mother, and Harrison, her
stepfather, and visited Travis, her father, one night a week and every
other weekend. One weekend, she refused to go with her father, but was
unwilling to explain why. There were two more subsequent refusals before Madelyn finally persuaded her daughter to talk about the problem.
Colleen had always been close to her dad and considered his approval to
be very much a part of her own confident self-image. But then Colleen
went through puberty. She gained weight and her hips widened too
much, and because she was short-waisted, the changes in her body
shape became depressing for the girl. No matter how much she dieted,
she couldn't lose weight. Her father started calling her "Chubby
Checkers." This made Colleen even more depressed, but angry, too.
Soon she began running to the bathroom after dinner to throw up.

Fortunately, Madelyn recognized the symptoms of bulimia and
took Colleen to see a psychologist who specialized in eating disorders.
Colleen made a quick recovery, because the problem was addressed almost immediately, thanks to a very attentive and knowledgeable mother.
But during those months of treatment, Colleen refused all contact with
her father. She cut herself off from him, and from her paternal grandparents because of their closeness to their son.

Again, it was Colleen's mother who broke the impasse. She repeatedly encouraged Colleen to begin seeing her father again, even though
she was as angry with him as her daughter was for his gross insensitiv-
ity. As she explained, "It was hard for me to push my daughter to see her
father—to convince her it was the right thing to do—because I wasn't
actually sure that it *was* the right thing to do, even though the psychologist said it was. But I decided to follow the doctor's advice, despite my
misgivings."

What further complicated this father-daughter relationship was the
father's resentment at having been shut out of his daughter's life. So much
so that he was unable to see that his sarcasm, during this most vulnerable time in her development, had had a profoundly negative effect on

Colleen. He denied being at fault, declaring that he had been a good and loving father who never missed a visitation and always provided his daughter with anything she needed. He was now ready to walk away from her, because he felt the divorce and its aftermath had already been too much for him. He had been devastated when Madelyn first had announced her surprise decision to divorce; plus, the financial setbacks he'd experienced as a result of the divorce had colored all his genuine feelings for Colleen.

When he finally agreed to see the psychologist who had been treating Colleen, he was made to realize that her rejection of him was his fault, not hers. Had there not been a wise mother and a psychologist involved in this situation, the father would have most likely faded completely from his daughter's life.

ARE THERE WAYS OF AVOIDING FADE-OUT?

Recognizing that noncustodial parents, particularly fathers, are at risk of fading out of their children's lives, are there steps that the families can take to avoid the problem? Several paths come to mind.

Shared Custody

When courts decide custody and visitation issues, they are usually guided by this principle: what is in the best interests of the child? In almost all instances, that means having the child in contact with both parents. Unless there is severe abuse or neglect, the children are emotionally better off by having a good relationship with their father. The child has half the father's genes, and deserves to be loved and nurtured by both parents.

If the divorced parents cannot get along, there is no easy answer for the fade-out-father problem. However, when the divorced couple can maintain a friendly relationship, family courts often recommend that they share custody of the children, rather than have the traditional award of sole custody to the mother with reasonable visitation rights for the father. Even if the original divorce decree did not provide for shared custody, the parties can always agree to modify their custody arrangements.

Joint custody comes in two forms: joint *legal* custody and joint *physical* custody. Joint legal custody offers fathers the right to participate in decisions regarding the child's welfare, particularly regarding the health and education needs of the child. Under joint physical custody, children alternate between the mother's and father's residences based on an agreed-upon schedule. According to the results of two studies, one done in 1989 at the University of Wisconsin and another in 1990 at Stanford University, joint legal custody failed to lure fathers into maintaining close contact with their children, whereas joint *physical* custody made a real difference.

Joint physical custody offers a high-risk/high-payoff strategy. It requires a great deal of communication and cooperation between the parents. Logistical problems are a constant. Johnny's at Dad's house, but the books he needs are at Mom's. The play date scheduled for Friday is in Mom's neighborhood on a day when Johnny is at Dad's house. Unless the parents can work well together, this arrangement can actually intensify conflict. Joint physical custody also assumes that the parents live close to each other (the same school district) and that the father wishes to share nearly equally the tasks of child rearing. When it works, it has the effect of keeping the father an active participant in his children's lives.

Shared custody may not be a panacea, but it can go a long way toward keeping the child in close contact with both parents, as opposed to having the custodial parent in charge of everything.

In any custody arrangement, a very real problem arises when one of the parents wants or needs to move away from the area where the other parent is living. Many family courts have prevented custodial parents from moving out of the state where their ex resides in an effort to keep both parents involved in the child's life.

Since 1996, however, courts in New York and California—states that are judicial trendsetters for the rest of the country, along with a handful of others—have been ruling that a custodial parent can live elsewhere because of remarriage, a job, or even the opportunity to further his or her education. For example, if the mother is the primary caregiver and she married a man whose company requires that he relocate, the court is now willing to consider that the move is necessary and that the terms of visitation need modification. Or perhaps the child spends half the week with his father and half with his mother, but the mother wants to move to another state to go back to school—and to be near her parents, who will provide child care. In these situations, courts have become more flexible. They can offer longer visitation periods to the parent who is not the primary caregiver than is stipulated in the original custody agreement.

Professionals who work in this area realize that one in six people in the United States moves every year, so it would be unrealistic to expect divorced parents to be tethered to the state where the divorce decree was rendered and where the child is living in close proximity to both parents.

To prevent legal complications, it's wise that a parent considering a move talk to his or her lawyer about the state's policy. Relocation by a divorced parent may require written permission either from a former spouse or from the court that issued the custody decision.

A mother who had primary custody should keep the visiting father engaged in the child's life as much as possible. Make sure he sees his child's report card, knows when his child is sick, visits his child's school on parents' night, is invited to his child's music or dance recitals or sports activities, and is generally allowed to participate in decisions that affect his child. In other words, don't treat him only as a financial resource but rather as a loving father who cares about his child.

The Role of a Therapist

Brian and Donna, knowing the damage divorce can cause, decided to seek the help of a therapist before the problems arose. Even in intact homes, couples often can't agree completely on sensitive, volatile child-rearing issues. It's much harder for a divorcing couple, who are in the throes of making life-altering changes in their lives and those of their children, to come to a meeting of the minds where their offspring are concerned. Brian and Donna were determined to get this part of the divorce right. Despite their own pain and turmoil, they agreed on one mutual objective: to avoid making the kind of mistakes they'd seen others make, to keep the love and respect of their children, and to be an equally essential part of their kids' lives.

So they went to a child psychologist. Not with the children. Just the two of them. And in session after session they came to understand what their children would be going through at various stages: right after the divorce, then months and years later. They also came to understand how the kids would feel and how their needs would change if either or both parents remarried. They learned to see the future of their children's lives *through* their children's eyes. Because a wise and objective child psychologist gave them the tools they needed to handle all the changes, there was less trauma for everyone. Brian always said that without this doctor's road map and insights, he and Donna would have never been able to co-parent successfully after their divorce.

One of the most important rules they had to promise (each other) to stick to was to always present a united front to their children. And to uphold each other's decisions and choices and not override, deride, or undermine what one or the other parent had said or decided upon, especially when it came to issues of discipline. Another rule: their disagreements (Brian and Donna certainly had them) were not aired in front of the children. And it was equally important that one parent never bad-mouth the other parent to the children. No brainwashing, no name-calling, no blaming the other parent. No turning the children into pawns or letting them develop an enemy-camp mentality, no matter how upset, bitter, or angry Brian and Donna might become with each other (for whatever reason).

If you and your ex agree to seek professional help for your family, each parent should have a say in choosing the therapist. Recommendations can come from your child's pediatrician, school, friends, your church or synagogue, or support groups you find in your area.

A Child's Tenacity

If the fade-out father doesn't want a relationship and the child is not yet old enough to take the initiative, it's almost impossible to repair the damage, but if the child is an adult and is willing to initiate the contact, good things can happen. Rarely do children lose their desire for their parents, and on that premise the relationship with the fade-out father can be restored.

Clyde and June divorced when Liane, their adopted daughter, was eleven years old. At first, Clyde and Liane saw each other every other weekend and on alternate holidays. Liane adored her father and always looked forward to seeing him. Though June had never wanted the divorce, she was not a vengeful ex-wife. Clyde's alimony and child support payments left him with a substantially reduced standard of living. A year after the divorce, Clyde met Stephanie, a divorcée with a six-year-old daughter. Gradually, Clyde began to skip visitation weekends with Liane in order to spend more time with Stephanie. He also began to delay his support payments, using the money to court Stephanie.

The missing support payments created real financial hardship for June, but she was even more upset by Clyde's treatment of his daughter. Liane would spend hours packing her things and getting ready for her weekend with her father, only to receive a last-minute phone call from him telling her something had come up at work and he wouldn't be able to get her that weekend. Often he'd arrange to take her out to dinner during the week as a substitute for the weekend visit that didn't take place. Then another phone call would come: "Honey, it's Dad. Something's come up. I hope you'll understand."

Liane was always hopeful, always devastated.

Two years after the divorce, Clyde married Stephanie, and they moved to a house two hours away where their combined incomes went a lot further. Clyde made it clear he resented the time it took to transport Liane for visitation. At age thirteen, Liane began to rebel, talking back to both her mother and her father, piercing her nose, wearing suggestive clothing, and skipping school. Because Liane was a bright child, she managed to keep her grades up. But Clyde's fading interest in his daughter grew into a real antipathy, fostered not only by Liane's behavior but also by his new wife's repeated objections to Liane's behavior and her refusal to have Liane around her daughter.

When Liane was in high school, she and her father lost all contact with each other. Eventually, Liane went to a community college, where she suffered a bout of depression. From intimate conversations with

Liane, June learned that Liane's depression was in large part related to missing her father. June decided to take an active role in trying to restore Liane's relationship with Clyde. At first Liane resisted the idea of initiating contact with him, feeling that it was hopeless, but she agreed to try if her mother would call first to test the waters.

"She's not the rebellious teenager anymore," June told Clyde. "She's a lovely but very sad young woman who misses you very much. It would be a great favor to me and to her if you could spend a little time with her so you could see the wonderful change."

"I don't have four hours to spend going to get her and bring her back," Clyde said in a flat voice.

"She can take a bus," June said, not allowing herself to express the resentment she felt at Clyde's dispassionate reaction. "Please, Clyde. This is important. She is your daughter, and she needs to believe that you care, even if you don't."

Sheepishly, Clyde said, "I do care. But you know how impossible the situation became. The way she was acting out . . . I need to think about it, and I need to talk to Stephanie."

A few weeks later, when Liane called her father, he agreed to meet with her, but not on his turf. He scheduled a dinner meeting when he had to be in the city. At the last minute, he cancelled the visit, excusing himself by explaining that his business meeting had fallen apart. Liane vowed that she would never see him again.

A month went by, and then one day the telephone rang.

"It's Dad. I'm going to be in the city tomorrow night. Would you like to have dinner with me?"

"I would, but I can't stand any more disappointment, so if you think there's a chance you won't be able to make it, let's end the conversation right now."

Clyde assured Liane that he wanted to see her and would keep the appointment no matter what happened to his meeting. They met and actually enjoyed their time together, though with some reserve on both sides. Over time and many cordial dinners, they resumed a warm rapport with each other.

Many alienated parents and children are encouraged by therapists to acquiesce to the estrangement, regardless of who brought it about.

They are advised to back off and give the relationship time, with the Pollyannaish prediction that eventually the person will renew their ties. But no one really knows if there will be a change of heart. What we can say for certain is that even if the relationship is restored, nothing can make up for the lost years, the shared laughter and tears, the pride of special occasions, and all the milestones that form the fabric of a parent-child relationship.

COPING WHEN FORCED TO LET GO

Not all relationships mend. If, as the custodial parent, you've done all you can do and the fade-out parent is unwilling to resume contact, you can't eliminate the hurt that the estrangement causes, but it's important to help the child overcome anger and bitterness. Don't let the trauma of the loss keep the child, no matter what the child's age, from achieving gratification in other areas of life. Encourage closeness between the child and other male relatives—brothers, uncles, stepfather, grand-father, cousins—so that the child continues to have a male role model and doesn't suffer such a sense of betrayal that he or she is afraid to trust and to make emotional investments in others.

Helpful Guidelines

- **Stay in touch with your children.** The self-imposed alienation of a father from his children can impede a child's ability to form trust-ing relationships as he or she matures. Although frequent interac-tion with the father seems to matter less for children's development than do an effective mother and an absence of conflict, nevertheless, where a child can have both parents in his or her life, that child is all the better for it.

- **Give the children a chance to adjust to divorce and remarriage.** Upon the trauma of divorce, children experience a sudden loss of self-confidence and self-worth. Sadness and disappointment often set in. Just because the children are not bouncing with joy when you are with them during visitation does not mean they're not reassured by the ongoing relationship. As their father, you should continue seeing your children despite any visitation problems.

- **Show children they can trust you.** As a noncustodial father who visits, try to always keep your promises: call when you say you will, arrive on time when you say you'll be there, don't cancel weekends or back out of attending sports events or music recitals.

- **It's normal for fathers to feel resentment, even anger, and guilt about their resentment and anger.** These feelings should not form the basis for discontinuing the relationship with your children. It's okay for you to express resentment, but do so with an explanation. In other words, you can tell your children that you understand their unhappiness with the situation, but that because of your love for them, you want to see them as much as possible. Remember, your children's support system has been pulled out from under them.

- **Spend some quality time alone with the children.** Despite the desire to have the children accept your new wife, you should make time to be alone with them. The presence of another adult, and one who may be viewed with resentment, can cause children to act sullen and rejecting. These feelings are normal and must be addressed very gently and gradually. Everyone needs time to adjust.

- **Enlist the help of other relatives.** Initially, if as a divorced dad you're not particularly good at providing a comfortable and nurturing environment for visitation, then take your children to the homes of grandparents or aunts and uncles if they live in the area. This will have the effect of added closeness between your children and relatives from your side of the family. If family isn't available, enlist close friends—other married couples with children, not girlfriends. These friends can serve as a substitute for extended family, and provide the warmth that your children require in the period immediately after the breakup of their original family.

- **A new family doesn't mean trading in old obligations for new ones.** The children from a previous marriage are entitled to be supported in accordance with the divorce decree. If you have taken on new financial commitments, those commitments will have to take second place. Even if you don't view it that way, the courts do. You should consider your obligation to support your biological (or adopted) children as both legal and moral.

- **The second wife is entitled to complete disclosure about the father's financial obligations.** Often the second wife feels hostile to her stepchildren because she resents the money being spent on their support. One way to minimize this resentment is to fully apprise her of these commitments before the marriage takes place.

- **Fathers are also damaged.** Experts find that fathers often suffer depression, sense of loss, and yearning for their children when they lose contact. But it's up to the father to insist on his visitation rights, not only for the sake of the children but also for his own sake. If a father fades out of his children's lives, he may find that happiness and fulfillment will fade from *his* life.

- **Don't buy your children's love.** Presents and constant entertainment are not required to maintain a close relationship with children, even if the mother has primary custody. Children want their father's presence, not presents. They want to do ordinary things together— cook a meal, shop for household items, watch TV, play a video game, take a walk, or just sit beside one another reading books. Ordinary activities make the relationship feel natural, easy, and comfortable, rather than contrived. This translates to less stress, therefore a greater likelihood that you won't fade out of your child's life.

- **Use experts in dealing with the problems of divorce.** Even if the kids were well-adjusted prior to the divorce, the parents need the expertise of a child psychologist so the kids will stay well-adjusted. This type of expert knows the extent of damage divorce can do to kids. The presence of an objective third party whose first concern is the well-being of the children can be particularly helpful to discourage embittered parents from using the kids as pawns.

- **Custodial mothers must play an active role.** To protect your children from the anguish of losing contact with their father, you must engage him in their everyday lives. Through your initiative, he should see their report cards, know what their health problems are, visit school on parents' night, and generally have a say in what the child is deciding about his or her future. Treat your children's father not as a paycheck but as a valuable participant in their lives. And even if you can't stand the sight of your ex-husband, your children can, and they need their father in their lives. Put your love for your children over your own biases, and in the end your children will be the winners.

- **Joint custody will minimize fathers' fading out of their children's lives.** This custody arrangement presupposes that the families live near one another—so that the children can attend the same schools regardless of which parent's home they're living in—and that the parents want to share the nurturing tasks. When divorced parents get along and share physical custody, fathers don't fade out. Where the parents have remarried, these arrangements require the additional cooperation of the new spouses. This is a tall order to fill, but if it can be done, it works.

- **Find substitutes for a fade-out father.** Enlist other male relatives to serve as role models for your children if you have not been able to restore the father-child relationship. Encourage your children to seek pleasure and gratification from other activities rather than withdraw from life because Daddy isn't there anymore.

four

The Wicked Stepmother: Fact or Fiction?

S e c r e t   F o u r :

Love between stepmothers and stepchildren is not automatic.

Melinda has been married to her second husband, Clark, for twenty years now, and they are the kind of comfortable couple we like to imagine has always been that way. Yet when she looks back on her experience as a stepmother, she describes a road with so many hairpin turns, so many inclines and declines, that it's amazing the family survived to see the children grown.

When Melinda met Clark, she was a divorcée with a three-year-old daughter, and Clark was embroiled in a nasty divorce that involved two young boys caught in the middle. Melinda's first marriage had been short-lived and left her with custody of her daughter, Suzy, and a big mortgage on a condominium in a bustling northeastern city. She was lucky enough to have her still young and energetic parents living nearby to help care for Suzy while Melinda worked as a buyer in a large department store.

Melinda and Clark decided to marry as soon as his divorce was final. Clark moved into her condo, and they were confident they could build a happily combined family with fewer problems than either of them had experienced in their first marriage. After all, they both knew a lot more about marriage, family life, and themselves than they had the first time around. They really believed that Melinda as wife, mother, and stepmother, and Clark as husband, father, and stepfather, together with the children as brothers and step-siblings, and the new children they would have together, would unite in one big, happy family. All their love for each other would carry them safely through stormy waters in a seaworthy vessel that could certainly negotiate the unknown.

Hello?

Melinda looked forward to mothering her husband's sons, Larry and Steven, ages nine and seven respectively. She wanted to befriend the boys, help them get over the trauma of their parents' divorce, and help them mature into well-adjusted, productive adults. She jumped right in, baking cookies, going to the zoo, renting movies, and making popcorn. The boys were reasonably well-behaved and appreciated Melinda's overtures. Happily, the two boys and Melinda's daughter got along well together.

At the end of their first year of marriage, Melinda became pregnant. Her condominium, which was already cramped when the boys visited, was now going to be much too small for a new baby. Clark, a computer analyst, was strapped financially because of his sizable alimony and child support payments, so he decided to do consulting work on weekends to pay for a bigger place. Because they both realized Melinda's job was not secure—now that she was pregnant and unable to do the amount of traveling that her position required—they tried being as frugal as possible.

It was at this budget-crunching time that Melinda's ex-husband remarried, moved to the West Coast, and stopped sending regular support payments for their daughter, Suzy. With Clark working most Saturdays, Melinda had to pick up his children for their alternate-weekend visitation.

"With my daughter, I drove nearly an hour to get the boys," Melinda said. "As usual, I would wait outside the large, two-story house where Clark used to live. I'd honk the horn. I never went inside, nor did Clark's ex-wife come out to bring the children to the car. When I first started picking up the boys, I could sense how much his ex-wife resented me as the 'other woman' who broke up her marriage, even though they had started divorce proceedings before I met Clark. I would often see her peeking out of an upstairs window, looking at me with pure venom. I realized my becoming visibly pregnant only underscored the fact that *her* husband had now become *my* husband. And my going there to get the children probably made her feel that I not only had taken her husband but was now intruding on her exclusive role as mother of his children."

Some weekends the boys weren't ready, and Melinda had to sit in the car and wait for them. "As I sat there," she said, "I could hear the screaming accusations that his ex-wife was hurling at me in front of the boys."

Melinda explained how difficult it was caring for the three children during the latter weeks of her pregnancy and for that first year after the new baby girl was born. After her maternity leave, Melinda decided not to return to her job, because, just as she had anticipated, travel was impossible. Losing her income only added more financial problems to their already stretched-beyond-the-limit budget.

"As I drove back to the city, I dreaded the coming weekend, the forced togetherness, the four children, Clark's added work, all of which left the two of us so physically and emotionally drained that we could barely tolerate any more demands from my daughter, the baby, or each other. Our sex life became nothing more than a vague memory."

Then the seas became very choppy. Clark's sons lost interest in visiting; they wanted to be with their friends. Melinda's daughter had developed such resentment for the two boys that she didn't want them sharing anything that belonged to her, including the extra bunk beds that cluttered her room.

"Some nights," Melinda said, "after everyone was asleep, I would go downstairs to the kitchen to sip a glass of wine and try to relax. As I sat there, I would think of how I once believed Clark and I, and all the kids, would be the happiest family this side of the Mississippi. What went wrong? *This family was refusing to be a family.* On those weekends when Larry and Steven visited, I was shrill, short-tempered, and angry. I was living up to the myth of the wicked stepmother."

Melinda couldn't overcome her resentments and her conflicted state of mind about the situation. By the boys not visiting, her workload was reduced but she could see that Clark was suffering not only from missing his sons and from guilt at having caused such upheaval in their lives, but also from the stress of ongoing financial troubles. On those occasions when the boys did visit, she asked Clark to take them out to dinner, then drive them home without her, so that he could have some time alone with them. This was merely a Band-Aid covering a deep laceration.

Serena, Clark's ex-wife, petitioned the court for an upward modification in child support, claiming she could not afford to continue living in her house, because she couldn't get a decent job that would pay enough to cover the costs of raising the boys. That meant more legal fees for Clark, whether Serena prevailed or not.

During their irregular visits, the energetic boys would race through the house. When they had first started visiting, to win them over, Melinda had failed to establish ground rules, a mistake she knew had to be corrected, because the boys were becoming more and more unruly. In the face of Melinda's new determination to establish rules, have some privacy, and not be overrun by the family, Larry and Steven became loudly belligerent on the rare occasions when they spoke at all, and finally revealed how much they resented Melinda, who "took their father away." All this occurred while the court case was moving forward, ultimately to a decision in favor of Clark.

"I was beginning to believe that I was the source of all the problems," Melinda said. "Clark was the favored parent, not only by his own sons but even by Suzy. The boys barely spoke to me except in anger, and Clark was put in the position of having to make choices about who was right, me or the children, when it came to cleaning up after themselves or whether they could watch a particular TV program."

These conflicts were compounded when Serena began to make late-night phone calls to their house, bitterly complaining about problems she was having with the boys when they returned home after a weekend visit, about financial matters, and even about complaints from Clark's parents that their son had made an awful mistake by marrying "that woman."

Melinda continued to struggle with her own self-worth, believing that everyone considered her the intruder, the home wrecker, the source of all that was wrong in the family. Still, she, Clark, and the children persisted, an unwilling and often recalcitrant group. Despite the difficulties, Melinda and Clark loved each other and wanted their marriage to work.

Finally, after a period of about four years, a degree of solidarity born of a hundred small interactions almost imperceptibly crept into the family relationships. The resentments became less overt, and happier moments became more frequent.

Melinda said, "The boys began including Suzy in their activities, even complimenting her for being a good baseball hitter, which she was. The children started getting along, even liking each other, though I knew they were still wary of me."

Melinda sought counseling. She wanted to know if Clark's children would ever accept her. The psychologist told Melinda she could expect the boys to continue their resentment toward her even into their early adulthood, that these were natural feelings that would ultimately work out if she could resist any retaliatory behavior and if she could continue to encourage the good rapport that the children were developing among themselves.

About that time, fate struck another blow. Serena got sick and needed surgery, but she had let her health insurance lapse. She asked Clark to pay the medical bills. When he told her he couldn't afford to pay the entire bill but would do what he could, Serena began a campaign to alienate the boys from their father. Just when Melinda and Clark thought the boys had been sufficiently turned against Clark to cut off their contact with him, they (by then ages fourteen and seventeen) did the unexpected—asked if they could live with Melinda and Clark. Though Melinda wanted to object, she decided not to and instead went back to work. Using most of her salary, she hired a full-time housekeeper to be there when the children came home from school, to clean the house, and to get dinner started. So the boys moved in, and—wonder of wonders, despite Melinda's apprehension about how they could all live under one roof—the new arrangement turned out to be the best one of all.

Eventually, the boys went to college and became independent. Suzy was soon off to college, too, and the youngest daughter was in high school. Melinda and Clark had endured, and grown even closer because of all they'd been through together. When their youngest child left for college, Melinda and Clark had the joy and satisfaction of finally having all the time for themselves, though they both admitted missing the sounds of kids playing, squabbling, and blaring the TV or radio.

"All we'd been through not only deepened our love, but really enlarged our understanding of each other and of all the children," Melinda said.

When asked what advice she would give to other women about to marry men with children from a previous marriage, she said, "There's no ideal role for a stepmother to play. She has to be adaptable, able to change according to what is possible and desirable at the moment for both the stepchildren and for herself. *She has to accept the step-relationship for what it is and not what she thinks it should be. And, of equal importance, she has to be an understanding partner to her husband, who is facing similar challenges in blending a family.* The only thing I wish I had was a few good signposts along the way to point out the dangerous curves as they came up, and maybe a checklist to find out whether I was doing it right or failing miserably, as I often thought I was. And for me, and maybe for others, going back to work and hiring a housekeeper proved to be the magic ingredient for a better rapport with all the children. I wasn't on their backs all the time."

She admitted that there were still problems with Clark's ex-wife, who never accepted his marriage to Melinda, as well as a bit of ongoing sibling rivalry among all four of the children—his, hers, and theirs. Melinda learned from her own self-education that a certain amount of rivalry is normal, predictable, and likely to continue. But most of all, Melinda learned that she is not and never had been "a wicked stepmother." She was just a normal stepmom who had normal kids who provoked in her some wicked thoughts from time to time.

"FAIRY TALES CAN COME TRUE" —
BUT THEY DON'T HAVE TO

The first stories we heard as children warned us about wicked step-mothers. These fairy tales reflected a time when many women either didn't survive childbirth or died before their children reached adult-hood, when a child was often just "one more mouth to feed," when "spare the rod and spoil the child" was the prevailing motif of the day. Cinderella's stepmother made her do all the dirty work in the house, while her own two ugly daughters went to the palace ball in finery. Snow White's stepmother sought daily reassurance from her mirror that she "was the fairest one of all," until one day the mirror spoke a different truth: "Snow White is the fairest of all." The stepmother immediately solved that problem by having Snow White taken to the woods to be put to death. And let's not forget the stepmother in "Hansel and Gretel": when there was not enough food for everyone, she sent the young children away to fend for themselves.

So, it is not surprising that stepmothers find they are tackling a hard crust of suspicion already set in the minds of their new children. These fairy tales have developed into a sort of collective uncon-sciousness for children (and adults as well, for they, too, were once children exposed to this litany of wickedness). As a result of this in-doctrination, it's easy to imagine the added trauma of the father's remarriage after divorce when the child is suddenly confronted with the father's new wife, the mother's replacement—the much maligned "stepmother."

A woman does not become a witchlike creature because she meets an attractive man, falls in love with him, and then agrees to help him care for his children after their marriage. Whether or not she is eager to mother his children, she is instantly confronted with the realities of par-enting: that children are a drain on the couple's time together and that they are ever present and in need of close supervision while they are in their father's care, not to mention the financial expense. Like most starry-eyed brides, and even as a previously married woman with chil-dren of her own, she walks down the aisle unappreciative of all the nu-ances of the role she is accepting. Yet as soon as she is pronounced a wife, she comes under the scrutiny of the outside world not as a new bride but as a stepmother.

Professionals in the field of family counseling, religious leaders, and social commentators have been slow to let go of the myth that the nuclear American family is the one, ideal kind of family relationship. *The ideal family is the one in which its members thrive and are able to reach their full potential.* Every family configuration is different. Some work, some don't. And for stepmothers, unanticipated circumstances are always arising.

As one woman said, "It's not easy explaining to a high school guidance counselor why you have two sets of sons the same age who are related through divorce."

And even today, finding a positive depiction of the stepmother in literature or movies is an almost impossible task. One 1998 film comes to mind: *Stepmom,* in which Julia Roberts plays the younger, new wife pitted against Susan Sarandon, the older, nurturing mother of the children. "The woman I play means well," said Julia Roberts in an interview. "She's a working woman who is trying to learn to be a mother and wife. At stake . . . are the two children. She wants them to like her." Eventually they do, and the family unites.

It's still a generally accepted belief that the mother symbolizes nurturing and affection and the father symbolizes authority. Yes, we expect more nurturing from fathers these days, but the mother is still the one who has primary responsibility for the emotional well-being of the family. This puts huge pressure on the new stepmother, whose stepchildren may already regard her with distrust and suspicion. Stepfathers do not experience the same degree of angst and erosion of self-worth as stepmothers, because their role is actually supported by a benign perception of males functioning as providers whose most important role is outside the home. They rarely have the responsibility of day-to-day care for stepchildren. And it's the day-to-day care and interaction that usually prompts the discord between the child and stepparent.

According to clinical psychologist Anne C. Bernstein, Ph.D., "Stepmothers often feel as if they've been put to work without a job description."

It helps to be clear that a stepmother is not and can never be the mother, even if the mother is deceased, except in the rare instance of a very young child whose mother has died. Every woman who becomes a stepmother has her own personality, so the situation in each family is unique, but there are certain rules of the road, particularly the one that requires each member to pitch in and help with the added responsibilities. The stepmother is the woman of the house that she lives in, and she should participate as an equal partner with her husband in establishing guidelines for a smooth-running household. This should not be construed to mean a rigid list of directives. Compassion and flexibility are essential, especially if the stepmother wants to avoid making her home a battlefield.

Too many stepmothers are living in an age of fear. Fear of failure. Fear of uncertainty. Fear of what everyone else is thinking about them. If only we could see more depictions of the many unselfish, long-suffering women who give of themselves to the children of their spouses. Movies and TV could go a long way toward that goal just as they have done in improving race relations.

DON'T EXPECT GRATITUDE

Many a new wife believes, as Melinda did, that the children will not interfere with the marriage, that she will be loved and accepted by the children, and that everyone will appreciate her efforts. These expectations are soon shattered by reality.

Jennie, a forty-year-old woman, virtually raised her husband's children. The children are now happily planning their visits to their mother, who left them when they were very young. Jennie has painful visions of what the future may bring. She imagines the children remembering their lives under her roof only as quarrels over her rules about keeping rooms tidy, no TV until homework is done, and eating a good breakfast before leaving for school.

"They'll think I was a total witch compared to their mother, who required nothing of them. She couldn't care less if they did their homework. She never even asked if they had any!"

One of Jennie's biggest fears is that her stepchildren will go off to live with their mother, forgetting Jennie and all she did for them. Now that the hard part of raising young children is over, the mother will reap the rewards that are in large measure the product of Jennie's hard work, love, and devotion. But Jennie admits that she has to prepare herself for that contingency. No matter what she has done for the children, Jennie knows they have a visceral bond with their mother that cannot be denied.

Hard as it may be to understand at times, this primal connection of a child with the mother is a force to reckon with. *Last One Home,* by Mary Pope Osborne, was written for young adults and shows a twelve-year-old girl, adamant about hating the stepmother who is kind to her, and who regularly calls her alcoholic biological mother on the telephone. The book describes the yearning the child has for her mother even though that mother has been both neglectful and abusive.

"I'm mindful," Jennie says, "of the fact that children rarely show appreciation for all the loving care and devotion they receive from their own biological parents, so it's certainly not going to happen with a step-mother."

Jennie is one of those unique people who truly accept human nature. She particularly knew that to extract gratitude from members of a stepfamily yields few truly satisfying dividends. Being honest with oneself and giving generously is a more reasonable way to proceed than keeping a tally sheet of obligations or insults. We all know people who have a benign way of handling injustice. They say, "Things have a way of balancing out in the end." And for the people who have this view, things usually do balance out. Maybe that's the reward for a healthy attitude.

Prospective stepmothers need forewarning of the issues that may collide with their hopes and dreams of domestic bliss. What Melinda said bears repeating here: *There is no one perfect role for the step-mother to play, but she must have the ability to change according to what is possible and desirable at the moment for both stepchild and stepmother.*

Ten Traps for Prospective Stepmothers

1.   Not knowing enough about the family you are about to marry into

2.   Expecting the children to automatically accept you into their lives

3.   Expecting yourself to love—or even like—the children immediately

4.   Failing to clarify your "job description"—the child care you are expected to provide for visiting or custodial children

5.   Competing with the children for the father's love and attention

6.   Resenting any lack of appreciation from the children, the father, and the extended family

7.   Failing to establish clear and reasonable rules and guidelines for the children in your new home

8.   Becoming overinvolved or vindictive due to problems with your husband's ex-wife

9.   Taking it personally when your new family regards you as an intruder or a scapegoat for the unhappiness due to divorce

10. Expecting to always have unconditional support from your husband, who may feel caught in the middle between you and his children

Remember that there will be many occasions in this blending process when the best thing to do is nothing. I'm not suggesting that you be a martyr, but don't be a nag, either. In private moments, get your feelings off your chest by talking (not complaining) to your husband, and then try to forget and move on. The passage of time may be your best friend.

TAKING CHARGE OF YOUR OWN HOUSE

Just knowing the issues that most stepmothers face is a good first step on the road to a happily blended family. Having *reasonable expectations* for your stepchildren's behavior is an essential next step. For example, any mother, biological or otherwise, has a right to expect good manners and personal hygiene. And what woman would tolerate the kids going in and out of her closet like it was their own department store? Or telling her to "get a life." Kids have to have reasonable expectations, too. They shouldn't assume that clean underwear perpetuates itself. Or that dirty dishes on the floor beside the bed is the latest in room décor. Or that it's not unreasonable for a stepmother to lose her cool when an admonishment to a teenage stepdaughter produces the kind of sarcastic retorts that are deliberately provocative. Knowing that these situations are likely to arise can go a long way toward defusing anger so that the stepmother can calmly deal with these problems. Can a stepmother tell her teenage stepchild, "For someone turned off by pollution, you sure contribute a whole lot to it?" Mothers can, so why can't stepmothers? Typically, new stepmothers restrain themselves when it comes to discipline, and rely on their husbands to handle these difficult situations. At first that's probably a good idea, but it can't continue that way. Eventually the woman has to take charge in her own house.

DEIRDRE'S DILEMMA

Long after a divorce, children may cherish fantasies of parental reunion. The presence of the stepmother destroys those fantasies. Torn by loyalty to their other parent, living or dead, children are loath to legitimatize the claim of this interloper, not knowing what to do with yet another parent and chafing at having to come to terms with a situation they had no part in choosing.

Deirdre was not prepared for sudden motherhood. After college in the Midwest, she moved to New York and became a paralegal in a Wall Street law firm. There she met and fell in love with a newly divorced lawyer who was the father of two children. The father had a joint custody arrangement with his ex-wife. After a one-year courtship, Deirdre and the lawyer married, and she moved from her cozy Manhattan apartment to a large home in suburban Westchester County, where she immediately became the stepmother to two resentful, undisciplined adolescent girls.

Though Deirdre became somewhat discouraged about motherhood as a result of her crash course, she still wanted her own children. Before she and her husband married, he had agreed that they would have a child of their own, but then changed his mind. He said he was "parented out" and reluctant to start another family. Despite the many long hours Deirdre now spends carting the girls from one activity to another, to and from school and to and from their mother's house in an adjoining suburb, they continuously remind her, "You're not our mother, so you can't tell us what to do." (Or, even more provocatively, "You're crabby. It must be that time of the month again.") Deirdre feels fatigued, unappreciated, frustrated, and shortchanged of the privacy and romance she expected from marriage. She is also forced to interact with the ex-wife and mother of the children, who does nothing to hide her contempt for Deirdre.

Deirdre never allows herself to vent her frustration in front of the children, rarely says an unkind word to them, and stoically carries on the functions of caring for these stepdaughters with more than mere tolerance. She forces herself to smile and remains in good humor most of the time. But how long can she keep up this cheery facade in the face of such a stressful situation? Her armor is bound to crack unless she can find a way to resolve these mounting conflicts.

Is she a wicked stepmother? The children, who reinforce the worst in each other, say she is but offer no concrete examples to support their view. Deirdre's husband can think of nothing that would qualify her as anything but a good person. Despite admonishments from their father, the girls continue to taunt her.

"They're too clever for words, those two," Deirdre said. "The minute their father is gone, they become incorrigible, even spilling things on purpose so I'll have to clean it up. And when they're told to clean up their own mess, they only make it worse."

Unfortunately, Deirdre's story is all too common. No adult should be forced to tolerate abusive behavior from children. So what can be done? Deirdre and her husband can establish ground rules. Deirdre's husband should impress his daughters with the need to treat Deirdre respectfully, or else.

And what is the "or else"? Visitation is intended for the children to be with their father. Deirdre does not have to be a constant presence. Her husband can start by eliminating the time Deirdre has to spend with the girls in his absence by picking up his daughters and driving them to his home, using the trip as added visitation time. And when they are visiting, he should always be there. If that fails to work, then Deirdre should begin to make herself scarce during the visits, but continue to spend short periods of time with her husband and the girls—hopefully using that time to improve their relationship.

If funds permit, another recommended change would be going out to restaurants more often to reduce Deirdre's workload. The presence of other people and a public place could serve as a buffer to discourage the stepdaughters' rebellious behavior. It's a demoralizing circumstance for all concerned, and should not be allowed to continue, even if it means taking some drastic measures, such as having the husband visit his girls on their turf, without Deirdre.

THE CRUX OF THE PROBLEM

Many women are now marrying for the first time when they are in their thirties and forties, and often marrying divorced men with children. According to statistics from the Stepfamily Association of America, as of 2000, there were twenty million stepmothers in the United States. Stepmothers usually arrive on the scene in a least propitious time— after divorce, death, or abandonment. *It's best not to act precipitously.* The new stepmother needs to take time to size up the situation. The children are used to a certain environment, and that environment is drastically changed not only by the different residence but also by the stepmother's presence in the family. Making changes too quickly, such as mandating too many new rules for the children, is bound to meet resistance. Gradual change, when necessary, is the better course. Keeping the children's lives as much the same as they're used to will work best toward establishing good relations and a new family unit. For example, setting an earlier bedtime than what the children are used to just because you want to spend more time alone with your husband can cause real resentment toward the new stepmother.

A first-time wife who marries a man with children comes to the bargaining table confronted by a team of people who see no need to negotiate in the first place. The personal wishes of one woman, however reasonable, do not have the weight of established practices that are part of a history shared by the team that sits across the table.

And when there are two teams, as is the case where both the husband and wife have been married before with children, the competition heats up, with each side lobbying for the adoption of their preferences. It can be discouraging, particularly for a stepmother who is hindered because she tries too hard to win over her stepchild. Be very selective about the rules you set. Make sure they're important ones.

YOU CAN'T PRESCRIBE LOVE

Fourteen-year-old Emily and her father had a close and loving relationship after her mother ran off and left them for another man. Father and daughter worked well as a team until the father became involved with Marlene, whom he married after a six-month courtship. While the couple was courting, Emily was reserved with Marlene, but polite. Despite Emily's reticence, there were no apparent problems, so Marlene assumed Emily would warm up as time went on. When the newly married couple returned from their honeymoon, Emily developed headaches, diarrhea, and nausea that seemed to intensify over a period of months. Marlene felt sorry for her stepdaughter, realizing that Emily had lost her father's exclusive attention when he remarried, so she fussed over Emily, buying her new clothes and taking her to museums, plays, and movies. She was sure that in time their relationship would grow close and Emily's physical problems would abate. Actually, for the most part Emily's health did improve, but her attitude toward her stepmother became increasingly hostile. The more Marlene did for Emily, the more Emily disliked Marlene. Soon Marlene began to feel frustrated and exhausted from her futile campaign to win over her stepdaughter.

The myth of the cruel stepmother is no more prevalent than the myth of instant love and devotion. A child's affection is not won quickly, no matter how dedicated and well-meaning the stepparent is. Many experts in the field of family counseling find that the father, his future wife, and the children often have wonderful relations and good times until the father and his girlfriend marry. Then suddenly, and for no apparent reason, the good times come to an abrupt end. Experts warn that it is unrealistic to expect stepchildren and stepparents to love each other immediately upon formation of the new family. Even the expectation that they *must* love each other is harmful to these relationships. Everyone soon discovers that sharing outings and doing things that are fun is very different from living together as a family under the same roof day after day.

Reasonably, stepmothers should not expect their stepchildren to accept and love them immediately. And just because the stepmother is kind and generous, as Marlene was, doesn't mean her efforts will be rewarded with love and gratitude. *Time is an essential ingredient of a good stepmother-stepchild relationship.* If Marlene could overlook Emily's hostility, not take it personally, and continue to be the same nurturing stepmother over a long period of time, the likelihood that Emily would respond with warmth and affection would grow.

It is crucial to keep in mind that the stepchild's hostility is a response to the stepmother in her official position rather than to her as a person. If the stepmother could realize that if she and the children had met under different circumstances, they would probably find things to like in each other, then it might make it easier for them to get along.

The relationship may be considered a good one if there is mutual respect and consideration. Real affection is the bonus that often comes over a period of years as it obviously did between Nancy and Maureen Reagan. Nancy Reagan became an instant parent to Ronald Reagan's two children from his marriage to Jane Wyman. Despite a rough beginning, Nancy and Maureen Reagan became close as the years went on.

This list could go on and on with stepmother-stepchild relationships that work, but they often don't start off that way.

In my own situation, I did not really get to know one of my husband's daughters until fifteen years after he and I were married. At the time, she was a freshman in college, then was off to a career, then moved from one city to another, and then had a family of her own. What I discovered was a wonderful young woman with warmth, wit, and talent, a great mother of two adorable boys, and soon realized that she was exactly the type of person I would have chosen as a friend had we been schoolmates. I only regret that her mother made it impossible for me to get to know this stepdaughter until so many years had passed. She was afraid to connect with her father, because her mother demanded that her children stay away from him, and of course away from me, too. To my stepdaughter's credit, she overcame her mother's influence and persisted, because she wanted a relationship with her father. I let her know that I wanted her to stay close to her father, that he wanted it, too, and that I wanted her to give me a fair chance. She did, and we're all the better for it.

EVELYN'S STORY

Two years into her new marriage, Evelyn is "ready to throw in the towel." Her stepdaughters, ages nine and fourteen, are with Evelyn and her husband, Ronald, every other weekend and one night a week.

"I've tried to do everything right," Evelyn says, "but nothing is working out the way I hoped it would. Nobody is happy with the situation. If my husband puts his arms around me, the girls glare as if they'd like to kill me. Either it's that reaction or they become sullen and moody. I have a ten-year-old daughter, Tricia. If I pay attention to her, my husband gets jealous. If I try to give him more attention, Tricia slinks off to her bedroom and shuts the door.

"To make matters worse, Ronald's daughters poke fun at Tricia because she has a slight curvature of the spine. I've asked my husband to reprimand his daughters for saying cruel things to Tricia, but he says it's just 'kid stuff' and they'll outgrow it, and that since he's hardly with them, he doesn't want to drive them away by being too critical. Frankly, I've come to loathe their visits, mainly because they are downright vicious to my child."

Evelyn often feels like a maid who is supposed to do the housework and stay out of the family's way. Ronald's ex-wife acts as if Evelyn doesn't exist. When she telephones and Evelyn answers, she immediately asks to speak to Ronald.

"I'm exhausted taking care of her kids," Evelyn says in a voice choked with tears, "and she acts as if I don't matter at all. Who does she think is mothering her kids while they're at our house? And then, of course, Ronald is forever worrying about his ex-wife's inability to manage on the alimony and child support he pays. She could get a job, but she won't. Now Ronald and I hardly talk to each other, because we're so afraid our conversation will gravitate to these issues, and then we'll have a shouting match. I know I sound like a bitch. I probably have become one, but believe it or not, I used to be a nice person. I never dreamed I'd be a stranger in my own home, either hated or tolerated by everyone. I don't know how much longer I can put my daughter through this ordeal. It's not fair to either one of us."

What Can Evelyn and Ronald Do?

Evelyn underestimated the profound effect that children and related issues from her husband's past life would have on their marriage. As with most stepmothers, Evelyn met her prospective stepdaughters under the highly controlled circumstances of courtship outings. She learned they were almost entirely different personalities once they all had to live under the same roof, even if only for weekends. What she also learned was that Ronald has been so fraught with guilt for having walked out of his first marriage that he can't see the real picture. He doesn't want to drive his daughters any further away than he feels they already are. He can't even bring himself to reprimand them for their cruel remarks to Evelyn's daughter, and this is the bone of contention Evelyn can no longer tolerate. She thinks Ronald is completely indifferent to Tricia despite Tricia's efforts to be kind and respectful to him. Evelyn isn't even sure she loves Ronald anymore, but hates the thought of another divorce, another failure, and another upheaval for the family.

"The kids are here to see their father, not me," states Evelyn. "They would prefer I not be there at all, even though it's my house. They curl up on the sofa and watch TV while I retire to my bedroom, where Tricia goes to escape the taunting. When the girls leave, Ronald starts to get amorous in an effort to appease my resentment. It doesn't work. I'm fed up."

The experts I consulted were unanimous in recommending counseling for the couple with an emphasis on Ronald's state of mind. At close range, this family dynamic includes a vengeful ex-wife; a guilt-ridden, passive husband; and children fueling hostilities between the natural mother, stepmother, father, and step-sibling. Ronald is unrealistic about his role as father to his daughters, unfair to his second wife and her daughter, and blind to his own failure to take charge. He needs to understand that because he (with the most influence and authority) opted out of the conflicts, he bears the primary responsibility for the disintegration of this new family. But that assessment will have to come from a trusted professional counselor, someone who can gently make Ronald go where he doesn't want to go, someone who can persuade Ronald to take charge of the mess that keeps growing.

According to Evelyn's description of Ronald, he is not mean-spirited or indifferent to her, but he is almost totally without introspection. Evelyn admits she is able to withstand the stepdaughters' and ex-wife's reaction to her, but rightly, she cannot accept the cruelty inflicted on her daughter. Ronald is not improving his relationship with his daughters by allowing them to torment Tricia. Experts suggest that his daughters need to be reprimanded *by their father*.

It's critical to the marriage and to the well-being of his own daughters that Ronald overcome his guilt and learn that he can still be a good father to his daughters and that they will continue to love him notwithstanding his divorce from their mother. During a healing period, their visits should include more outings without Evelyn and Tricia so that father and daughters can improve their own relationship, followed by a long-overdue father-daughter talk. Ronald needs to let his daughters know that Evelyn and Tricia are as important to him as they are and that he wants a peaceful relationship for all concerned. According to experts, Ronald needs therapy that is geared primarily toward helping him overcome his guilt, and by so doing, enabling him to assume his many roles as husband, ex-husband, father, and stepfather.

Professional intervention is the only sensible course. Though Ronald believes Evelyn is being overprotective with Tricia, experts will be better able to convince Ronald that Evelyn's defense of her child is appropriate because of the lasting ill effects that torment could have on a child with a physical problem and because it is in fact mental abuse.

It is the first responsibility of any parent to protect his or her child's mental and physical well-being. In those situations where the remarriage is causing serious mental or physical harm to family members, the marriage cannot take priority. It is a clear exception to the rule.

As this book goes to press, Ronald and Evelyn are living apart, but as a result of therapy and Ronald's new sensitivity and awareness of his role in the family, they are intending to try again.

THE WHOLE TRUTH, NOTHING BUT THE TRUTH . . .

Not one woman whom I interviewed had known what to expect from marriage to a man with children from a previous marriage, even in those cases where the woman had also been married before with children. They were all bewildered to a greater or lesser degree by the new family dynamic, particularly because our society does not offer enough support for stepmothers in their stigmatized role. Women should talk freely to their second husbands-to-be in order to find out what the future is likely to hold. The couple should discuss their expectations, and what each of them needs to know about the other, especially from the vantage point of the prospective stepmother, because her role will be the more demanding one.

What Women Need to Know: A Checklist

✓   What are the expectations of the man you are about to marry, with regard to the marriage, his prospective stepchildren, career goals, finances, prenuptial agreements, the possibility of having children together, interaction with extended family, where to live, whether he expects you to work, and anything else you think you should know about your future husband's expectations that will affect your relationship?

✓   What kind of family life did he have during his previous marriage?

✓   What kind of person is his ex-wife, her good traits and bad traits?

✓   What can the new wife expect from the ex-wife? Will there be cooperation or terror?

✓   Was it an acrimonious or amicable divorce?

✓   Does the ex-wife work?

✓   Does the ex-wife want the children to have a close relationship with their father?

✓   How much of the husband's income is committed to the former family? How much is left for the new family? How will the families be provided for in the event of his death? Or disability?

✓   What is the relationship between the ex-wife and her former in-laws, the ex-husband's parents and siblings?

✓   What are his children like, and how do they relate to him and to their mother? Are there any physical or emotional problems that are out of the ordinary? How does he think his children will relate to the new stepmother?

✓   What kind of relationship does he have with his parents and his siblings?

✓ What are the goals you each have for a happy life? Where do they conflict? Where do they mesh?

✓ How do you both feel about his children's coming to live with you? (You should let your betrothed know if you have strong feelings against his children's coming to live with you, because they might do just that.)

✓ Are you willing to perform the mundane tasks of housekeeping and mothering someone else's children, knowing there will be very little demonstrative appreciation? (Bear in mind that over time that *might* change, and you and the children may develop a strong bond.)

✓ If there has been a bitter divorce and custody battle, are you willing to be extremely tolerant and understanding while the children recover from the trauma? *(These children of bitter divorce do not need the added trauma of living with a person who resents being a stepparent.)*

✓ Are you willing to be kind toward and tolerant of children who are going to take much of your husband's weekend time away from you?

✓ If you also have children, are you willing to *risk* having their lives negatively impacted by your new marriage and the presence of a stepfather and step-siblings?

✓ Are you prepared to deal with emotional outbursts, hateful and sarcastic diatribes against you, and spiteful behavior from your husband's children? Can you be calm and firm without being vengeful?

✓ What are the religious convictions of the various members of both families? How is religion observed? Who attends services?

✓ How will you feel if your husband and his children attend a church that is different from the one you attend?

✓   Will there be enough space either for the children to live with you or for visitation? If they are going to be space invaders, how will that be dealt with?

✓   What kind of reception can the new wife expect from the rest of the family—grandparents and siblings?

Becoming fully informed means getting to know the family you are about to marry into. Even if it's not feasible to meet the entire extended family, meeting the children, spending time with them, and getting your children together with his children is not only advisable; it's a must. This should occur as soon as you commit to the marriage, if it hasn't already—unless, of course, the children are adults and live on the other side of planet earth. If the man you are planning to marry is stalling or denying you an opportunity to get to know his kids, get paranoid! It's a bad signal, and it should become a time for you to stall on setting a wedding date. During the engagement period, the couple needs to talk about the matters raised in the checklist. Talk and talk and talk. It's also a good idea to take a trip with all of the children. Spend a few days together, but be sure to stay in separate rooms. If you observe even a hint of problems, it would be wise to seek premarital counseling. (In fact, this is recommended under any circumstances.) Bear in mind that before marriage, contact doesn't present the whole picture that ultimately comes into focus once everyone is living under the same roof. But the more the new wife knows, the better she is likely to be at handling the problems as they arise. For they surely will.

During my interviews, too many women expressed their disappointment with their lives once the honeymoon was over and the stepchildren moved in, either permanently or for scheduled visitation. Confronting truths before marriage could prevent, or at least minimize, real disillusionment and future indignation.

One woman said, "It was as if I bought a particular item from a store, only to come home and find out the package contained something else."

"A ROSE IS A ROSE IS A ROSE"

What a child calls a stepmother is an important aspect of their interaction. One stepmother said her nine-year-old stepson called her by her first name while she was dating his father. When she and his father married a year later, she asked him if he would like to call her "Mother" because she knew he called his biological mother "Mommie." The stepmother was trying to convey that she wanted to be close to him, and she thought using "Mother" would be more familial. The boy nodded silently, but for a long time afterward he never addressed her by any name, which meant he couldn't speak to her until he had her attention. She could see that he was uneasy that he had tacitly agreed to call her "Mother." She told him he could just go back to calling her by her first name, because he seemed to like that better and it didn't matter to her.

Experts in dealing with family problems recommend a basic rule—confer with the children and follow their lead in what is comfortable for them. In their effort to make the family a more cohesive unit, stepparents often push for relationship names rather than what they believe are impersonal first names—Mom versus Janet. What they aren't considering is that in older children this can create a feeling of disloyalty to the biological parent, whether living or not. Using any derivative of *mother* or *father* can be viewed by children as symbolizing a replacement or loss of their biological parent, which means that instead of unifying the new family, it may backfire and create a barrier.

One mother who heard her child calling the stepmother "Mom" tore into a rage.

"*I'm* your mother," she shouted. "Don't you dare call *that woman* Mom!"

The message in this outburst is quite clear and creates conflict and unhappiness for the child. At the point where this occurs—and it often does—the stepparent has to offer the child the comfort level that was taken away by the natural mother. She will have to put her arm around the stepchild and say, "Don't worry about any of this. I'll be happy if you just use my name."

Most stepchildren start out calling the stepparent by his or her first name, and may continue to do so throughout their lives together, or they may come up with something else, like Mom Louise or Dad Joe. They may even choose to call the stepparent Aunt Louise or Uncle Joe, to establish that there is a family connection even though it isn't comparable to Mom or Dad. Hopefully, the stepparent will graciously accept what the child chooses—after all, it is not a measure of what the relationship is or can become.

STEPMOTHERS' RULES OF ENGAGEMENT

As soon as the children have had an opportunity to get to know their new stepmother (and stepfather), and are living together or are visiting, the couple should coordinate their efforts for managing the family with the notion that children usually feel more secure in a structured environment. That should not be interpreted as military discipline or boot camp. The couple should discuss and agree to a set of rules with mutually acceptable consequences and rewards.

Always bear in mind that visiting children have another home and another set of rules to follow. Learn (from your husband and from the children) what is expected of them in their custodial home, and try to avoid extreme differences whenever possible. If it isn't a critical matter, let it go. Just because you don't like elbows on the table doesn't mean it has to be so if they're allowed to put elbows on the table in their custodial home. On the other hand, if you have a houseful of kids, his and yours, and you need everyone to pitch in by picking up after themselves and bringing dishes to the sink, chores not expected of the visiting children, you and your husband need to explain why the different rule applies in your home: "We all want to do fun things, but we won't have time if we have to spend hours cleaning up."

Even with rules, there should be an atmosphere of gentle formality. After all, this is the birth of a new family. Most important, with children or stepchildren, the cornerstone should be *consistency*. Consistency builds trust. We all want to know where we stand and what to expect from the people around us. Even if we don't like a rule, we want to know where the boundaries are so we can function without surprises.

Though rewards and consequences are required, the emphasis

should be on *rewards* as positive reinforcement for desired behavior. *The desire for praise is stronger than the desire to avoid punishment.* Everyone wants attention, but love, kindness, and praise is the preferred attention. If the only attention is negative, the child will take even that rather than no attention, so rewards become an essential ingredient to good behavior. No matter what age we are, when we are rewarded for listening, our hearing automatically improves.

And finally, if there are too many rules, the impulse will be to find ways to avoid them. Anyone who has ever been around a child knows this. Although the following list is not comprehensive, it does establish some basic guidelines for building a good relationship, with manageable discipline, in a loving home.

- Consistent rules are the best rules.

- Rules a child helped formulate will be easier to follow.

- Rules with related rewards and consequences are the only real and enforceable rules.

- Children will do anything—even behave—to get what they want.

- The fewer rules, the better.

NAVIGATIONAL AIDS

Being a stepmother can be a lonely and perplexing journey through uncharted waters. Our close friends and family don't always understand the struggles, and too many families plunge into remarriage without preparation for the challenges they have to face. There is a trend toward premarital counseling by clergy for young couples about to marry. However, there are problems with finding clergy who are willing and able to counsel those who have been divorced and are about to marry again. And even the professionals who normally help embattled families— therapists and clergy—are often ill-prepared to deal with the unique problems that confront blending families, particularly after the traumas of death and/or divorce.

In many traditional denominations, there is still such a stigma attached to divorce that clergy from these particular denominations are often reluctant to help stepfamilies. One minister, Ron Deal, planned seminars for the increasing number of stepfamilies he was seeing at his Jonesboro, Arkansas, church, but some members of his congregation accused him of supporting the breakup of marriages. An Atlanta minister who didn't wish to have his identity known said, "I'm not going to help people with their stepfamily problems. When you abandon your family, this is what you get. I have no intention of condoning people jumping out of one marriage and into another."

Because the Catholic Church forbids remarriage after divorce, a Catholic priest may not be willing to help stepfamilies except when the stepfamily includes a parishioner who remarried after the death of a former spouse. And then, one would have to question the extent of the priest's expertise in handling stepfamily problems—family problems of any type, for that matter—unless they involve religious issues.

Of course, there are always members of the clergy who want to be helpful, and some of them are quite knowledgeable, but finding the right one can be difficult.

Where there is access to a good support group, it is completely worthwhile to take advantage of what they have to offer, sooner rather than later. Support groups are also good resources for finding a professional counselor who specializes in remarriage problems. (The resources section at the end of this book offers links to support groups.)

One stepmother who attends a support group said, "I feel validated, supported, and have a place to learn positive approaches to stepparenting. Nothing I've ever done in my life could have prepared me for how hard it is to be a stepmother." Another stepmother, who regularly attends a support group in her own neighborhood, said, "To be a good stepmother means reconfiguring your expectations. It's the place where hopes and dreams collide with reality."

Barbara Perlmutter is the founder of Stepfamily Consultation and Counseling, in Seattle, which holds regular group sessions for stepmothers. She finds that the most common challenges for stepmoms are feelings of competition, shame, and rage; dealing with ex-wives; financial issues; self-care; and discipline.

"Stepmother groups are the highlight of my practice," Perlmutter says. "I am constantly reminded of the generosity of their spirit, understanding, and problem-solving skills. The courage, humor, emotion, and resilience that I witness reflects what each stepmother is called upon to provide." Perlmutter is uplifted by what she sees—the level of integrity, commitment, truthfulness, and energy of the women who take on the awesome task of mothering someone else's children.

Helpful Guidelines

- **Know what you're getting into before the wedding.** Refer to the checklist in this chapter, study it, and make sure you have answers to the questions raised in the list.

- **Lean on the husband you love and who loves you.** Without the full support, encouragement, and understanding of the husband, nothing will work in blending the new family. Attention and major concern for the marital relationship, the presentation of a united front that provides structure and security, and clear guidelines for appropriate behavior are vital requirements for a happily blended family. When the wife is secure in her new position with full spousal support, she will best be able to fulfill the stepmother role. Only by performing optimally will the stepmother receive the recognition and status she deserves. In other words, a wife who knows she's loved and respected by her husband will be able to meet the challenges of being a stepparent and feel good about it.

- **Insist on courtesy and respect from the get-go.** No matter how conflicted the family is, no matter how resistant the children are, no matter how vicious the ex-wife is, it's perfectly proper and sensible to demand that the family members extend courtesy and respect to one another and to the new stepmother. It's hard to retrench once the stepmother has taken the path of least resistance and allowed a breach of these fundamental aspects of civilized family life.

- **Don't be a martyr.** The stepmother is a person as well as a new wife. In these roles, she is entitled to have her needs, wants, and well-being considered by everyone in the family. She must make her desires known. To be too self-sacrificing will mean that the step-mother ends up feeling so much resentment that she will be of no value to anyone, including herself.

- **Understand your stepmother role as being that of a "caring adult."** As previously said, a stepmother is not and can never be the mother even if the mother is deceased, except in the rare instance of a very young child whose mother has died. Even though being a stepmother may include "mothering" responsibilities, the children will not feel the same way toward her as they do about their biological (or adoptive) mother. The stepmother is the woman of the house that she lives in, and she should participate as an equal partner of her husband in establishing guidelines for a smooth-running household. This should not be construed to mean a rigid list of directives. Compassion and flexibility are essential. Remember that one cruel act or comment can be remembered forever by people who don't have an instinctive love for one another.

- **Accept and cherish your husband, not only as your partner but also as the father of his children.** Before your marriage, your husband had a family. The husband's love and loyalty to his children should be viewed as a positive aspect of his manhood. The strong bond he feels for his children is now extended to the new wife. He, like most of us, has the capacity to love all the members of his family. By having a full understanding of the points made in this paragraph, you can avoid jealousy and competition.

- **Don't take stepchildren's resentments too personally.** The many challenges encountered by stepmothers are usually the result of her place as the successor to the first wife and mother of the children. She may be viewed as the intruder, not as the woman she is but as the new wife and stepmother. You might even be the sort of person they would really like if you weren't their stepmother.

- **Enjoy your marriage.** You are his wife. You are not "number two." Even if it feels that way because of the children, and because their needs have to come before your wants, you're still number one.

Remember that he's with you. Don't push him away. Don't make your entire relationship about the exes and the stepchildren. Yes, he was a package deal, as perhaps you were, too, but you don't want your private moments together primarily focused on the children, and all those others. She is his ex-wife, not yours, just as your ex-husband is your ex. Men are often better at compartmentalizing their lives than women are. But women, too, need to learn that skill.

- **Don't insist on being called "Mom,"** but do try to build a kinship with your stepchildren. Perhaps your stepchildren would be comfortable calling you *aunt* instead of just using your first name. "Aunt" conveys a feeling of kinship and connection, and we all respond to such symbols, particularly children. The basic rule is to talk names over with the children and find out what they prefer. Bear in mind that the biological parent may have strong feelings on the subject, and his or her desires need to be considered, too.

- **Try to establish a working relationship with the children's mother.** You may laugh or grimace at this suggestion. Believe it or not, it's the best thing you could do if it can be done. It's time to discredit the notion that the mother and stepmother are natural adversaries. If the stepmother wants to have an easier time with her stepchildren, she will do better with their mother in her corner. What better way than to let her know you have no intention of usurping her role, but you want to give the children a warm and hospitable environment when they visit. Tell her that she is vital to the children, and only with her help and advice can you offer the children good nurturing that is appropriate for their individual needs. Some ex-wives will scorn these efforts at friendship, but there will be others who are pleasantly surprised and will welcome the opportunity to be involved. You have nothing to lose by trying.

five

Ex-In-Laws, and
Other Extension Cords

S e c r e t   F i v e :

The extended family is always with you.

Parents expect certain events to occur in their children's lives—going away to school, getting a good job, marrying, and having children. Just when they think all their dreams have come true, the doorbell rings, and their daughter (or son) is standing there with a pained expression: "Mom, Dad, I'm getting divorced."

Extended family, particularly grandparents, may not view divorce and remarriage the same way you do, especially if they believe their relationships with your children are in jeopardy. In such instances, they can be quite visceral in showing their anger or disapproval, sometimes to the extent of shunning their own son or daughter.

The term "extended family" applies to not only your own family members but also to those of your ex-spouse and your new spouse. People who are family, or who were once considered family, can behave in ways that are harmful to the new marriage, because they fear that valued relationships may be lost or diminished. So why are these people, who should be supportive and helpful during a crisis, behaving destructively if they want to maintain contact with the children? For the moment, let's just say people who are afraid of what is about to happen aren't always in control of their behavior. Fear can prompt any of us to do things we normally wouldn't do. Unfortunately, extended family members may not be thinking about events they will want to attend—children's religious confirmations, school graduations, weddings, and even births of grandchildren, who may be the in-laws' great-grandchildren—and how their behavior during these times of trouble will affect whether or not they will be included in future times of joy.

Rejection and disapproval from friends may also occur with harmful comments such as: "How could you break up your family like that?", "What did you expect, marrying a man with custody of all those kids?" or "You sure didn't wait very long to remarry." (We all know the implications of that statement.)

Ideally, the adults involved in divorce and remarriage will anticipate some of these problems and prepare for them. But when difficulties do ensue, most of the time it's wise to let relatives and friends calm down, and to do nothing to exacerbate the situation. This can be a difficult challenge, because their about-face is often unexpected and painful, but staying calm and courteous may very well defuse some of their anger. In many cases, family members affected by divorce and remarriage do want to maintain a relationship with in-laws and former in-laws. And if you're the former in-law, remember, although the other set of in-laws are no longer a part of your family, they are still as much a part of your children's family as they were prior to the divorce.

WE NEED TO TALK

You and your spouse chose each other. It's a good bet you didn't choose his or her family. And it's an equally good bet that they didn't choose you, but once the wedding takes place, you *all* have one another "for better or worse."

Divorce and subsequent remarriage create a big change in all of the relationships involved, and grandparents may feel a particularly keen sense of loss of the grandchildren. That loss will be intensified if the family plans to move a distance away or if the mother now has the means to stay home with the children or hire help to care for them. And if the son or daughter is marrying someone who has children from a previous marriage, the grandparents are also being asked to adjust to the presence of "instant" step-grandchildren at the same time.

How to avoid the worst? It's advisable to open communication as quickly as possible with a heart-to-heart talk.

Talk! That's right. Talk!

Right from the beginning of the new marriage, it's best to realize how confused the extended family is, dealing with all these new people all at once. My best advice is that the wife should speak to her family and the husband should speak to his, keeping this thought in mind: decent folks are prone to do the right thing when they know what is expected of them. Speaking to your own family insures a better reception. Most people don't want someone they regard as an intruder—sort of like "the new kid on the block"—telling them what to do.

You're talking to your family. It's a given that every family has their own set of expectations. One grandmother might expect "children to be seen and not heard." Another might think there's something wrong with a child who doesn't speak up. Another might love little babies, but not adolescents. Some people are more openly affectionate and use words of endearment like "sweetie" or "honey." Others are more reserved and seemingly unapproachable. Getting everyone used to the others can be an awesome task, but one that can prevent serious misunderstanding down the road.

This *talk* serves multiple purposes: it enables everyone to have their say, to express how they want to relate to this new family, to learn more about these new people who are suddenly thrust on them, to get some idea of what the future holds in dealing with everyone else, and to set some ground rules both ways. Just figuring out how everyone is going to fit together is a good beginning and provides a necessary preview before the drama actually gets started.

With the exception of deliberate saboteurs, your own family wants you to be happy and to succeed in your new marriage. What they need to know is how they are expected to deal with all the children, the biological relatives, and the step-relatives.

One person who has a brother who just remarried a woman with three children had this to say: "My brother's perception of how we should be with his new family doesn't take into account the tenor of our lives. My parents are getting older, have less energy, and can't walk up and down steps like they used to. Their house has three bedrooms upstairs but they hardly ever use them, because Mom has trouble climbing the stairs. She and Dad have converted the first-floor family room into their bedroom, so my brother's expectation that the kids can use these bedrooms is unrealistic, unless he wants to pay for a maid to get the rooms ready and then clean them after his whole tribe leaves. When I suggested that, he got angry, reminding me how my children used the bedrooms when they were young and came to visit. I explained that Mom was younger then, plus I helped her take care of the children and the rooms. At first, he didn't buy that. Instead, he interpreted what I said as a rejection of his new wife and her children. But we kept talking until we reached an understanding about getting help for our parents on those occasional visits."

Here are ten topics that need to be aired at an early stage in the remarriage, before the onset of problems. Getting these issues out in the open in a positive and loving tone will go far to forestall difficulties. Let your family know:

1. That you don't expect immediate affection for your new spouse and children, just kindness and hope that with the passage of time, affection will develop. Ask them to be patient and understanding with these new children and your new spouse, and tell them how much you will appreciate their kindness. Assure them that you will be asking your new spouse and stepchildren to show the same understanding.

2. That you expect the appearance of equal treatment of all the children—the biological offspring and the stepchildren. Ask them specifically to give holiday gifts of comparable value to each child, even if it means spending less on each gift. Explain that this will help you and them to nurture better relationships with your new spouse and his or her children.

3. That you will be expected to spend time with your new spouse's extended family, so you will have to see your family on alternate holidays, as you probably did during a first marriage if there was one.

4. If your remarriage means moving a distance away, this is the right time to discuss it with the family, assuring them that you will make every effort to visit as often as time and money will permit and that they will be welcome in your home.

5. Discuss how your parents would like to be addressed by the new family members, and remind them that it will have to be mutually comfortable.

6. If there are religious, racial, or cultural differences, or even important political differences, explain them up front. Whatever your family's initial reaction, implore them to be tolerant and understanding for your sake and for the sake of their grandchildren.

7. If there are financial differences, this is the time to let the family know it. For example, if you and your new family are going to have to live more frugally than you were living during your first marriage, and even during the time you were divorced, talk about it. Perhaps the remarriage means giving up alimony from your previous marriage, and that sum of money will not be replaced in this remarriage, because your new spouse has support obligations to his first family. It's better to get it out on the table than to have to hear them complaining about what you had to give up for "that man."

8. Give them a chance to express their own reservations and anxieties. Tell them you want the families to be comfortable with one another so that you, your children, and your parents can be together as much as time permits. Explain that if tension develops, it will have the effect of lessening the number of family get-togethers. Assure them that you will do everything possible to avoid tension, and explain that you expect them to do the same.

9. If your family is close to your ex-spouse and wants to remain close, be open about how you feel. It might be fine with you as

long as they don't carry tales back and forth. Let them know that.
If that ongoing relationship presents a problem, try to explain
your rationale. If you're asking them to curtail the relationship,
they are your family and deserve to know why.

10.   Let your family know that *you* want to hear about problems be-
       fore they become tidal waves and damaging to relationships. A
       good way to end a conversation of this type is to remind your
       family that the love you feel for your new spouse in no way di-
       minishes the love you have for them. You just want another
       chance for happiness. And even if your family knows you love
       them, during these times it's a good idea to reassure them of your
       devotion.

WHAT'S MINE IS MINE

Grandparents usually transfer their loyalty to the current spouse of their
son or daughter, unless there is a risk to their relationship with the
grandchildren. In that case, they may decide that rapport with the parent who has primary custody is critical to their ongoing relationship
with their grandchildren, and forsake their parental loyalty to their own
child. Sometimes the problem is solved by only the passage of time and
the assurance that the grandchildren are not lost to them. This fear of
loss can even be felt by the parents of a daughter who has primary custody of her children from a previous marriage, but who is remarrying
and moving these grandchildren a distance away.

Maryanne had been married for ten years and had two children, Tom and Nanette. After Maryanne's divorce, every day after
school Tom and Nanette went directly to their grandparents' house and
waited there until their mother picked them up at the end of her workday. Maryanne's parents loved having the grandchildren around on a
daily basis.

Three years after her divorce, Maryanne developed a serious relationship with Alan, a man who worked for the same company she did.
Alan lived in another town and had custody of his teenage son from his
first marriage. Maryanne's parents were very cold toward Alan, and

made no attempt to welcome him or his son. When Maryanne told her parents that she and Alan were getting married, they were devastated, particularly when they learned that Maryanne and the children would be moving to the town where Alan lived because his son was just one year away from high school graduation.

After the marriage took place and the family relocated, the grandparents felt as if their lives had been shattered by the loss of contact with their grandchildren. Twenty-five miles became a real barrier to the grandparent-grandchildren relationship.

Maryanne's ex-husband, who had the children every other weekend, was still living a few miles from Maryanne's parents. As maternal grandparents they immediately strengthened their bond with their former son-in-law, and for the next couple of years they froze Maryanne and her new husband out of their lives. Maryanne knew that the reason for the acrimony was not a personal dislike of Alan or his son but rather her parents' devotion to their grandchildren and their loss of day-to-day contact with them. Eventually, by assuring her parents that they would always be a major part of the children's lives, Maryanne was able to mend the rift. Alan was a wise enough man to understand his wife's parents' sense of loss and not take it personally. Moreover, Alan's son was old enough at the time of the remarriage to not be harmed by the coldness of the step-grandparents.

IN-LAWS OR OUTLAWS

Sometimes for the sake of family harmony, and to prevent hurt feelings or harm to a child, adults need to make certain sacrifices—as did one outcast father I interviewed. George and Celia had been married for twenty years when George announced that he wanted a divorce. He also told Celia that he wanted to marry a woman he had been seeing on his out-of-town trips. George and Celia had three children, ages eighteen, seventeen, and thirteen. Celia was the betrayed wife who didn't want a divorce. She begged George to give up the "other woman" and to see a marriage counselor. Celia turned to her own family for solace. They intervened and tried to persuade George to reconsider, but he refused.

However he and Celia did attend counseling sessions for three months. The outcome: George proceeded with the divorce. Two months after it was final, he married Teresa, the "other woman."

Celia's family was furious with him for having broken up what she believed was a happy home. In fact, the "happy home" had been purely a facade. George had been miserable with Celia for years. Celia had been concerned primarily with maintaining her social position in the town where she and George grew up. She was punctual about getting to the hairdresser, the seamstress who altered her designer clothes, the charitable committees on which she served, and her tennis games at the club. She was always soft-spoken and seemingly agreeable with George, but when it came to the warmth and emotional support he needed from a wife, she was unable to provide that. Her emotions ran from polite to polite. Appearances were what mattered most to Celia and to her family. George's children were old enough to understand how unhappy he had been in the marriage, but they sided with their mother because of their father's infidelity.

After George's marriage to Teresa, the children refused to visit him at his new home, but agreed that they would see him elsewhere. Those visits lasted about two months, until Celia's family began to influence two of the three children to shun their father. Celia's sister and mother began to gossip about George's new wife, calling her "a low-class gold digger." George's eighteen-year-old son refused to be brainwashed against his father, and actually did have a realistic picture of his parents' marriage. When this son was graduating from high school, George was faced with the prospect of seeing his former wife and all of her immediate relatives. George resolved to keep his contact with his ex-in-laws to an unemotional minimum on his son's special day.

Other than a perfunctory greeting to the former in-laws, George and Teresa barely spoke to anyone except his son. Celia and the other two children avoided eye contact and said not a word to George and his wife. When the family disbanded after the ceremony, everyone, including George and Teresa, was invited to his ex-wife's parents' home. George's own parents, the other set of grandparents, agreed to go back to the house for the family get-together. Though George wanted to attend the celebration, Teresa thought it would not be a good idea. Finally,

George agreed with Teresa and chose instead to bid a warm farewell to his son and explain that he didn't want to create an uncomfortable atmosphere for him on this occasion. He invited his son to come over to his home for dinner on another night. After a warm embrace with his son, George and Teresa left the school auditorium.

George kept his thoughts positive and centered on his child and on the occasion. He avoided any appearance of resentment and behaved civilly to everyone, but wanted to be certain there would be no embarrassment to his children or discomfort for Teresa, so he politely declined the invitation to the home of his former in-laws.

This situation is typical of divorce and remarriage with children, even with the additional complication of adultery. It's difficult for parents not to feel resentment toward their former son-in-law or daughter-in-law if the divorce was painful for their own child and grandchildren.

THE GRANDPARENT CONNECTION

Grandparents often provide critical love, support, and understanding to the children who have had to undergo the trauma of divorce and the upheaval of remarriage by one or both of their parents. They can offer unconditional love as well as a sense of continuity for children experiencing the chaos of a broken home. It's best for all concerned that the grandparents not take sides or if they do, avoid revealing that bias to anyone. But sometimes this advice is easier to hear than to follow.

Annette and Fred were devoted grandparents, but they never expected to have to deal with step-grandchildren. When their daughter married the first time, and eventually had two little girls, Annette and Fred were delighted, because they lived in the same town and had easy access to their two granddaughters, ages seven and nine.

Sadly, their son-in-law died of cancer in his late thirties. Their daughter decided to go back to school and get a teaching degree. There she met a professor, who was a widower with two sons. When the daughter and the professor decided to marry, Annette and Fred were overjoyed and looking forward to having their new son-in-law's two boys, ages thirteen and ten, join the girls.

During their daughter's first year of marriage, Annette and Fred got to know the boys well enough to have all four children stay with them on occasional long weekends so that their daughter and her new husband could have more time to themselves. Soon Annette and Fred began to regret the frequent visits, because the boys were getting unruly and difficult to control. The grandparents continued to try to treat the children equally, but they found themselves yearning for the way it had been when they had relaxed visits with their granddaughters. Those days of baking cookies and having little tea parties or picnics in the park were gone.

The boys had to be watched every minute. Not only were they boisterous, but they had become verbally rude and insulting. Fred tried taking the boys out separately from the girls, thinking they needed to expend some of their energy playing ball or going bowling while Annette spent time with her granddaughters. No matter how much Fred tried to entertain the boys, he was unable to keep them from getting bored and misbehaving. Annette and Fred began to resent their daughter's stepsons. They gradually cut down their contact with all four grandchildren, not knowing how to continue visits with the granddaughters without creating friction with their daughter and her husband if they were to exclude his boys.

This whole situation left Annette and Fred feeling guilty, ashamed, and worried, especially about the damage to their relationship with their beloved granddaughters. Annette and Fred were also aware of how much effort their daughter was putting into the blending of the new family. They wanted to support her and give her some of the extra time she badly needed to nurture her marriage, but they couldn't seem to love the boys the way they did their granddaughters.

Finally, Annette spoke to her daughter about the problem. Initially, her daughter eased the situation by having the boys visit their other grandparents, but that didn't work out as well as they hoped it would. The other grandparents were much older than Annette and Fred and didn't have the energy needed to babysit the boys for more than a few hours at a time. The families rocked along and tried to juggle the children as best they could. Fortunately, Annette and Fred were decent, sensitive people who forced themselves to conceal any hostility toward the two step-grandsons. They knew that in a few more years the problem would resolve itself, because teenagers eventually grow up.

Annette and Fred's story is not unusual. With blended families surpassing biological families as the norm in the United States, more grandparents than ever are in the same predicament. It's an ongoing challenge to sort through feelings of partiality, resentment, and guilt. Even in the best of situations—such as Fred and Annette's, where there was no divorce but rather a remarriage of a widow and widower (both with children from prior marriages)—the involvement of extended family has its inherent problems. So, is it any wonder that the presence of divorce, particularly an acrimonious split, will create even more turbulence?

GUIDELINES FOR GRANDPARENTS

What if you're a grandparent who has been cut off from your grandchildren because the custodial parent is carrying on a vendetta, and depriving you of access to the children as a means of punishing your divorced son or daughter? What if your daughter-in-law or son-in-law has sent out a notice of divorce thanking all the in-laws who helped make the *glorious event* possible? You can still repair the relationship for the sake of the children, as well as for yourself. If you've done nothing to justify the estrangement from the grandchildren, it's best to have a talk with the former daughter- or son-in-law. Explain that you understand the anger that exists between the once-married couple, but you want to continue to maintain the grandparent-grandchild relationship and will do whatever you can to be supportive of the children, whom you love. Also set the record straight—make it clear that you do not want to get in the middle of the problems that the former husband and wife have, nor do you want to have the children hurt in any way.

In *Grandparents/Grandchildren: The Vital Connection,* Arthur Kornhaber and Kenneth Woodward advise grandparents to "let everyone in your family know that they have you to rely on in a family emergency." Divorce and remarriage are sufficiently stressful to be considered emergencies, particularly from the perspective of the children.

This is the time for grandparents to offer support that children need in time of loss and uncertainty. They can be the most wonderful resource that a family can have during these traumatic changes in their lives.

In *Surviving the Breakup,* Judith S. Wallerstein and Joan B. Kelly report on a landmark study of how children and parents cope during the first five years after divorce. The authors stress strong extended-family relationships as a crucial variable in the children's adjustment. They note that those children "who had extended families, especially grandparents, who were close by or who kept up a continuing interest from a distance, were very much helped by this support system."

How to Avoid Estrangement from Your Grandchildren

- Don't be too hasty and aggressive. If the custodial parent remarries, give him or her plenty of time to make the new marriage work.

- If you are denied visitation, don't run out and start a lawsuit. First open dialogue with the parent or parents. Try to find out what the problem is.

- Where direct communication is difficult, ask another family member to serve as a neutral conduit. Most experts in divorce counseling believe that it is not harm to the child that is feared by the parent but rather that the grandparent will disparage the parent in front of the children. Offer reassurance on this score. Discuss ground rules for visitation with parents beforehand. For example: You agree to request convenient times for visits and to stick to the arrangements made for pickup and delivery of the children. You promise not to make disparaging remarks about the parents in front of the child. You will not undermine the parents' wishes with regard to the children, nor will you buy expensive gifts for the children without first discussing them with the mother/father. You will go to whatever lengths necessary to insure that the children will be safe and happy in your company. If the children want to telephone the parent at any time, you will make sure they are able to do so.

- Then, of course, follow these agreements!

- If talking directly or through a neutral family member is not working, try to enlist the family into counseling. Where that's not feasible, professional mediation is a helpful alternative. Family courts are a useful resource for mediation professionals.

- When all else fails, legal action may be the only remedy, but with this caveat: it is an emotionally wrenching and financially expensive pursuit that may not accomplish the goal you want—namely, a loving relationship with a grandchild.

To proceed with legal action, it's wise to locate an attorney familiar with family issues in the state where the grandparent is seeking visitation. The lawyer referral service of state bar associations can be a useful resource for locating attorneys who specialize in this area of the law. Or consult Grandparents United for Children's Rights (see resources).

That said, and knowing the downside of court action, what else can be done to remedy grandparent alienation? If possible, have grandparent visitation rights included in the divorce decree. When it's too late for that to occur, find alternative ways to continue the relationships advises Arthur Kornhaber, M.D., a Lake Placid, New York, psychiatrist and president of the Foundation for Grandparenting. Write letters, call—let the kids know you're interested. Send gifts for birthdays and holidays. And never make them feel they have an emotional conflict of interest.

CAREFUL—GRANDPARENTS HAVE RIGHTS, TOO

Now let's put the shoe on the other foot. What happens when you're a former son-in-law or daughter-in-law and you want to exclude the grandparents from the family because these parents of the ex-spouse are a constant reminder of the person who has been eliminated from your life?

Think again. Tossing out your former mother-in-law with the wedding album is not fair to the children. She is their grandmother, even if she's no longer a part of your own life. If you exclude the children's grandparents (the good ones, not the ones who drink too much and act inappropriately in front of the children, not the abusers or criminals), you are depriving your children of a source of love and support that they need and deserve. *There can never be too many people to love a child.* Let's face it, even if you have a former mother-in-law who halts traffic to help salamanders cross the road, if she's good to the children, she should be a welcome part of the family.

In recent years, the question of grandparents' legal rights to visitation has become a controversial issue. On the one hand, why should grandchildren be denied time with a grandparent just because their parents are divorced? Conversely, at what point does the intervention of the courts infringe on the parents' rights to decide who their children may see? During divorce, people often feel that they have little or no control over their lives anymore. The courts may tell them how to live, where to live, and how much money to live on. Now custodial parents are being told that their child must be made available to the grandparent on a specific day for a specified amount of time? Add to that legal obligation the personal obligation to a new spouse who also has expectations for visiting his or her parents, plus obligations to visit your own parents. Why should you have to add mandatory visits to the parents of your ex-spouse?

Lawsuits can be ugly. Detailed and public airing of family secrets is a consequence of the adversarial court process that may ensue. For everyone concerned, it's important to remember that every aspect of the conflict will be magnified and will leave a residue of anger, humiliation, and distrust. So why provide fertile soil to grow a lawsuit?

Nevertheless, grandparents can and do sue for visitation. Each state has its own laws in this regard, and not every grandparent denied access to the grandchildren will qualify for court-ordered visitation. Fortunately, many state laws now provide reasonable visitation rights for maternal and paternal grandparents. In addition, a federal law passed in 1998 mandates that a visitation order granted to a grandparent in one state must be recognized in any state where the grandchild is living.

A 2000 decision by the U.S. Supreme Court *(Troxel v. Granville)* implicitly acknowledged the right of grandparents to sue for visitation. However, it also affirmed the right of "fit parents" to make decisions about the "care, custody and control" of their children. A grandparent's case will be stronger if he or she has been denied visitation altogether, as opposed to simply wanting more time with the child.

THE HARMFUL GRANDPARENT

All grandparents are not warm and fuzzy. Sometimes a grandparent can be harmful to young children, not only because of wrongdoing but because of age and infirmity. The latter situation can be overcome by having visits with another adult present.

When grandparents have serious behavior problems, the parents must protect the children, even to the extent of denying the grandparent access, but that action should be reserved for the most extreme situations, such as severe alcohol or drug addiction or physical or sexual abuse to the child, or for cases where the grandparent is seriously upsetting the child because he or she is unwilling to stop making degrading remarks about the child's parents or stepparents.

When these situations arise, it's best to have discussions with other family members who are close to the offending grandparent. Explanations for denied access can often be a benefit to all concerned. It can even be the trigger for getting professional help for the problem grandparent.

MIXED BLESSINGS

A divorce often changes the balance of the adult child's relationship with his or her parents. One divorced son was genuinely grateful for his parents' welcome and warm support of the children. However, as he discovered, there can be a downside to such arrangements.

Brian is recently divorced and has alternate-weekend visitation with his two young children. Brian cannot afford an apartment large enough to accommodate his kids, so he visits with them at his parents' house. Brian's mother is the consummate nurturer and loves the visits with the grandchildren. But she also wants appreciation and gratitude for providing the space, food, and continuous attention that young children require. When she began to remind her son to wash his hands before coming to the table, he began to feel like the older brother of his children. This was not the role he wanted to present to his children. Luckily, he had the kind of close relationship with his mother that allowed him to tell her to back off and let him be the parent. Once the problem was resolved, the visits became comfortable for everyone, so much so that Brian actually moved back home with his folks until he was able to reestablish himself financially.

SEEING THE BIG PICTURE

Julie's former in-laws had always been good to the children, both in nurturing them and in providing some financial support. In addition to wonderful birthday and Christmas presents, they paid for the children's music lessons and summer camp and made annual contributions to an education fund that they had set up when the children were born.

It was no secret that they resented Julie's decision to divorce their son, but they continued to treat her decently. Three years after the divorce, Julie met another man and fell in love with him. When she announced her decision to marry again, her former in-laws grew cold and distant, but continued their contact with the grandchildren. Then, Julie began to find excuses why the children couldn't see their grandparents. Eventually, the relationship between the grandparents and the children depended entirely on their son's visitation with his children. He would bring the children to his parents' house, and they would all visit together. After a time, Julie realized that she was being unfair to her children, and admitted that she really liked her former in-laws and that her behavior was selfish and destructive.

Soon after Julie married, she telephoned her former mother-in-law and apologized for not having been as loving and grateful as she should have been for all the good things they'd always done for her and the children. The relationship was mended, and the children happily began to spend more time with their grandparents.

But what happens if the grandparents continue the acrimony because of the divorce? The custodial parent has a difficult decision to make, because no parent wants their children to hear disparaging remarks made about them. This is a time for a direct conversation. It's worth the effort to try to resolve these differences for the sake of the children. Either by phone or letter, or preferably in person, tell the grandparents that you want them to continue to be a part of the children's lives, but that it upsets the children to hear negative comments about their mother/ father. And don't make this a threat, though there is certainly a threat implicit in the request that they stop their bad-mouthing. If the remarks continue and the children are still upset, tell the grandparents they can't go on seeing the children until they stop their unkind commentary to the children about the parent.

WALLS OR BRIDGES

Suddenly there are step-grandparents. Generally that's the way it happens. Biological grandparents usually have several months to get used to the idea that their son or daughter is having a child. There's time to buy a crib and a layette or paint the walls of the baby's room. Some may even be lucky enough to be right there in the delivery room when the birth occurs. The baby is a joyful part of the family and may even resemble one or more of the grandparents.

The son or daughter's remarriage to someone with children means that those children are now a part of the family, whether the grandparent likes it or not. And sometimes they don't like it, don't even like the spoiled, hyperactive stepchild that their adult child must now live with. There is the added worry about what he or she has gotten himself/ herself into. And where does this step-grandchild fit in with the "real" grandchildren? How should the child address this new step-grandparent? When there are hugs for the other children, does the step-grandchild get hugged, too?

Maybe there are education funds set up as Christmas or birthday presents for the "real" grandchildren. Does the step-grandchild have to have one, too? There is certainly another alternative that draws attention away from the disparate treatment. These funds can be set up and money added to them quietly without focusing attention on this type of gift during holiday celebrations.

Of course, the inequality will emerge when the grandchild is given educational opportunities that are not available for the step-grandchild, but still, there is only so much money to go around. Providing funds for education depends on each family's unique situation: for example, just how much money is available, and how many step-grandchildren are there? These questions need to be addressed honestly. Parents and children, too, need to understand that grandparents who are not wealthy but do have some resources for helping to educate their own grandchildren may not be able to do the same thing for step-grandchildren.

The age of the child when he or she becomes a step-grandchild is another factor to consider. Older kids may want equal treatment, but may not be particularly close to the step-grandparents, especially if they have a relationship with grandparents of their own. Perhaps parents can spend more of their own money on the children who are not receiving grandparent funding. In all other respects, holiday gifts should be reasonably equal for all the children, and when there is glaring favoritism, hurt feelings are bound to follow.

A Christmas Rebellion

Wendy and Lance had been married for four years. Each one had a teenage child from a first marriage. Since Wendy's parents were living overseas and came to the states every spring, the family spent Christmas visiting Lance's parents. Mindy, Lance's daughter, always received lavish gifts of clothing, jewelry, books, and cash from his parents, while Karen, Wendy's daughter, received a $25 gift certificate from a local department store. Karen always left Lance's parents' house feeling hurt and depressed because of the gross inequity of the gifts received. Eventually, she began to resent her entire stepfamily, including Lance, his parents, and Mindy. Finally, she didn't want to spend the holidays with this family. One Christmas, Karen's adamant refusal to go to their house caused a tense standoff between Wendy and Lance. The holiday was ruined for everyone, because Wendy, in support of her daughter, also refused to go to Lance's parents' home until the problem could be resolved. As of the writing of this book, the two families are still at odds, because Lance doesn't want to upset his elderly parents.

Children cannot appreciate the complexities of these types of situations and should not be expected to understand such disparate treatment. In fact, despite the advanced ages of Lance's parents, he should have found a way to talk to them in order to salvage what was left of the family togetherness, and hopefully, in time, repair the relationships. He could have explained to his folks that they weren't being asked to feel the same way about a step-grandchild as they did about their natural grandchild, but that to be considerate of the step-grandchild's feelings, the gifts should have been comparable. If Lance's parents failed to respond, he and Wendy might have to make other plans for the holidays. They could spend alternate holidays elsewhere, either in their own home or with other family members, or on a holiday trip.

A WILLING HEART

In these difficult situations, it's imperative for all concerned to remember that *the step-grandchild is first and foremost a child.* Every adult must do whatever he or she can to avoid hurting or offending any child. That doesn't mean the step-grandparent has to love the new step-grandchild. Love isn't automatic. It may take time to develop love for someone else's child who is not related by blood. But if the time is given with a willing heart, most young children are fairly easy to love. I don't think that necessarily applies to teenagers, but then, there are moments when we don't even love our own teenage children!

Sylvia described the situation with her parents and her husband's daughter (from an earlier marriage) as reserved at best and rejecting at worst. "After five years, my mother and father are unwilling to make even a pretense that my stepdaughter is as welcome in their home as their biological grandchildren are. I've begged them to try to show some warmth to this nine-year-old girl, who is really quite a lovely child. If I can love her—and I do—why can't they? It's not that they do anything mean, but it's just an attitude that comes across when they're around the little girl. She's still calling them Mr. and Mrs."

The chilly relationship is bound to hurt the child. And, as a result, the new son-in-law is bound to respond unfavorably—if not at first, then certainly in time.

The cohesiveness of a family depends on everyone's feeling that they are welcome, loved, and treated fairly.

In-laws and step-relations may not have the right to expect love, but they have the right to expect to be treated fairly and welcomed into the newly blended family. What can Sylvia do to persuade her parents to be kinder and more accepting of their step-granddaughter? First, she needs to make them aware of the situation from her perspective. If that doesn't produce the desired results, then she should caution them that they are going to see less of her if they continue to reject their step-grandchild. Most grandparents want contact with their families more than almost anything, so Sylvia's words of caution are likely to work.

One simple way to start repairing the rift is to suggest the grandparents put their arms around the child and say, "I think it's time that you called us Grandma Alice and Grandpa Jim."

Hopefully, the child won't respond by saying, "You aren't my grandparents." If that were to happen, as it does occasionally, the best response is "We may not be your real grandparents, but we'd like to feel as though we are, and we thought by calling us Grandma Alice and Grandpa Jim, you might get to feel that way, too."

By adding first names, there's no confusion, the identification is clear, and the titles don't appropriate those of the child's actual grandparents. Of course, what children call their grandparents can be as varied as children are creative. Some call their grandparents Grandma and Grandpa Smith or Papa and Nanny. Whatever the title, the purpose is to establish a warm, familial relationship. My own grandchildren have combined Grandma and Barbara to call me Baba. In fact, whenever possible, I spend Friday with one of my grandsons, and he refers to the day as his "Baba day." I couldn't be more thrilled.

One step-grandparent went to pick up her step-grandson at soccer practice. When she arrived, the coach asked her who she was, since they had never seen her before. She stammered, not knowing what to call herself. Finally, she blurted out, "I'm his granny." When the boy appeared, the coach watched as he ran to her and hugged her. Because there was a warm and loving relationship between them, she didn't feel comfortable identifying herself as his step-grandmother. "It's too much of a mouthful," she said, "and it really doesn't express the way we feel about him." And what child wants to address someone as "step-grandmother" or "step-grandfather"? It sounds and feels unnatural.

When a child spills cherry soda all over the new sofa or breaks a piece of your fine china, it shouldn't matter that the child is your step-grandchild. An accident is an accident. It might be more difficult to be forgiving when it's someone else's kid who did the damage, but if the family is to remain close, that child must be treated the same way a natural child is treated. In such circumstances to forgive is really divine. And this applies to everyone, grandparents and parents alike—aunts and uncles, too.

PUT IT TO THEM

Okay, let's say it's a bust. The new spouse and his or her children are not being accepted. This is an extremely painful situation for the remarried parent, who now feels torn between his or her parents and the new spouse. This is as close to an impasse as it gets, but it doesn't have to be that way. The power comes from taking a firm position and making it clear to parents and the extended family that you'll never be happy in their company if they can't accept your new spouse. When a strong stand is taken, even if the parents are angry and upset at first, they usually will come to the realization that the alternative is losing their child, and that's something they won't want to do.

Sometimes the new spouse is accepted, but not the new step-grandchildren. If the children are late teens or older, it doesn't matter very much, but with younger children it matters greatly. Not only does it hurt the children, but it puts the marriage in jeopardy. It's only natural to avoid contact with and resent people who are rejecting your children. If the people who are hurting your stepchildren happen to be your parents, then you can expect a rippling effect that will create real family strife.

As a key rule of thumb, the primary responsibility for action falls to the spouse whose parents are causing the problem.

Let the parents know that their lack of acceptance of innocent children is harmful to the children and cannot be tolerated. Let them know contact will be at a minimum if it continues.

Tips for Step-Grandparents

- Accept your role as a bit player, not the star of the show.

- Bringing two families together is difficult under the best of circumstances. Do what you can to minimize conflict, versus creating more.

- Don't get nosy about the past. Don't pry.

- Remember birthdays and special events. Just being there encourages a relationship.

- Do things with the children, even taking them to a movie if you can't stand on your feet for very long.

- Support the parents' rules and expectations.

- Find opportunities to praise the child, and be slow to criticize.

- Don't say unkind things about the child's family members.

- Always give the appearance of equal treatment.

- Tell the children about the world when you were a child. It's a neutral subject and all kids love hearing about Grandpa's military service, the first television shows, the days before computer, and the myths about the moon until we finally got there.

GRANDPARENT SABOTAGE

Some parents go to great lengths to punish the son or daughter who has broken up the family by divorcing. They may threaten to disown their son or daughter if he or she remarries. They may cut off contact with their own grandchildren. They may discriminate in their treatment of family members, giving more to siblings in intact first marriages. They, like the children of divorce, have the unrealistic hope that but for this remarriage, the son or daughter would have returned, and still might return to the first spouse, and the original family would be whole again.

It's hard to believe that parents will do things that are so damaging to their own adult children, but they do. They are quite capable of nasty gossip, of talking disparagingly about you to your children, of aligning themselves with your ex-spouse, and, as described, of rejecting your new family. Why do they do these mean-spirited things? These are ways in which grandparents, in their frustration and hurt, sometimes try to compensate for their feelings of loss and helplessness. In a perverse way, they are trying to regain control of a situation they believe has gone awry. Perhaps the grandparents received many benefits from a wealthy son-in-law that they are now losing. There may even be a religious component, with a belief that divorce is sinful and what God brings together "shall not be torn asunder." Or they may believe, as is the case of some religions, that the sacrament of the original marriage cannot be violated. For example, in the absence of annulment, the Catholic Church does not recognize remarriage as long as the ex-spouse is still living.

However, religious beliefs do not justify sabotaging a marriage. Putting the marriage first may require severing ties with those trying to destroy it if, after a warning, they persist in acting destructively. Control what you can, and know that relationships ebb and flow over the years. Family alliances alter due to many unforeseen occurrences. The children grow up and they leave. In time, things usually correct themselves.

WATERING THE FAMILY TREE

Janette's in-laws welcomed their son's ex-wife, Janette (his current wife), stepchildren, and ex-in-laws with warmth and camaraderie at a big Thanksgiving dinner. This didn't happen immediately. It took a couple of years. Of course, Janette's in-laws had the advantage of knowing that their son and his former wife and current wife, as well as all the kids, hadn't suffered through embittered divorces.

"My mother-in-law is a jewel," Janette said. "She and my father-in-law rented a room at their country club, because they didn't have enough space in their condo for the combined families. My two kids from my first marriage were there, as well as my husband's former wife, their two kids, her current husband, and her daughter from that marriage. Her parents, my parents, my husband's sister and her family, and her husband's parents were all there. It has started a Thanksgiving tradition. Now when we sit down to eat dinner, the oldest living member says the blessing. It always includes gratitude to God for all of us being there to enjoy each other and the holiday together, rather than being apart. Even if it means everyone has to chip in to pay the costs, I recommend it."

Of course, the key to this family gathering was the fact that there were no ugly divorces to drive the families apart. Obviously, when one or both members of a marriage that failed are left feeling betrayed, rejected, angry, and bitter, as a consequence there will be enemy camps, with families being forced to choose sides. Whether this could work when that degree of resentment is present is doubtful. But in time, usually in two or more years, the heightened emotions cool off, and when they do, it's worth trying to reconnect the families. Grandparents are in a unique position to do this if they have been able to maintain a position of neutrality.

Depending on how the family is approached, how realistic expectations are, and how patient everyone is in allowing the families to get acquainted the family can be a steady support and a kind of haven when the rest of the world seems unreceptive. It's worth the time and effort to mesh the extended family into the orbit of the newly created family.

Helpful Guidelines

- **Within reason, be tolerant of differences in new family members.** New family members, just like your first set of in-laws, might be radically different from people in your own extended family. They may have a different set of morals, values, and histories, and expectations of their own. They may want to do things in ways that you find unacceptable or that are even strange by your standards. Differences need to be tolerated without any visible signs of anger or resentment. But you don't have to tolerate criminal, depraved, destructive, or dangerous behavior. For example, if they keep guns around and you have children, talk to your spouse and ask that the guns be locked up in a safe place.

- **Be as honest as possible without being hurtful.** Stay close to grandparents. Even if there are moments of contention, try to be as direct as possible about what you can and can't do. It's preferable to pent-up resentment. As the son or daughter who is the parent of the grandchildren, there has to be a conscious effort to ease the grandparents' fear of loss and to strengthen their ties to the stepchildren. For example, if you want to foster equal treatment of children at gift-giving time, provide gift suggestions within the appropriate range. Most grandparents would be deeply grateful for hints of winning gifts.

- **When there are conflicts, enlist the help of other family members if talking to your parents isn't working.** What you are feeling is probably what others are feeling. Encourage the members of the family to discuss their concerns so that you can address them. Enlist the help of other family members who may be walking a parallel path. They can be a source of empathy, strength, and guidance in understanding these conflicts.

- **If grandparents are reasonable adults, have a family conference that includes the children.** Biological and step-grandchildren can benefit from the opportunity to contribute their ideas and strategies for successful visits. Tell the children that because of the age of the grandparents, time to rest is needed. Work out ways to give rest breaks during the visit. There should be no embarrassment in asking for cooperation from everyone so that the relationships are close and enduring.

- **When you sense a problem between your parents and the step-grandchildren, invite them to talk to you about it.** Love for a blended grandchild is not automatic, but it can develop, given time and a willingness to embrace the child. A point of connection needs to be found and nurtured. The entire relationship doesn't need to be forged immediately. The parents must set the tone for what happens in the broad sense of family, but the grandparents should have input. If a rambunctious child needs stronger discipline, the parents should know what is happening, with the intention of working with the grandparents to correct the misbehavior so that the visits can continue, not end. Always keep in mind that a too hasty reaction can inflict lasting wounds in what may be described as a precarious situation. Extended family should be encouraged to reach out, and the children will eventually respond.

- **Talk to grandparents about the loss children feel as a result of the trauma of death, divorce, and remarriage.** Many grandparents have no frame of reference and need to be informed of what the children are experiencing. Spending time with a new stepparent's parent can stir up ambivalence or even resentment in a child who has either just lost a parent to death or has been traumatized by the divorce and remarriage of a parent. Even an otherwise happy child may slip into a funk or become sullen for no apparent reason. If nothing has been done to provoke the sudden change of mood, it shouldn't be taken personally. Most children of divorce and/or remarriage need time to work out feelings of divided loyalties, grief, fear, anxiety, and confusion. They didn't bargain for this new family any more than the new family bargained for them, but now they're thrown together by the choices of others over which neither side had much control. A period of adjustment is needed, and adults must be gentle with the children and let them know that they understand that change within a family can be difficult to handle.

- **Arrange get-together times.** Arrange for grandparents and grandchildren to do things together as they may have done before the remarriage. The same scheduling should be done for step-grandparents and step-grandchildren so they have the opportunity to get to know one another, starting with short visits. From time to time, all the adults should get together without the children. Even the two sets of in-laws should have opportunities to get to know one another. And don't burden elderly grandparents with too many rambunctious children. Their nerves won't take it.

- **Recognize the limitations of aging.** Just like the rest of the members of the new household, the older folks need time to adjust to the changes that have taken place. Even in very extreme situations— such as when a remarried son or daughter has been disowned or disinherited by a hurt and angry parent—slow reconciliation is very likely to occur over a period of time, as long as everyone knows the door has been left open for this to happen. Memory loss can also be a problem for older folks. Making sure Grandma knows the new stepchild's birthday might silently convey the expectation that she send a card or gift.

- **Create a new family history.** Most families have albums of photos to look back on to provide a sense of stability and reminders of happy times. Often there is at least one member who loves to organize, collect, photograph, and document. Enlist that person to work with the grandparents and all the children to begin a new photo album that includes everyone in the newly created family—with both group and individual shots. This activity, if done with a sense of family spirit, can help the new stepfamily initiate a concrete record of their new family history.

The Pleasure of Your Company . . .

Secret Six:

Holidays and celebrations call for flexibility and creativity.

Face it—deep down, we suspect everyone else is having a better holiday than we are. Their turkeys are more golden, their trees more beautiful, and their entire holiday season is crammed with parties and good cheer. Everything is fueled by images in the mass media and our personal recollections, real or imagined. We tend to assume that under every roof is a happy, harmonious family more love-filled and more satisfying than our own. But this is a very skewed picture of reality. People don't suddenly and magically get along during the holiday season, especially if they're not getting along the rest of the year. If there are problems, as there often are in blended families, the holidays and other celebratory events frequently are the ideal settings for new (and old) conflicts and frustrations to surface.

In the early years of a blended family, special-occasion conflicts can be opportunities. Blended families should view conflicts not as negative events but as opportunities to develop their own traditions. Learning to negotiate with one another is part of developing intimacy while maintaining independence. The main task is not how to avoid conflicts but how to deal with them effectively so that as they occur, hostility and resentment will be minimized. Ultimately, patterns will establish themselves and conflicts will lessen.

Countless times we've heard that there's no place like home for the holidays. But which home? For millions of blended families, the annual question is fraught with anxiety and contention. Whose home will be the center of activity? How many turkey dinners can anyone eat in a day? Should you force children to visit during the holiday break when they want to stay home and be with their friends?

And what about the other special events and celebrations that should bring families together? Now that the biological father has faded from his children's lives, who walks Pammy down the aisle? And if divorced parents decide to remarry, whose children, if any, will attend the wedding? Or that all-important college graduation, milestone anniversary, baptism, or bar mitzvah?

At their best, these ceremonies and traditions happily reinforce commitments to family, community, and shared beliefs. And therein lies their importance—and difficulty—for blended families.

PUT THE CHILDREN FIRST

In our culture, holidays are especially geared to children. Christmas is all about family togetherness—brightly lit trees with gifts from Santa Claus, roasts baking in the oven, and the familiar lyrics of Christmas carols. Hanukkah is eight days of lit candles and a gift for the child on each of the eight days. Passover is built around the reading of the Haggadah, a narrative dedicated to family interaction at the dinner table, with a special focus on children. And to children, Easter is all about bunnies and egg hunts.

So, on these days, *I suggest an exception to the rule of putting the marriage first.* Plan with the children's comfort level and happiness in mind. You have the rest of the year to put your marriage first.

Since stepfamilies are a way of life for more than eighty million people in the United States, the kids are too often shuffled from one feast to another, collecting piles of food and gifts at each stop. These children are uptight, because they're not sure exactly where their base of security is. These problems arise even in first marriages—but the logistics of scheduling often dominate the holiday season for blended families.

Sometimes the kids just refuse to go along with the program. How can noncustodial parents reason with children who want to be home for the holidays with their friends and in the comfort of a familiar setting? It hurts to know that you are not as important as you believe you should be. It doesn't seem fair, nor does it seem right. More than anything, you want to be with that child you rarely see, and sometimes it means making sacrifices and asking others you love to also make sacrifices. But sometimes it also means putting your child's priorities at the top of your holiday list.

The first Christmas after his father remarried, Robby, a twelve-year-old, decided that he didn't want to visit his dad for the holiday. This was after months of his parents' battling for control with proposals and counterproposals of how Robby would get to his father's house and for how long. And there was also the overeager stepmother, who wanted Robby to become a part of her family. "I don't want to be with her or her kids when I visit Dad," Robby said. "I just want to be with my dad. Why can't she just leave us alone?"

Typically, everyone blamed the others for Robby's attitude. Mom blamed Dad. Dad and Stepmom blamed Mom. In truth, it was Robby who wanted to avoid feeling intruded on by his stepmother and her family when he was with his dad. Because he didn't think it would be possible to have his dad to himself, he preferred to stay at home with his mom.

Sometimes strong feelings are cloaked behind what appears trivial. Just decorating a tree can be emblematic of the problem faced by two families trying to have a happy holiday together. In a December 2003 *New York Times* article, Gloria Clark related how each family decorated opposite sides of the tree: "My family just threw [tinsel] on for a natural effect," she said, "while they put each piece on one by one." Eventually, they could laugh at what they did.

It comes down to wanting what you're used to. Traditions are important, because they communicate our identity as family, and their predictability provides security to your life when everything in your life seems up for grabs.

CLEARING CUSTOMS

The renowned sociologist Amitai Etzioni, in his recent book *The Monochrome Society,* devotes a whole chapter to the important ritual of holidays. He recognizes the expanded kinship structures of remarried families, and he speaks of the "increasing complexity of roles and relations reflected in the inclusion in family holidays of a large number of people who are related neither by blood nor marriage, but by former marriages, what one sociologist half-jokingly calls the 'x-kinship structure.' "

Most significantly, Etzioni observes that our society is struggling to come to terms with holiday rituals for these new x-kinship family structures, which is why holidays often hinder rather than serve their needs.

When a stepfamily tries to form their traditions, one result is that previous traditions are broken or changed. No matter what the intention, when traditions are altered, something dies inside us. Most people have no idea how important traditions are to them until they can't do them anymore. People fight to keep traditions alive.

Conflicts are structurally embedded, because there are more people with whom to be in conflict, more rivalry and competition that leads the way to family strife, and what makes it especially difficult is the fact that there are no right answers. Etiquette books might present some guidelines, but not extensive ones, and they certainly don't address the intense feelings of the participants, the awkwardness of these situations, and the intricacy of diverse backgrounds. The family members have to decide not only who will celebrate with whom which part of each holiday but which rituals to adopt for celebrating, what foods to serve, who will be there, and how will they get there. These are complex and sensitive issues that can take a heavy emotional toll on family members.

One mother with primary custody agreed to allow her former spouse visitation for all holidays, and now resents it. "Why should he have all the pleasure of every holiday with our children? I didn't know that I'd be miserable on every Thanksgiving and Christmas because I was missing my children."

A divorce agreement that requires a child to be with the noncustodial parent during all holidays is a difficult situation for the other parent, even if that parent has the child almost all the time. Of course, the parents can renegotiate the terms of their agreement if both parties are willing. If the noncustodial parent refuses to be flexible, however, there is always the option of petitioning the court for a modification of the agreement. But everyone should realize that the minute the petition is filed, the adversarial system comes into play and relationships are at greater risk. This is where a reasonable approach and good communication are vital.

To juggle children among the various households is no easy task, not if you care about how they feel versus how you feel. Just when the kid is scoping out the new cousins, it's time to pack the bags for the changeover to Dad's new in-laws, and there's a whole new set of not-quite relatives to be met. It's a particularly challenging task when the children live in a different state with their custodial parent, because the other parent sees the children only during holidays and school breaks. Alternating years would mean long periods of little or no contact.

THE NEW WORLD ORDER

Family counselors, sociologists, and researchers are seeing a significant change in the way ex-spouses are relating to each other. Baby boomers recognize what their parents' generation didn't always recognize—that the kids are happier when the divorced parents get along. Today in many households there is a new tolerance for former spouses so that families can be together for holidays.

One divorced couple, both remarried to other people, gather around one table for Thanksgiving with all their children. One of the mothers said, "This is not 1950. People are more relaxed today. And we can't just think of ourselves. We need to think of the children."

Another woman, a lawyer in Philadelphia, said she spends Christmas

Day with her husband, their child, her former husband, and his wife and their child, plus the daughter she had with her former husband. It is this last child who didn't want to be with only half of her family for the holidays, so she orchestrated this Christmas Day celebration. All the grandparents are also invited.

In a December 2001 *New York Times* article, "Guess Who's Coming to Dinner Now?" a Manhattan writer revealed the guest list for her own holiday celebration: "There is her immediate ex-husband, James. And her first ex-husband, Andrew. There is her 9-year-old daughter, Sasha, by her first husband, and her two children by her second husband, Zarina, 6, and Jahanara, who is almost 3." Her first husband's girlfriend and one of the writer's ex-boyfriends were also invited, along with other members of the writer's extended family, her brother, his wife, and their new baby. Remarkably, it is one big, happy family, and they intend to keep it that way.

"There are certainly growing numbers of stepfamilies, and many more exes than in the past," says David Popenoe, Ph.D., the co-director of the National Marriage Project, a research institute at Rutgers University. "Now you routinely have third and fourth marriages. And every year there are more and more cases of people spending Christmas with their exes who, in times past, would not be talking to each other, let alone spending Christmas together."

"And within these new blended families, many are forging closer bonds with former spouses than in the past," said Harvey Ruben, M.D., a family therapist and professor of clinical psychiatry at the Yale School of Medicine. "A new norm . . . is becoming a part of the culture."

Fran and Jennifer are the wife and ex-wife of one man, Albert. They are all in their early forties. Before they divorced, Fran and Albert had two children, Louise, age fifteen, and John, age thirteen. The families have joint custody of the two children and live close enough to each other to be in the same school district. Fran is now remarried to Bob, and they have Richie, a three-year-old. Jennifer was previously married and has Sabrina, a ten-year-old. Jennifer's ex-husband has faded out of their lives. The first year the families spent together—Christmas Eve in Jennifer's house and Christmas Day in Fran's house—was the most awkward, but the two women were determined to get along for the sake of all the children. The older kids figured out that Christmas stockings in both houses would mean two sets of stocking stuffers. The stockings turned out to be the icebreaker—the children's triumphant laughter relieved the initial tension.

Fran said, "The reason this works is because we're flexible, open with each other, and we love all the kids. Frankly, it was my kids' idea to share holidays so that they wouldn't have to be carted all over to see the grandparents, plus go from Mom's house to Dad's house."

"It's hard for people to believe it," Jennifer said, "but Fran and I have become friends. We cover for each other, even babysit for each other from time to time. But now that Louise's older, she usually does the babysitting."

For those who haven't yet been able to reach this level of harmony, be patient and at least entertain the possibility. Let's face it; divorce is a regressive process. Everyone slides down the maturity scale for two or three years, so holidays and celebrations in the remarried families soon after divorce are likely to be less harmonious than they will be in the future.

Occasionally, to overcome a sense of guilt, spouses will try to outdo each other by overspending on gifts for the kids. All that does is teach the children to exploit the parents and to mistake material things for love.

Fran and Jennifer shop together for the children, and they stick to a budget, with each child receiving approximately the same number of gifts of similar value.

Usually, it takes a few years after divorce and remarriage for people to realize that it's worth making the effort to get along rather than to have sad and lonely separations during holidays. Depression is greater in the general population around the holidays, and it's greater in stepfamilies, too. Remarried couples don't expect that holidays will be perfect and that everyone will be blissful, but they want to provide as much joy for all the children as they can, and in so doing, they make everyone much happier.

When geography doesn't permit more casual sharing of holidays, it may be worth having the whole family travel to alternating locations, even if this means staying in a hotel and cutting back on the amount of money spent on gifts. Kids tend to love hotels, especially ones with indoor pools and spas, and long hallways where they can race each other to the room.

NO SURPRISES, PLEASE

Family counselors offer a guiding principle: Make holiday plans well ahead of time so that everybody has a chance to adjust to the schedule. The greatest pain and anger and confusion come from last-minute jockeying.

Counselors emphasize the need to keep the children aware of the plans. "It's also important to be amiable, with a willingness to acknowledge a child's feelings," says Linda Brawn, executive director of Families First, in Massachusetts.

Yet meeting children's wishes does not mean saying yes to their every demand, according to Jeannette Lofas, founder and director of the Stepfamily Foundation, in New York. She, like so many who are working in this area, believes parents are too lenient because "they're afraid of losing the child's love."

A little tough love goes a long way toward establishing the right patterns early in the relationship with a child who sees the noncustodial parent only during court-decreed visits. Every parent has the right to say there are certain things in life that you have to do. What's wrong with a father (or mother) expecting that the child should be with him (or her) during holidays? On its face, there's nothing wrong with that expectation, but to be assured that the visit will be a loving one and not a battlefield, it's advisable to start this arrangement immediately after a divorce, and then be sure to remind the child every year well in advance of the holiday or summer visit. This is definitely a circumstance where surprises are not a good idea.

HOUSE RULES AND RITUALS

Remember, it's not easy for children to adapt to an officially new family with a stepparent, step-, and maybe half siblings. It's a big adjustment—

not only the separation from their custodial parent but the unfamiliar environment made even more so by multiple, temporary relationships with new people. While the children fumble their way through this maze, they are expected to do all the right things at the right time. But what is right? Is it right to give the "dad present" that you made in school to the natural father you see infrequently or to the stepfather you see daily?

In the new environment, often, there are new rules and new rituals. Bear in mind how comforting it was in your own childhood to have the same, familiar rituals for holidays. These rituals are something that children grow up relying on, and maintaining them from biological to blended families can go a long way toward helping a child adjust. Even if the Passover dinner at your brand-new in-laws means noisy kids, a long religious service, and a case of indigestion from five-thousand-year-old recipes, adopt the tradition for the sake of the family. A child who has always received a small present every day of Hanukkah may not want to switch to a bunch of presents on Christmas morning. Or maybe they will if they get both. Or the child who always goes to church services on Christmas Eve may feel a void if that practice is not followed in the blended family.

In celebrating holidays, be particularly aware of the loss that an older stepchild may feel because of the presence of a new stepparent, especially if this child has been carrying heavy responsibility in the family. A teenage stepdaughter who has helped run the household may have been handling holiday celebrations and may rebel against a new stepparent who wants to do things her or his way. It's only natural that a child feels some jealousy and resentment toward the stepparent who appears to be taking over. In these circumstances, the addition of new rituals should be gradual; no changes should even occur during the first year of the remarriage. The relationships are more important than the rituals.

And what about the remarriage where there are older children on both sides? Whose rituals get left out? To solve the problem of dueling rituals, it might be a good idea to have a powwow or make a list, put each ritual on a slip of paper, and have the children pick from a grab bag of rituals. However it turns out, try to have a good laugh. Gradually, you can add or subtract rituals, but make these changes with the children's participation. To prevent overload, alternate households for holidays, providing parents agree to the schedule. Whatever you do, don't ruin the holidays by quarreling over who goes where, as long as children have time to be with both families, even if it's not the actual day of Christmas or Thanksgiving. If you live close to each other, make Halloween a big holiday on the year it's not your turn to have Christmas. The key is to allow children to enjoy and celebrate the magic of the season—the spirit of the holiday should govern everyone's behavior.

HAVE A S'BLENDED HOLIDAY

Callie presents a typical problem of a family trying to blend successfully. "My husband wants to be with his family, and that's where his children want to be. I want to be with my family, and that's where my children want to be, so what do we do?"

Though some families get off on the wrong course, it doesn't mean the problems can't be corrected. Glen lives in New Hampshire with his second wife, Lilly, and their two-year-old son, Mitchell. Glen's children from his marriage to Callie—Carl and Claire, ages twelve and ten respectively—live in California with their mother and stepfather. Glen has the right to see his children for a month every summer and for alternate Christmas holidays.

The first year that Glen's children visited for Christmas was a bona fide disaster for everyone. When his children arrived, they dropped their things in the entry hall, headed straight for the den, and flipped on the TV. Any effort at conversation was useless. Their attention was entirely focused on the TV. Whatever Lilly asked of them was met with passive resistance. When Lilly tried to enlist the children's help in setting the table for dinner, they ignored her. When asked if they wanted milk or juice with dinner, they said, "Neither." Lilly asked them to help her bring their bags upstairs so they could unpack their clothes. Later that evening, Lilly went upstairs to turn down their beds and found all their clothes strewn about the bedroom.

When Lilly told Glen what was happening, he reminded her that the kids were there for such a short time, she should let it go. To which Lilly replied, "Why should I have to do everything for your kids when they won't even speak to me?"

Lilly admitted she began to brood over the situation. "I'm the one who had to shop, cook, serve, clean up, buy Christmas presents, do the decorations, plus get up with the baby at the crack of dawn. And on top of that, I was expected to be the affable stepmother to two kids who didn't even want to be with us."

Glen acknowledged he wasn't doing his share, but as an accountant, he always had a busy end-of-the-year work schedule that afforded him less time than he would otherwise have to help Lilly prepare for the holidays. Both Lilly and Glen knew that his children preferred to be home in California for Christmas, and resented having to be with their father and stepmother. When the week was over, Glen became depressed about the mess he felt he'd created for Lilly and for his children. He vowed to make it up to all of them that summer by taking his own children on a white-water rafting trip, just the three of them. Lilly admitted she was offended at first but at the same time relieved of the added burden of caring for the two stepchildren for at least one of the four weeks they would be visiting.

This arrangement worked and soon became the tenor of the summer visit. During the week Glen was with his children, Lilly and the toddler visited with her own family on Cape Cod. Over the next several years, Lilly developed a genuine affection for Glen's children, though she couldn't quite explain why, except that they had matured and were happier about the visit. Another important reason for the change was Glen's own realization that he had to spend a lot more time helping Lilly when his children were visiting in the summer to make up for the long hours he was away from home during the Christmas visit. Gradually, the difficulties were ironed out, but mostly because of Glen's extra input and Lilly's willingness to allow the children to become accustomed to her. It took four years of patience, cooperation, and reasonable behavior to work through the problems and toward better relationships.

KEEP BIRTHDAYS HAPPY

Birthdays are especially important to a child, because it's the one day of the year that he or she alone is the honoree. If the tradition is to give a large party, it's best to try to continue that practice, and if possible, the noncustodial parent should be included, with his or her spouse. If that isn't possible because there isn't an amiable level of personal contact between the parents, then the noncustodial parent should make sure to commemorate the child's special day either by a gift and telephone call and/or by doing something festive with the child as soon as it's feasible. Because birthdays come every year, it would make sense to alternate years if both parents live in the same area. Stepparents should participate as much as it's convenient and gratifying to do so. Again, parents should make the effort to let bygones be bygones and get together on the child's birthday if location permits.

GRADUATION DAY

Graduation exercises present another special occasion when divorced (also remarried) parents need to be there. Gavin related the importance of having both parents participate at his graduation from an exclusive prep school in the East. Nine years earlier, Gavin's parents had had a bitter divorce, and never wanted to have to deal with each other again. The father actually borrowed money in order to pay for Gavin's education, because he believed his son needed and deserved the benefit of a challenging educational environment. Gavin's mother objected to her son's going away to school, and viewed the father's willingness to go into debt to finance the educational costs as a ploy to alienate Gavin from her. Ultimately, she changed her mind when she saw that Gavin loved being at this particular school and when she found out that her son would be graduating with honors.

It was devastating to Gavin, however, when his father told him he didn't want Gavin's mother to attend the graduation ceremonies. "I'm the one who went into debt to make sure you had the best possible education, and had to fight your mother all the way to get her to allow you to attend the school. Why should she be there to gloat and make my wife and me wish we'd never invited her?"

"Because she's my mother, and I want her there."

Gavin's father finally relented. Gavin was barely able to eat or sleep the week before his graduation, not knowing what to expect when his parents came face-to-face for the first time in years. Actually, the day went off quite well. The parents didn't sit near each other, though they did all go to a restaurant together after the graduation. Fortunately, enough other relatives were there so the parents were able to be at the same table but manage to avoid conversation.

Gavin's desire to have both parents attend was entirely normal, and parents and stepparents should do whatever is necessary to avoid any display of animosity for the sake of the child. This means acting like grown-ups, in which case everybody wins.

WEDDING BELLS FOR THE SECOND (OR THIRD) TIME

A wedding is a time of celebration—for the caterer, the florist, and the bridal consultant. Actually, it's a wonder that some weddings—first or second—ever take place at all, considering the clans of complete strangers coming together in this artificial and awkward setting. We have to be grateful for the soothing effects of good food, good drink, good music, and, most of all, the elixir of love.

Your initial impulse may tell you that getting ready for a second wedding is not that complicated. After all, you or your spouse-to-be, or maybe both of you, have been down this aisle before. Not so. This is not a new beginning with a clean slate, especially where children are involved. But it is another chapter in your life, and one that requires more patience in planning, more resilience in handling last-minute changes or even unpleasant scenes, and a strong desire to be together even in the face of adversity.

The obvious needs to be repeated: Your wedding offers the first opportunity to forge new ties with the relatives who will form the blended family after the celebration is over. Impressions made at the wedding can and do spill over to the relationships that arise from the remarriage. Open-mindedness and adaptability should be the watchwords of the day.

If you're planning a ceremony any more elaborate than a visit to the town hall, you need a book like Martha Woodham's *Wedding Etiquette for Divorced Families.* Woodham answers questions of protocol for the most convoluted family relationships—from the wording of invitations and announcements to bridal showers, to gifts, to the marital vows. She also addresses what to do about jangled nerves, vengeful ex-spouses, renegade stepchildren, resistant families, and shrinking bank accounts—not to mention seating arrangements that will keep feuding parents apart at both the ceremony and the reception so that your special day is not ruined.

If the bride's been married before, at least there's no controversy about who gives her away. In most second weddings, the bride simply walks down the aisle without a male escort and joins the groom at the altar. Or the bride and groom can walk down the aisle together.

One survival tip offered by a third-time bride: given the multitude of parents, stepparents, in-laws, and former in-laws who may be involved, skip the receiving line, or the food will get cold and the champagne will lose its sparkle before you can raise a toast.

What about the Kids?

Whether the children should attend their parent's wedding requires some serious thinking. Because the wedding makes a new person a permanent part of the children's lives, they may resist playing a role in the event. This is particularly true if there is an angry ex-spouse orchestrating from backstage. Even if the children have agreed to be part of the ceremony, they may back out at the last minute. Children of the bride and groom should be the first to be told about the wedding plans, and they should be included in the celebration if they *want* to be there. Use common sense—a child who is often unruly should not be permitted to ruin your special day.

If children don't want to be in the ceremony, don't pressure them, but do try to keep a place for reasonably well-behaved children if they change their minds. Being sensitive to the moods and thoughts of the children is necessary in working through the early stages of the wedding. Encourage them to talk openly about their fears and doubts; however, that shouldn't translate into veto power over your plans to wed. Even with all the obstacles, couples can enjoy a happy wedding experience by talking and listening to each other and, most of all, by tempering decisions with a view to the future and a full awareness of each other's needs and desires.

If Your Young Children Will Be Included . . .

- Whether you are planning an at-home, outdoor, or small chapel service or an elaborate church or synagogue wedding, consider the comfort level of the children and the expense.

- Think about the time of day. Kids get cranky in the evening when they're tired. Young children do better at daytime weddings. And if you really want to avoid chaos, don't have young children, either yours or his, as attendants. The minute the flower girl or ring bearer is about to walk down the aisle, more likely than not you'll hear, "I have to go tee-tee."

- For the reception, think about a buffet rather than a seated dinner. Even adults are apt to fidget if they have to be seated for several hours. Buffets are more kid-friendly.

- Hire a babysitter to be in charge of the children at the reception. The babysitter can escort the kids outside if they are getting in the way or they become unruly.

- Let your photographer know in advance that you don't want a wedding album filled with pictures of only "cute kids."

- If it is an evening wedding with a band and dancing, arrange for the babysitter to take the children home at a reasonable bedtime hour.

Resistant Relatives

Dealing with resistant relatives at what should be a joyful celebration is one of the many challenges in this blending process. Even if your new father-in-law tells you his daughter has a built-in jerk detector that led her to her first husband and now to you, use this occasion to test your self-restraint. Don't make a scene. Instead, make another vow on this special day—to win the old codger over. Even in first-time marriages, the planning stage leading up to the wedding, the wedding itself, and the immediate aftermath usually set the tone for how the respective families get along in the years ahead. It's even more so in second weddings with new, but seasoned, in-laws and children from prior marriages. On the other hand, don't let happiness cloud your vision—some of these people are not wishing you well, but you still have to deal with them. After you've taken your wedding vows, vow to yourself that you'll make a sincere effort to convince these detractors that you're okay. Still, there will probably be times when a perfect solution cannot be found, so it's best to focus on the celebration and joy of the marriage.

When Children of Blended Families Marry

Too often there is real heartbreak when two intact families must come together for the wedding of their beloved children, so imagine what complications can arise when there are weddings that involve the strained relations of blended families—when there are four or five mothers or fathers to contend with. You begin to believe the only safe seating arrangement for the wedding dinner is a hundred tables for two.

Many divorced parents will use their children as pawns in power plays when the family comes together in celebration. With their childish antics and resentments for each other, they whipsaw these adult children at the very time when a warm embrace is called for. The father who pays for the wedding may decide that entitles him to dictate what little, if any, part his ex-wife will play in the event. And she's the mother of the bride. The divorced mother may send her son or daughter on a guilt trip by giving an ultimatum: "If your father intends to bring that home-wrecking wife of his to the wedding, then I'm not coming."

The bridal couple should politely ask their families to put aside their animosities for this one important day, their wedding. Remind the whole family—his, hers, and everyone involved—that they don't want their wedding to be a battlefield. If nations in combat can achieve détente, then the bridal couple should be able to do the same, at least for that one day. Urge them to stay home if they can't be civilized to each other.

(Step) Daddy's Little Girl: Who Gives the Bride Away?

One mother of the bride said, "My ex-husband isn't paying for our daughter's wedding. Her stepfather is paying, so who should walk her down the aisle?" What happens when the natural father has been a loving and responsible parent, as Nelson was? At last, the day arrived when Nelson's daughter, Isabelle, called to tell him that she was getting married. Nelson had an immediate vision of himself escorting his beautiful daughter down the aisle. But then he realized that Brett, Isabelle's stepfather, had also been devoted to Isabelle. So he adjusted his vision to include both him and Brett walking on either side of Isabelle. When he and Isabelle went to lunch to discuss the wedding, Isabelle was hesitant, as if there was something she had to say but she couldn't seem to get the words out. Finally, she blurted them out. "Dad, I know this is going to be hard for you to accept, but I've decided that Brett will give me away."

Nelson could hardly believe what he was hearing. This joyous moment, stolen from him. How could she? Why? Hadn't he always been there for her, expressing love in every way a father could? He remembered the many times he'd dropped what he was doing to take Isabelle to a piano lesson, buying her her first car, paying for her support and her college. And now Brett had volunteered to pay for the wedding, though Nelson had been willing to pay. Was this why Brett was paying, so he could be the one to walk down the aisle with Isabelle on his arm? Nelson could barely speak.

Isabelle assumed that Nelson's silence meant he was okay with the arrangement. He wanted to tell her that he wasn't going to be there, so it wouldn't matter who gave her away, but he couldn't hurt her that way even if she had hurt him so profoundly. He simply nodded.

A couple of weeks later, Isabelle called him. "Dad, I can't get your face out of my mind. I don't know what I could have been thinking. I want both of you—you and Brett—to give me away. Is that okay with you?"

Nelson was almost too choked to speak. When he did, he said, "Anything you want is fine with me." When Nelson put the receiver down, he felt elated and relieved that he had never said or done anything hurtful to mar his daughter's happiness, despite his own hurt.

A considerable litany has developed about who "gives away" the bride, the natural father or the stepfather? According to Woodham's *Wedding Etiquette for Divorced Families,* the choice comes down to one basic premise—it's up to the bride, though Woodham decidedly favors the natural father regardless of who pays for the reception. There is a caveat to this rule of thumb: ". . . The true test here would be [for the bride] to ask herself which man she thinks of as her father in her heart of hearts." Woodham offers many options to accommodate the changes in family relationships—one dad can walk the bride halfway down the aisle before handing her off to the other. If both dads get along, they can escort the bride down the aisle, one on either side. And when asked who gives the bride away, they can say in unison, "Her family and I do." Again, the rule of comfort should prevail.

If there is no dad or stepdad, an uncle, a brother, or a good friend can give the bride away. And who says she has to have a male escort? One young woman, whose father died when she was a teenager and whose relationship with her stepfather was merely polite, elected to walk down the aisle with her mother, to the delight of all her guests.

There is even the option of going solo. One bride said that walking down the aisle alone made her feel like a queen, and furthermore, she was big enough and old enough to give herself away. Good for her.

Helpful Guidelines for Holidays

- **Put the children first.** In the context of holidays, children come first.

- **Make plans early.** Organize details carefully. Work out exact dates and times of arrival and departures. And try to keep things as simple as possible.

- **Write out the itinerary.** Make a written schedule for both the children and the adults who are involved in their travel. Ask the other parent for written confirmation of travel schedules so there will be no misunderstanding.

- **Involve everyone, especially the children.** Make sure everyone participates and knows what the plans are. Consider the concerns of the stepparents, the grandparents, the children, and anyone else who will be a part of the visit. Ask each family member to name three of their favorite holiday activities. You might be surprised at what the children tell you. Take their priorities into account when making your plans. Compromise and flexibility are key in working things out.

- **Consider the issue of location.** If a child doesn't want to go to a new house for the holidays, find out why, and try to work it out. Usually, younger children don't want to decide where they'll spend holidays. Adults should decide, to save the child from feelings of guilt at having to choose one parent over the other. In some cases, the matter may already have been decided in court by a holiday clause in the divorce agreement. If not, alternating holidays may be the fairest away of resolving the location problem.

- **Equalize sleeping arrangements.** If it looks as though children from two families will be sharing the same living space, make sure that one child, or set of children, is not favored over another. If not everyone can have a bed to sleep in, use sleeping bags. Kids are resilient and won't mind the "sleepover" arrangement.

- **Be fair and reasonable about gifts.** Just as no favoritism should be the goal with sleeping arrangements, the same goal should govern the matter of gifts. Gifts should be planned for. Set standards for gift giving. Discuss financial limits. Make sure all the children are treated equally. Everyone should have an equal number of gifts to open and a stocking of their own.

- **Avoid competition.** In blended families, stepparents, former spouses, grandparents, and other adults may compete for the time, favor, and attention of the children in the family. Sometimes children take their cues from adults and do the same thing—compete for the favor of others, too. Realize that the competitiveness is usually rooted in jealousy and feelings of personal inadequacy. Try to appreciate your own positive qualities and those of your family. Enjoy yourselves and sidestep feelings of unhealthy competition.

- **Do less, but do it better.** Three complete holiday meals in one day is too much for anyone's stomach. Keep celebrations manageable. End family get-togethers before fatigue sets in, and plan activities that leave everyone relaxed when they're over.

- **Put your best smile on and get along.** Children in blended families are relieved and adjust best when the adults are at least pleasant to one another. What is most important to children is that the adults they love get along. View challenging relationships as a test of your inner strength. Don't bring baggage from the past into the present.

- **Add new family traditions.** Establishing traditions for this new blended family will help to make the holidays a little more special and meaningful. For example, kids love to decorate holiday cookies, so that can be something they do at your house. In fact, wonderful foods added to the meal can be neutral added traditions. For the holiday meal, serve something special for dessert, like a gorgeous English trifle smothered in whipped cream.

- **Be flexible about the day of celebration.** If children will be away for the holiday, celebrate with them on another day. It isn't necessary that the day of the celebration be the actual holiday. What's wrong with Christmas in July, if that's the only time you have an opportunity to see the children?

Helpful Guidelines for Weddings

- **Wedding protocol—don't be a slave to it.** It's best to search the etiquette books for answers, but treat what they have to say as mere suggestions, and focus on doing what's best and most comfortable for your family situation. Because of the complicated relationships that arise out of remarriage with children, the first order of business is to do what will be least awkward for the couple and, secondly, for the children. In short, the rule of comfort should control. Unless the wedding is a first for the bride who wants an elaborate wedding, try to keep it simple.

- **Don't pressure the children.** If the children want to be in the wedding, include them; otherwise, let them attend or not. They may change their minds at the last minute. Be flexible enough to accommodate those changed minds. There are many inner conflicts at work with children of divorce, so don't pressure them to do something they don't want to do.

- **Provide guests with a cast of characters.** Weddings are more fun when you know the players. If the bride and groom have seven or eight "parents" between them, offering guests a family map, whether informally or on a program, will help them identify the stepparents, siblings, half siblings, and step-siblings they are likely to meet.

- **Be direct with troublesome relatives.** If there's a relative who is likely to cause a scene, ask for a promise that there will be no outbursts or active antagonisms. If the relative won't give that promise, urge that he or she not attend the wedding. If despite the promise an outburst occurs, don't get into the fray. Ask someone else (not the bride or groom) to step in and defuse it.

Dollars and Sense

S e c r e t   S e v e n :

Get money issues out in the open as soon as possible.

For most remarried couples when it comes to money, what's yours, what's mine, what's ours, and when we die who gets what are the questions that stew in the background until they boil over. If "problems with the children" is the number one reason remarriages fail, money problems run a close second. One man on his second marriage said disputes over money caused his first divorce. "Every time the subject of money came up, we fought. My first wife was from West Virginia, where dish throwing is an Olympic event." The number one way to *not* fight about money is to calmly discuss money issues in anticipation of problems and then continue these discussions as questions arise. When two families are trying to blend into one, the emotions of love, guilt, anger, and deprivation often find expression through the uses and abuses of money.

Root Causes of Financial Discord in Blended Families

- Men who feel they've been "wiped out" by their ex-wife are unwilling to let their present wife know exactly what the financial picture is.

- With so many more individuals involved and with alimony and child support obligations, there is often a reduced standard of living for everyone concerned.

- Career women who have had the autonomy to handle their own financial matters are unwilling to relinquish that independence.

- A father who feels guilty for breaking up the family may feel that he owes his ex-wife and their children more than he can afford, considering his new obligations. He may pay even more than is required by the divorce decree, to the detriment of his new family.

- Either or both wives have inherited money of their own but refuse to allow its use for the support of the family, while the husband struggles to meet his obligations for everyone involved.

- Grandparents of one set of children are well-off financially and bestow luxury on these grandchildren, while the other children (step- and/or half siblings) are not getting the nice things the others are getting.

- When there are lavish gifts and trips from a wealthy father, the stepfather may feel devalued and emasculated and may take out his feelings of insecurity on his wife and stepchildren.

- The new wife has to move into the house where her husband lived with his ex-wife, but because of financial setbacks, there isn't enough money to redecorate the house, so the new wife feels like an intruder.

- The remarried mother continues to live in the house she lived in with her former husband. The new husband feels like he is living on the charity of his wife's ex-husband, and doesn't want to spend any money on a house that not only doesn't belong to him but is a constant reminder of his wife's life with her former husband.

- The husband and wife keep all their money in separate accounts, impeding the blending process and impeding family unity and trust.

- The ex-wife lives extravagantly on alimony and child support, while the new wife and children must cut corners just to make ends meet.

CHILD SUPPORT OBLIGATIONS

"Kids and money are the biggest problems," said Diane Milne, human development specialist with University of Missouri Outreach and Extension. Milne teaches classes for divorcing parents. She specifically keys in to the emotionally charged issue of child support as the battleground for remarriages. If Dad is mad at Mom, the child support check may be late, insufficient, or withheld. That has an immediate consequence on the new marriage and the household budget.

"Only about 50 percent of all custodial parents who are supposed to receive monthly child support receive the full amount," Milne said. "And seldom is child support adequate to pay half the expenses of child rearing." Typically, the first family and the second family are engaged in constant competition for the same source of funds. Supporting the stepchildren while still supporting biological children can create a real money crunch for blended families.

It's important to understand the subject of child support from both sides: the perspective of the custodial mother (or father) who depends on receiving those payments and the viewpoint of the remarried father and his wife who have to live on less because of those monthly payments going to another household. *Today many women are also paying child support to ex-husbands who have primary custody of the children.* According to the most recent data available from the U.S. Census Bureau, only 56 percent of custodial parents actually had child support agreements, and 59.1 percent of custodial mothers with child support agreements were not receiving the payments they were due. The average annual amount of child support received by those mothers who received any payments was $3,700; the vast number of custodial mothers received nothing at all. Custodial mothers were three times as likely as custodial fathers to be poor (32.1 percent versus 10.7 percent, respectively).

No matter what your second spouse says before the wedding, expect resentment when that alimony or child support check is written, even when the largest portion of the income is still available for the new family. If there isn't a lot of money to start with, the problem grows even worse, with hopes and dreams shattered by the realities of supporting two families on the same, or substantially the same, income. To compensate, spouses and ex-spouses have to go to work or to school to hone skills they will need to return to the job market. Child care is costly, and often those costs must be paid for while the mother also has to pay her education and retraining expenses.

So it should come as no surprise that these couples often fight over pocketbook issues that range from when to buy a new car, to weekly allowances, to getting braces for the kids' teeth. Who keeps the checkbook? Who controls investments? When a new spouse wants to know what it costs to run the house and asks for an accounting, the reaction often is "You mean, you don't trust me." Or maybe one spouse has always paid cash for slightly used cars, as compared to fully financed new cars. These and other attitudes toward money can erupt into the kind of heated arguments that can destroy a second marriage.

For a second wife, the potential danger is that her husband's money matters are so entangled with his past, she may feel that he values his previous family more than her and the new family. Usually, there are financial traps over which the husband has no control and that work a gross injustice on the new family. To put this dilemma into sharp focus, here are a couple of striking examples from my interviews.

The Changed-Circumstances Trap

Janey is married to Chuck and has a daughter with him, but he was previously married to Anna, with whom he had one son, Donald. Although Chuck and Anna were awarded joint custody at the time of their divorce, Donald now lives full-time with Janey and Chuck. When Anna decided to move to New York City for a major career opportunity, though without much of a salary increase, she voluntarily gave Chuck full physical custody of their son. With the cost of living so much higher in New York and her salary not sufficiently adjusted to take care of the added costs, Anna also petitioned the court for an increase in alimony so that she could continue to live there and advance herself professionally.

In the determination of Chuck's ability to pay, his second wife's income was taken into account to make the judgment. Janey had income both from investments and from her earnings as a pharmacist. Because of Janey's income, Anna's lawyer was able to persuade the court to increase Anna's alimony.

"I was furious," Janey said. "I work hard, not only at my job but also at home, raising her kid as well as ours. I certainly have no incentive to increase my own investment income and salary, because it's just taken away from our family and given to Chuck's ex-wife so that she can live where she wants to, and live better."

Knowing the provisions of your new spouse's divorce decree before you marry helps to prepare for potential disruptions, but be forewarned that divorce settlements, unless they include a "no modification" clause, are not written in stone. If an ex-wife believes her former husband is not paying her enough to live on, she has a right to use every law at her disposal to receive the amount of money she believes she is due.

Of course, there are some ex-wives who are never satisfied with the amount they are receiving. These exes use the money issue as a means to keep their unresolved anger going indefinitely. As a consequence, many couples live in a perpetual state of fear, afraid to spend money on real necessities because they expect the ex-wife to sue for more alimony and/or child support based on "changed circumstances." Those changed circumstances may (and often do) include the second wife's increased income even though she may have children of her own that she is helping to support. Until our legal system becomes more sympathetic to the needs of the 85 percent of divorced couples who remarry, these upward modifications will continue to work havoc on the remarried families.

The Lack-of-Accountability Trap

An offshoot of this situation involves the lack of accountability that persists in payment of alimony and child support. Is the custodial parent spending child support money on the child, as directed by the court?

"My husband pays exorbitant alimony and child support," reports Felicia, "but whenever his kids come to visit, you'd think they were living in poverty. His ex-wife lives in a big house in one of the best neighborhoods, and she doesn't work. Both of us work and live in a modest house in a middle-class area. She buys herself designer clothes, takes luxurious vacations, and belongs to an expensive health club. When we take a trip, it's a camping-out long weekend. I'm really tired of the unfairness. This lack of accountability drives me crazy, but there's nothing we can do about how she spends all my husband's money. Instead of buying the kids new shoes, she buys herself a new outfit."

A father who remarried despite his heavy alimony and child support obligations said, "I wouldn't mind paying if I thought the money was going for my kids, but they get shortchanged while my ex-wife buys clothes for herself and plays tennis at a country club. According to the law, I don't even have the right to ask where any of the money goes."

At present there are no means within the courts for ensuring that child support money goes for supporting the children.

It's hard for legislators, lawyers, and courts to admit that the same laws that have worked for years to help some women are now being abused and are penalizing other women and children. With a growing awareness of fathers' rights, many legal experts want to see Congress amend the Uniform Reciprocal Support Act (which as it currently stands enables courts to cross state lines in order to enforce child support agreements), namely by adding a provision to allow accountability for the parent who is making timely payments of child support, when there is reason to believe child support money is not being used for its intended purpose.

The Financial-Aid Trap

Another example where the law has failed to keep up with the changes in the structure of the family involves the matter of college financial aid. Children of divorce and remarriage are being penalized because courts are *not* requiring parents to pay the cost of college expenses for their children from prior marriages. By law children are no longer minors when they reach age eighteen, so the parental obligation for support ceases at the precise time that college expenses usually begin. And too many fathers check out of their responsibilities for education, only too glad that their obligations end at eighteen. This transition from the age of minority to the age of adulthood precludes courts from ordering either parent to pay college expenses. Only when the parent agrees to pay college expenses is it made a part of the divorce decree. As college expenses skyrocket faster than most other items in the cost of living index, it is becoming increasingly difficult for families to afford these hefty burdens.

As children of blended families turn to the colleges and universities for financial assistance, they find themselves in a catch-22 situation. To receive such aid, the children must come from families below a certain income level—and that's the catch, because the level of income often includes the sum of incomes of parents and stepparents who are neither willing nor obligated to pay. In effect, the combined incomes of all these adults eliminate the child's entitlement to financial assistance. The timing is particularly cruel because if the father refuses to pay, the mother who may want to pay is now faced with a reduction in her income because child support payments also end when the child turns eighteen. The children lose while the families fight over a lack of money needed to take care of a most important matter—education.

More Education Dilemmas

Education costs present one of the largest future expenditures faced by all families, but they present a special problem for blended families. What if the father of the wife's children worked his way through college and expects the children to do the same? If the stepfather is not wealthy, is it fair to expect him to pay for her children, as well as his and theirs? And yet is it reasonable for some of the children (who can't qualify for financial aid because of incomes that are *not* available for their benefit) to have to live at home and work their way through a local, state-supported college while the step- and half siblings go off to expensive private universities with money made available to them from other sources—grandparent participation and/or inheritances?

Because income is derived from so many different sources, children within the same family are often offered different education opportunities. If there are no trust funds set up to take care of education costs, the husband who is paying for the support of his children from a previous marriage and his current wife will end up paying for the education of probably all the children: his, hers, and theirs. In talking to many families paying hefty education expenses, I heard the common complaint that the ex-wife doesn't help or plan to help with the college costs of her own children. Many mothers and fathers who are willing to pay don't have the income to contribute much, but there are also plenty of mothers and fathers who have means but don't view college expenses as *their responsibility*.

Ironically, too many children don't seem to believe they should contribute to the cost of their own education by working. Family therapists believe many of today's children have developed a sense of entitlement, passed on to them by one or both parents who have used money to overcompensate throughout their childhood. If neither the mother nor the child is contributing for whatever reason, it places a heavier burden on the father and stepmother. Paying for these continuously escalating college costs requires real sacrifice no matter how it's done.

Of course, one has to look at the specific family situations and take into consideration that even with hardworking, self-sacrificing ex-wives and students who also work, college costs are beyond what most families can afford.

LOVE, LABOR, LOSS

Consider the situation that occurred in the household of Sam and Eleanor and their five children. Sam had three children from his previous marriage: Cassie, Marilyn, and Shirley, ages nineteen, eighteen, and sixteen. Eleanor had two children from her first marriage, eighteen-year-old Phyllis and seventeen-year-old Brad. Suddenly, Sam and Eleanor were confronted with four children in college and one attending a private high school, all at the same time. As part of Sam's divorce decree, he had voluntarily agreed to pay college expenses for his three daughters, with the girls having the responsibility of obtaining their father's approval on their choice of colleges.

Although Sam had agreed to pay the college expenses for his children, Eleanor's ex-husband had not agreed to assume that burden for *his* children. To make matters worse, Sam and Eleanor were confronted with the financial aid problem described above. The incomes of both of their ex-spouses (including the alimony Sam paid to his ex-wife) were added to the total income for the family, thereby making the family income too high to qualify any of the children for financial aid. Four incomes comprised the total income for the family, but only two incomes were actually available to pay the cost of education for all five children.

Eleanor's two children were accepted at expensive Ivy League schools. They decided to work part-time during the school year and summers to help pay their expenses, but that did not begin to cover the high cost of the prestigious universities. Eleanor persuaded her parents to help, and her children took out student loans. Sam's children went to local state schools.

Sam's children felt enormous resentment toward what they perceived as betrayal, believing that their father was willing to give more to his stepchildren than to his own children. Sam's attempted explanations to his children—"I'm paying a huge alimony to your mother, and I'm not paying anything toward college for Eleanor's kids"—fell on deaf ears. Even though they were told about the student loans and the money from Eleanor's parents, they continued to see the situation as grossly unfair to them. These feelings of resentment led to an estrangement from their father and his new family, creating another layer of tension between Sam and Eleanor, and her children.

Children who are caught in the crossfire are damaged by what they perceive as favoritism. Sometimes they are placed squarely in the middle of the manipulation that takes place in blended families, so they come to view money as a scorecard—a measure of their parents' love.

If the regulations governing who gets financial aid create these un-fortunate results, then why do these restrictive guidelines persist? At some colleges, as many as one-third of financial aid applicants have parents who are divorced, but when the parents remarry, the percentage of applicants who receive aid radically decreases.

For public colleges and universities, usually it is only the income and assets of the custodial parent that are required, but now, with joint custody arrangements becoming more and more prevalent, the income and assets of both parents are required.

Private colleges and universities take things a step further. Arguing that biological parents have at least *a moral obligation* to help educate their children, private colleges routinely require information on the fi-nances of absent parents and stepparents, and many include grandpar-ents' net worth. Even if it's unrealistic to expect a former spouse, a grandparent, or a stepparent to contribute toward the child's education, their individual income and assets are included in the formula for de-termining entitlement.

In the last few years, some colleges and universities have begun al-lowing parents to provide information when the absent parent has had no contact with the child for many years and cannot be counted on to contribute. There are more and more instances where these facts influ-ence the school's decision. To some extent, the decision to grant or deny aid has to do with how much the college or university wants the par-ticular student.

Ellen Frishberg, director of student financial services at Johns Hopkins University, says that "a lot of our decisions are made on a sub-jective basis, taking into account the student's individual family rela-tionships, as well as the financial circumstances of the various family members."

Though the courts may not require parents to pay for college ex-penses, Congress can mandate fairness in determining who is entitled to financial aid. Since most colleges and universities receive federal money, the mandate would apply to them as long as they continue to re-ceive those federal funds, usually in the form of grants. By such man-date, students who come from blended families would have a better shot at getting the help they need.

FOR LOVE OR MONEY

Some wives are astute enough to see what financial dependency can do to women who have not only lost their husbands to divorce but continue to rely on them for their survival and that of their children.

Francine is married to Jeff, but she nearly left him over the issue of money, more specifically his constant willingness to give money to Lois, his first wife, who has managed to play the game of emotional ransom.

"My husband's ex-wife is a leech," Francine laments. "They've been divorced for sixteen years and have one daughter. Jeff has supported them both all these years, and put the daughter through college. He paid alimony until Lois married again four years ago. When that marriage ended a year ago, she came right back at us to get money from Jeff. The second husband left her and paid her nothing, so she lost the alimony from Jeff and now wants a loan to put a down payment on a condominium. We were about to do some remodeling on our house, but Jeff said, 'I can't leave her stranded. She's the mother of my daughter.' I told him if she didn't get stranded, he was going to get stranded by me."

When Jeff came to the realization that his marriage was really in jeopardy, he told his ex-wife that he was unable spare any more money, because of other commitments.

"He finally cut the cord," Francine says, "and Lois has finally weaned herself from him. As for me, I took a good look at my husband's ex-wife and realized that the last thing I would ever want is to be in her shoes. So I decided to go back to work, especially since our kids are now in school and I have the time. Fortunately, I hadn't allowed my professional contacts to evaporate. If anything ever happens to our marriage, I don't want to be dependent on Jeff. I have too much pride for that."

An important aspect of this story is the ages of the two wives. Francine is in her late thirties. His first wife is fifty years old. She is one of those women who derided feminism and women's working outside the home, whereas Francine believes women should have the same rights and obligations as men.

When a man marries a woman who is almost a generation younger than his first wife, the significant age difference is likely to cause the women to see the world in different ways. Attitudes about a husband's obligations in marriage and divorce fall right into the generation gap.

FATHERS WITH GUILT

Just as Francine wanted financial independence, Ruth considered herself to be a self-reliant woman. An accomplished violinist, she loved playing in a symphony orchestra and teaching children how to play the violin. She had no desire to have children of her own. When she met Reid, he was still married and had two children, ages six and eight.

When they fell in love and decided to marry, Ruth thought she had found the perfect situation. She would have a role in mothering Reid's children without having children of her own who would interfere with her career.

As is often the case, Reid felt a tremendous sense of guilt when he left his wife of nine years. When his children begged him to stay with them, he was torn. "I'll be good if you'll stay with us," his six-year-old son said. Reid wanted his ex-wife and children to have everything, since they couldn't have him, and so he agreed to give them a substantial part of his salary, leaving himself an inadequate amount to live on comfortably without Ruth's contribution.

Although he felt strongly that the children belonged with their mother, he missed them terribly. They visited every other weekend, every other Christmas, and for a month during the summer. His ex-wife suffered a bout of anxiety and depression as a result of the divorce but still had to work part-time to continue living in the house, because of a property tax increase.

Ruth was convinced that Reid was unreasonable about what he owed his previous family. She and he rented an apartment with two bedrooms, and the children got the bigger one, even though they were there only on alternate weekends. When they were visiting, Reid was up at dawn so he could prepare breakfast for the children. He never asked Ruth to do anything alone with the kids. Whatever outing they took, he was there. Ruth felt that Reid stood in the way of her forming a close relationship with his children. He was miserable when the children had to leave.

After three years of marriage, Ruth decided she wanted to have a child of her own. She and Reid borrowed money to build a house with four bedrooms, one for them, one for the baby, and one for each of his children. Ruth had to continue working in order to pay for the house and the added cost of another child. When her own son was born, she stayed at home for six weeks, then hired a full-time housekeeper so that she could go back to work.

Having her own child made her realize what Reid had been going through. Being separated from them, he had so few ways to show them love and protect them, so spending money on them became his primary method of expressing love for his children.

Ruth admitted that although she and Reid had worked through many problems, she still found herself looking at the price tags for items he bought his two children. She kept figuring out how many hours she had to spend working and away from her son in order to pay for everything Reid bought for his children. She could also see, after having her own child, that her need to protect her son far surpassed any protectiveness she felt for her stepchildren. She liked them well enough, but her need to ensure that her own child had everything he needed was paramount.

THE PROTECTION DILEMMA

How much money is enough to make up for a parent's absence? In effect, this is the question that haunts many fathers whose children are weekend visitors. Increasingly, it's also a question that haunts working mothers.

We all try to provide what our children need—it can take the form of getting dental care, hiring tutors, paying for a new bicycle, or buying them cars when they're old enough to drive. The expenditure of money is a form of expression, but the basic desire to protect is much stronger in a natural parent than in a stepparent. It's not the same as "buying love." It's the desire *to give to loved ones*. A parent who wants to give and protect should not be made to feel guilty for these normal parental desires unless the giving becomes excessive and causes deprivation for the new family.

However, when a man uses money as a means of assuring his former family that he is really a good guy in spite of the fact that he left them for a different life, he is setting himself up for a big disappointment. He is not going to achieve his aim, and more than that, he is raising expectations in others that will become impossible to fulfill. If anything, the expectation level should be lowered to help the first family base their requests on reality rather than on pipe dreams.

Men who spend beyond reason on ex-wives and children often compensate by being stingy within the present marriage. When a husband's feelings of guilt tilt in the direction of a former wife and children from his first marriage, the fragile balance of power in the new family is fractured. It's difficult to know how guilt will play itself out, but once the issue of overspending arises from a guilty conscience, it's critically important to bring the subject to the fore. The success of the remarriage is at stake.

And to be fair, it's wise for the second wife to ask herself whether or not she believes that a money request from a stepchild is valid. Rather than second-guess her response, she can ask herself how she'd view the request if it were coming from her own child.

When stepchildren and half siblings are living under the same roof, it's actually easier to manage, because the guilt factor is not present. They share the same food, the same household items, the same pool of money. But there will usually be inequities to a greater or lesser degree. And *perceived* inequities are always present where children are concerned, even when they are biological siblings. These rivalries can make both children and teenagers seem excessively selfish and manipulative.

One stepmother remembers how her stepson acted at the dinner table. "He was frantic to be sure he got the first helping so that he could get all he wanted. If I baked a cake, he would take two pieces even though he rarely ate that much. There was no reason for him to worry that there was not going to be enough food, but he acted like every meal was the last."

As children become teenagers, their behavior grows more nuanced. They can become particularly facile at manipulating their parents for money. They grow much more aware of the emotional content of money. In addition, their financial needs are usually greater than those of younger children.

In any family, a child is conflicted by the need to be independent while still being entirely dependent on the parents' money. In stepfamilies, these conflicts can become particularly frustrating and destructive.

No matter how philosophically a stepmother views alimony and child support, every penny that goes out to the husband's former family is money taken away from her needs and the needs of her children. In the end, no one is really satisfied: the ex-wife feels that the payments are inadequate to meet her needs, the stepmother feels the strain of seeing money leaving her own family coffers, and the father is truly caught in the middle. The children invariably feel that they are getting short shrift in the money department. Everyone becomes like that child grabbing for the first helping of food to be sure of getting all he wants. Of course, the ideal aim of every couple is to know at the outset of a remarriage how much money is available over and above previous obligations, and how it is going to be spent, but unforeseen expenses are bound to arise. As I said before, though it bears repeating, when your spouse spends money on his or her child from a previous marriage, before criticizing, consider whether you would spend that money on your own child. If it really is a frivolous expenditure of money that you don't have, don't rant and rave. Discuss it calmly.

SHOWING YOUR ASSETS

In any marriage, but particularly in remarriage, there is an aspect of financial planning that needs to be addressed—how will assets be held and invested? Couples in remarriages are more likely to own property than those entering first marriages. These assets were probably acquired through past working and savings or through inheritance or a divorce settlement. Ownership of assets at the time of marriage is usually not equal. And then there is the touchier matter of earning power and the ability to acquire assets greater than what the other partner would be able to acquire. In a healthy marriage, the less affluent spouse should have the right to participate equally in the long-term planning process, because assets form the foundation of the couple's financial security.

Second wives are prone to make the mistake of using up their assets quickly after remarriage. If the husband has come through a recent divorce, he may not have much in the way of property, because chances are he has given his first family his major asset—the home. And his savings are usually gone, because he has had to pay legal fees, not to mention the monthly payments of alimony and child support. However, the husband who has arrived somewhat empty-handed may have the greater earning power. This means he will be in a position to acquire assets over the years. To maintain financial equity within the marriage, the second wife should *try* to secure the assets and savings she brought into the marriage, particularly if she has children from her previous marriage.

The first joint investment is usually the purchase of a home. Should the wife use her prior assets to help purchase a home? That should depend on whether the couple lives in a community property state.

What does the term "community property" mean? In simplest terms, it means that husband and wife are deemed to equally own all money earned by either one of them from the beginning of the marriage until the date of separation, usually a date that occurs when one spouse moves out. In addition, all property acquired during the marriage with "community" money is deemed to be owned equally by both husband and wife, regardless of who purchased it. To know whether you live in a community property state, check with your lawyer, specifically a lawyer specializing in wills and trusts.

Like community property, all debts contracted from the beginning of the marriage until the date of separation are community debts, and each spouse is equally liable for these debts—unpaid balances on credit cards, home mortgages, and automobile loan balances. We've all heard of wives who, with handy little credit cards, went on binge shopping sprees as soon as they found out that a philandering husband was planning to divorce them. That unpaid balance on the credit card is his debt, too, and if he's the only wage earner, it's likely he'll be paying all of it.

Separate property, on the other hand, is everything that a husband and wife *own separately,* and does not need to be divided between spouses at date of divorce. Separate property is:

1. Anything owned prior to marriage.

2. Anything inherited or received as a gift during the marriage.

3. Assets (such as a vacation home) acquired *solely* using money owned prior to the marriage or from inheritance.

4. Anything either spouse earned after the date of separation.

Separate property can also include anything that one spouse gives up to the other spouse in writing.

It is easy for separate property to become mixed with community property, and for that reason it's important to be able to trace the payments and show where the money came from. For example, if a woman uses her money to put a down payment on a house, and then pays off the mortgage with community property, she would be entitled to reimbursement for the amount of the down payment, but without interest on that sum.

Similar to separate property, debts incurred before marriage are separate debts and belong to one spouse—for example, educational loans or medical and dental bills.

Under community property laws, a house may be viewed as jointly owned, regardless of who holds title. As a rule of thumb it can be stated: *Assets brought into the marriage are not viewed as community property. However, assets acquired during the marriage, whether titled jointly or not, are community property.*

If one person comes into the marriage with significantly greater assets than the other, then there will be greater disparity in discretionary income. Since most people who have acquired assets prior to the marriage have worked hard for them, it would seem counterproductive to insist that all assets be held jointly. But even when some assets are held separately, there should always be discussion between the couple before purchases and investments are made, regardless of the source of funds for these new acquisitions. It's a matter of respect for each other.

When the couple is able to discuss distribution of assets and act on their joint resolutions, they will learn to trust each other's financial motivations. The financial partnership is strengthened whenever decisions are mutual and equitable.

BEFORE MARRIAGE—TALK!

Be honest with each other. Discussing money issues can be one of the most volatile conversations you will ever have, but also one of the most important. "Don't you trust me?" is bound to creep into this discussion. At the outset, make sure each of you knows that *trust is not the issue,* but rather the need to fairly *provide* for all parties. Whose home should you live in, yours or your spouse's? Should you buy or rent a new home? Most of all, you both want to avoid surprises concerning financial matters.

Either we think about money the way our parents thought about it, or we think the opposite of what they thought, but it's still *because of them* that we think the way we do. Those attitudes become entrenched and difficult to change. Some people believe in paying cash for everything except a house: "If we can't pay for it, we can't afford it, so we don't buy it." Others have a different creed: "I don't want to wait until I'm too old to enjoy it, so I'll buy it now and pay for it with a credit card." Whatever the philosophy, it's important that the spouse knows it and can live with it or that there can be compromise.

Discuss all the options and your feelings about each of them.

Talking Points

✓   Will you each keep your own financial accounts, or will there be joint accounts or both?

✓   Scrutinize all assets. How much do both of you have in real estate, stocks, bonds, cash, fine jewelry, art and antiques, and other items? Now that you're combining assets, evaluate what to keep and what to sell. Allocation of assets is an important investment strategy. Seek expert advice for larger estates.

✓   What are your incomes? Will both of you work?

✓   What are your financial liabilities—what is owed on credit cards, auto loans, mortgages, and other debt? Who will have the responsibility to pay off the debt? Will it be one of you or both of you?

✓   Who will have the responsibility to make alimony or child support payments? Will it be one or both spouses? What are the details of these obligations? Are there any provisions for increases or decreases in the future? Are there agreements to pay higher-education expenses for the children? Bear in mind that unless divorce agreements contain "no modification" provisions, the amount of alimony and child support is subject to change.

✓   What are you both going to receive from pensions and inheritances? Will you share this money? It's best to state your feelings right at the start.

✓   What kind of life, health, and disability insurance do you each have? Is it economically advantageous to have both of you on the same health insurance policy? Are there prior commitments about naming life insurance beneficiaries? If so, put that on the table. Be attentive to beneficiary designations on all insurance policies and retirement plans. Most companies will provide beneficiary change forms for insurance, annuities, and qualified retirement plans, so there's no excuse for some horrendous oversight.

✓   What will each of you be obligated to pay for the support of your new family? Of course, take into account that circumstances may change—for example, the birth of another child.

✓   How much does each of you plan to leave to an ex-spouse and any children from a previous marriage? How much will each of you leave your new spouse and children?

ESTATE PLANNING

Consider two real-life situations described by a prominent estate-planning lawyer in Atlanta. "Though this is not a common occurrence," he said, "it can happen to anyone who has not taken the time to carefully review all assets at the time of a remarriage or the birth of a child."

In a tragic moment, a second wife who had been married to her husband for over twenty-five years, and had a child with him, learned that her husband had neglected to change his beneficiary on his pension plan. The first wife, whom he hadn't seen in twenty years and who had no children with him, received slightly over *$1 million* at the time of his death. The lawyer said, "If that had happened to me, I'd come out of my grave."

Unlike the first tragedy, the second one occurs all too frequently. When a recently widowed father was about to get married again, his son urged him to do a prenuptial agreement. The father refused. "No, that would be like saying I don't trust her. Besides, she knows my wishes."

The wedding was lovely. The marriage was a happy one, though it lasted only until the father's death, four years later. His entire estate, worth slightly more than *$3 million,* went to his second wife. When she died, five years later, her children from a previous marriage received everything. The son from the first marriage never saw a penny of his father's estate.

Where There's a Will, There's a Way

At the time of marriage, whether it's the first, second, or third, a couple should make new wills. Certain types of trusts are also useful instruments to provide for children from previous marriages.

Until recently, a will was considered the cornerstone of any estate plan. Even now, a will is vital if your children are minors, since it's in a will that you nominate guardians for them should they be orphaned. And a will is probably all that's necessary if there are few assets to pass on to heirs. No matter how large or small the assets involved, *estate planning is of great importance to couples who have children of any age from previous marriages.*

Each partner should have a will, preferably drafted by an attorney who understands the *practical and emotional* issues involved for blended families. It should not be assumed that verbal agreements with your spouse during the marriage have any bearing on what happens after the death of either one of you. Wills are the primary means of ensuring that assets will be distributed as each spouse desires after his or her demise.

A remarried couple should arrange not only that minor children will be provided for but that the surviving spouse will be financially secure.

Joy's husband's will failed to do that. He left his wife 20 percent and left 20 percent for each of his four children, who lived with them.

Joy says sadly, "My husband was determined that I would not profit from our marriage unless we were married for a long time. We had been married nine years when he died. I was terribly hurt when I first read his will, but he refused to change it. It really had a chilling effect on our marriage and my role as the children's stepmother, especially since their natural mother was dead."

Wills can send a strong emotional message that ought to be considered, particularly since the documents are usually read by the spouse at the time they are drafted. Of course, wills are a private matter, and there's no way of stopping a spouse from redoing a will *without* the knowledge of the other spouse.

If a wife shares her husband's financial obligations to a first marriage over a period of many years, she should share equally in any accumulated assets during the same span of time. This rationale should help a husband resist the pressures of ex-wives, older children, and grandparents, who will want to offer their advice on the subject of inheritance. The same should be true if the wife had financial obligations from a previous marriage.

Splitting Heirs

A husband or wife in an original family typically leaves all his or her assets to the surviving spouse, with the understanding that the survivor will then arrange to convey the estate to the couple's children. But can you safely assume that your spouse will provide for children who are not his or her biological offspring? We've already seen what happened to one son from a previous marriage; the second wife didn't leave him anything. This area is one that can be dealt with very successfully with the help of knowledgeable lawyers who specialize in the field of wills and trusts.

The question of how to provide for children from previous marriages worried Jeremy and his wife Cara, both of whom had recently retired. When the couple married, fifteen years earlier, Jeremy and Cara each had two children from first marriages. With an estate now worth slightly over $1 million, they wanted to be certain that all four children shared equally.

"We've seen situations where family members start out with high ethics and good intentions, but somehow the children of the first to die get cut out, and the surviving spouse's children get the lion's share of the assets," Jeremy said.

"Or what if I go first, and you remarry someone who winds up with all of it?" Cara said.

Jeremy laughed. "That won't happen, but we want to avoid these kinds of problems."

QTIP Trusts

To resolve these worries, their lawyer advised Jeremy and Cara to include QTIP trusts in their estate plan. "QTIP" stands for Qualified Terminable Interest Property. According to Robert Petix, a Providence, Rhode Island, attorney specializing in wills and trusts, "QTIP trusts have the chief advantage of allowing an individual to place assets in a trust and to decide to whom the assets will pass after the surviving spouse's death. Furthermore, the assets will be entitled to a substantial tax saving—a complete marital deduction for estate tax purposes. In brief, a spouse—say, the husband—puts property intended for the wife in a QTIP trust. When the husband dies, the wife is entitled to all of the trust income. In addition, the trust may allow for encroachment on the principal for the wife's support in reasonable comfort—that is, if she needs it to pay for health care, further education, or maintenance." After the wife's death, however, the trust principal passes to beneficiaries, often the children of the first marriage, who were named by the husband when the trust was established.

There is a potential downside, however. According to Petix, "QTIP trusts can present unforeseen complications, so it's always important to consult with the attorney who is drafting the trust instrument to understand fully the real-world effects QTIP trust planning may have on a family." As discussed above, the main feature of a QTIP trust is that none of the assets placed in the QTIP trust will be subject to estate taxes at the first spouse's death, but Congress exacts a "cost" for this advantage—that all income be paid from the trust to the surviving spouse. This can cause conflict between the children from a first marriage and the surviving second spouse.

In one case, Petix represented a surviving spouse who had been married to the now deceased husband for about fifteen years. There were grown children from his first marriage who, under the terms of the QTIP trust, were entitled to all the assets after the death of their deceased father's second wife. Unfortunately, the father's estate consisted largely of undeveloped land, which the children regarded, not unjustifiably, as their father's legacy. They thought of the land as theirs.

This did little to comfort the surviving wife—their stepmother—who was entitled only to income from the QTIP trust. Undeveloped raw land produces no income, and the children, who were serving as cotrustees of the QTIP trust, along with their stepmother, were reluctant to sell "their" land to benefit the stepmother. Resentment grew. Even though federal tax law requires QTIP trust assets to be made income producing for the benefit of the surviving spouse, this did not prevent the stepchildren from blocking every attempt made to sell the land in order to acquire income-producing assets.

Consider also the case of the "trophy wife." If the husband of a trophy wife expects to solve his wealth transfer planning problems through the exclusive use of a QTIP trust, he should think again. Often, the trophy wife will be as young as, or even younger than, the children from the first marriage. She may well outlive the children, in which case they will never inherit anything from dear old Dad.

The lesson is simple: couples should consult with their legal advis-

ers to make sure that they have fully contemplated the results of the decisions they've made in their wills.

Revocable Living Trusts

For transferring sizable or complicated estates, estate-planning attorneys often favor revocable living trusts, so named because you place your property in a trust created while you're still living. You can change the trust terms at any time, and even serve as the trustee so that you're not giving up control of the assets during your lifetime. When you die, the trust assets are distributed to the beneficiaries you named, according to instructions you set forth in the trust document. Or you can instruct that the assets flow into a different type of trust, such as a special-needs trust for a disabled heir.

The Kennedy family has used revocable trusts for many purposes, not the least of which was to avoid having public disclosure of their financial assets. Since these types of trusts do not become a part of the marital estate, they are not made a part of the public record.

Bypass Trusts

While QTIP trusts are included in the surviving spouse's estate, bypass trusts are not. The issue of what is and what's not included in the estate may become moot because of changes in the law.

Because of estate tax changes in the 2003 Tax Code, the value of an estate transferred without tax consequences will keep escalating annually until the year 2010, at which time no taxes will have to be paid, no matter how large the value of the transferred estate. No one knows if Congress will extend these tax-free transfers after 2010.

In the simplest bypass arrangement, the deceased spouse's will establishes a trust funded with a prescribed amount of estate assets and names a trustee other than the surviving spouse to administer the trust. If, under the terms of the trust, the surviving spouse is given no general power of appointment over trust property (except the right to receive trust income for life, with the remainder to be paid to the couple's heirs), for estate tax purposes none of the trust property will be included in the surviving spouse's estate. The bypass trust (also called the exemption-equivalent trust) may allow a portion of the principal to pass to the surviving spouse, but this is not required. At any point decided by the testator, that is the deceased person who executed the will, the assets are distributed to whomever the maker of the trust designates.

Gifting Strategies

Another way to distribute your estate fairly is to use the annual federal gift exclusion during one's lifetime. The Tax Code allows everyone to transfer $11,000 per year per beneficiary free of federal gift taxes. Over a period of years, this strategy can significantly reduce a taxable estate while allowing distribution of assets to selected family members—such as children from a previous marriage. For those with larger estates, which might include a home or a family business, up to $1 million over the annual gift tax exclusion can also be transferred tax-free. A similar exemption ($1.12 million in 2003) exists that allows generation-skipping transfers up to that amount to grandchildren and great-grandchildren tax-free.

Compare Trusts and Wills

In deciding which type of instrument you prefer, it's necessary to understand how wills and *living trusts* compare in five key areas:

- **Probate.** Assets you transfer via a will must go through probate, the potentially costly and time-consuming court process of administering your will. Assets you transfer via a revocable living trust avoid probate.

- **Cost.** An estate-planning attorney can draft simple wills for a husband and wife for considerably less money than it would cost to draft a living trust. So it's important to weigh the benefits and costs before you decide what's best for your family.

- **Privacy.** When a will is probated, its contents are made public. This does not necessarily mean, however, that the assets of the estate will be made public. Since living trusts are not probated, there are no public records of the trust terms.

- **Incapacity.** With a living trust, you can name a successor trustee to manage the trust assets if you become mentally or physically unable to do so. If you don't have a living trust, you will need to draw up a durable power of attorney to name someone to take charge of your assets if you become incapacitated.

- **Hassle.** With a will, you simply bequeath your separately owned assets that do not have a named beneficiary. In contrast, *the property you want to put in a living trust must be retitled to the trust.* Anything not so titled when you die will have to be probated.

PRENUPTIAL AGREEMENTS

There is a certain emotional component related to prenuptial agreements that offends the sensibilities of people in love, because it's unpleasant to think about the prospects of divorce or death when you're in love and about to get married. But the "prenup" is a way of eliminating uncertainty about what a court may decide is an equitable distribution of property. It's about clarity, about how the couple is going to live, how they are going to spend, and how they are going to save. It also has the added benefit of allowing the parties to avoid costly legal battles over the issue of distribution of property during a divorce. If you have a substantial amount of money compared with your second spouse, or vice versa, discuss the issue of prenuptial agreements.

Prenups are becoming an acceptable means of good estate planning. They certainly are favored by the rich and famous.

When dating developer Donald Trump, Marla Maples vowed never to sign a prenup. She held out even after she discovered she was pregnant. But for Trump, it was no prenup, no nup. Only when their baby was born did Maples acquiesce. According to Trump's lawyer, Stanford Lotwin, "She signed a week or two before the marriage."

So did Melinda French Gates, the Microsoft employee who married the founder of the company, Bill Gates. In 1993, Bill Gates told a journalist that he would never ask his wife to sign a prenup. In a literal sense, he kept his word. He didn't ask her to sign one, but he had his old friend, Microsoft president Steven Ballmer, talk her into signing a prenup. And she did.

Trump had children from his previous marriage to Ivana, but Gates had never been married before, so why the prenup? Like many states, Washington is a community property state. In the unhappy event that the Gateses' marriage failed, absent a prenup, half of his 24 percent holding in the company could fall into unfriendly hands.

According to Stanford Lotwin, "It is very difficult to set aside a prenuptial agreement if each person to the agreement is represented by counsel." But it's not impossible. Miami lawyer Denis Kleinfeld says that he recently negotiated a hundred-page prenup to protect the client's children's inheritance, only to have the bride's lawyer announce cheerily, "Don't worry—if this marriage falls through, we'll crack this thing." So Kleinfeld advised the client to salt away his assets in a foreign trust. He says he's never seen a foreign trust fail to protect a client's assets from her or his ex-spouse. The Cayman Islands are a popular locale for such trusts.

Once viewed as a legal strategy for a wealthy spouse, typically a husband, to exploit the other party, usually a less wealthy wife, prenups have evolved into a legal tool to protect the financial interest of both parties. Supported by case law developed in the late 1970s and early 1980s, prenups are no longer perceived as an affront to family values but rather as a tool to create a fair and practical way to handle the dissolution of assets in the event of divorce or death. My main reason for including this extensive information on prenuptial agreements is their usefulness in protecting and providing for children from previous marriages even when the estates are not huge.

While the courts initially resisted the idea of such agreements, operating on the premise that marriage was forever, today courts recognize that both men and women are able to negotiate with each other and enter into agreements that they want the courts to enforce.

Over the past twenty years, more women have entered the workforce than ever before. And many of these women have enjoyed financial success in their careers and in their own businesses. Another aspect of the contemporary scene is the later-in-life marriages by so many of these women. They have as much of a reason as men do to protect their individual assets.

Carole, a college professor, credits a prenuptial agreement with saving her finances from complete disaster when her second marriage ended. She had plenty of debts, thanks to legal fees and a court-ordered payment to her husband. But, she said of the agreement, "it did protect the house and my retirement, and it shielded the royalties I earned from books I'd written. Without the prenup, I would have had to give him half of all of it."

Naturally, planning for the *end* of a marriage, through divorce or death, is a sensitive issue, but the prenup is a way of eliminating uncertainty about what a court may decide is an equitable distribution of property. Additionally the prenup allows the parties to avoid costly legal battles over the issue of distribution of property during a divorce.

EIGHT STEPS TO AN AIRTIGHT PRENUP

1. Make sure there's no hint of coercion. Time the execution of the agreement so that it will not appear to have been signed under duress. It should be signed at least thirty days before the ceremony. The closer to the wedding date the agreement is signed, the greater the danger it will not be upheld.

2. Both husband and wife should have separate attorneys. If one person selects the attorney for both of them, that person is open to the charge of influencing the other. It's best for the person asked to sign the agreement to have his or her own attorney read and advise on what the terms of the agreement mean.

3. Both husband and wife must disclose their financial assets. The most frequent reason for invalidating prenups is that one party failed to disclose *all* assets.

4. The agreement must also be perceived as fair and reasonable when it is presented to the court for enforcement. It must contain a sufficiently clear description of the property affected by the agreement.

5. Don't get nasty—like the provision in one prenup that imposed a $1,000 penalty for every pound the wife gained. The lawyer persuaded his client to remove the penalty provision, pointing out that it could spur a judge to toss out the whole agreement.

6. See that your spouse stands to inherit a reasonable amount if he or she survives you. It shows fair play.

7. Once you are married, don't mix premarital and postmarital assets. "Commingling is the kiss of death," counsels New York matrimonial litigator Harriet Cohen. Why? Because if you cannot absolutely prove what belonged to you before the marriage, you might lose it.

8. The document must be signed and recorded with the probate court in the county where the document is signed, witnessed, and notarized.

If you're determined to protect your cash but still flinch at the unromantic notion of a prenup, in some states you can always secure your money in an irrevocable trust—a solution that can really be forever.

REMEMBER WHAT MARRIAGE IS ABOUT

While this chapter sounds a cautionary note on the matter of finances, you mustn't lose sight of the love and trust that brought you together in the first place. When my husband and I first married, he had alimony and child support obligations that he could not meet because of a cash flow problem due to hefty legal fees from his divorce and, at the same time, a temporary downturn in his business. For a year, on my own initiative and from my earnings, I paid all of our expenses, including his alimony and child support obligations. Though each of us had children from previous marriages, we have always combined our incomes into a joint checking account and paid all bills from that account. Many years later, I was pleasantly surprised to learn that my husband had quit-claimed to me a half interest in all of his commercial property, almost all of it debt-free. I offer this as an example of what a real marital partnership is about, providing for each other through good times and bad times. It's the sum and substance of marriage.

Helpful Guidelines

- **Be understanding of your spouse's legal obligations to his/her former family.** Don't punish the person you love for doing what he or she is legally and morally obligated to do. Respect your spouse for being the kind of person who honors commitments. (That doesn't mean tolerating excessive spending to the detriment of your new family, however.)

- **Talk openly and candidly.** Discussing money matters was once considered impolite. That is no longer so, particularly between husband and wife. Talk about every aspect of the financial picture. Understand exactly what is coming in and what must go out. Know all financial liabilities—credit card debt, auto loans, mortgages, and other debt. Decide who will have the responsibility to pay off the debt. Decide how each spouse will keep financial accounts—as individual or joint accounts or both. Let your feelings be known on every aspect of the financial picture, including the issue of inheritance for your children from a previous marriage.

- **Get professional advice.** Since no one has all the answers to each unique problem, don't be afraid to get help along the way. Financial advisers and lawyers who specialize in wills and trusts can help insure financial security for the family you cherish. Make sure that everything is in writing and that an attorney who specializes in the area of wills, trusts, and estate planning is the one to draft all documents. New wills should be made soon after the marriage takes place. Certain types of trusts are useful instruments to provide for children from previous marriages.

- **Assign one bookkeeper at a time.** For the sake of order and accuracy, only one person should pay bills, but the other spouse should be kept fully informed of the details of household expenses. If one of you has a particular proficiency at handling the family accounts, that should be the person who does it. If neither of you have the inclination to do this, alternate on an annual basis. Toss a coin to see who goes first. Keep good records, especially with regard to alimony and child support payments. You may need these records for tax purposes.

- **Scrutinize all assets.** How much do both of you have in real estate, stocks, bonds, cash, fine jewelry, art and antiques, and other items? Now that you're combining assets, evaluate what to keep and what to sell. Allocation of assets is an important investment strategy. Seek expert money-managing advice for larger estates.

- **Discuss who will work.** Will one or both of you work? Discuss how the birth of another child might affect the issue of who will work and how this event might impact your financial circumstances.

- **Be prepared for changing circumstances.** Bear in mind that unless the divorce agreements contain "no modification" clauses, the amounts of alimony and child support are subject to change—up and down. Your ex can use this clause to increase the amount. But so can you—to decrease payments. If you can show changed circumstances either in your financial situation or in that of your former spouse, you may be able to decrease your alimony and child support obligations. For example, if your child decides to come and live with you, that's a changed circumstance in your favor. If your ex goes back to work, that may also be a basis for reducing her alimony. If a costly serious illness occurs, that is also a changed circumstance.

- **Plan early for college expenses.** Know who has either a responsibility or a desire to pay for higher-education expenses for the children. Determine how these expenses will be paid on the income that will be available. Make provisions as soon as it's possible to do so. Consider setting up college accounts that will be beneficial to your income tax picture. Ask your accountant to explain how IRS 529 accounts can be a tax benefit.

- **Determine beneficiaries for pensions and inheritances.** Heated emotions can surround these issues, so it's best to state your feelings right at the start.

- **Determine the extent of life, health, and disability insurance you both have.** Decide if it's economically advantageous to have both of you on the same health insurance policy. Find out if there are prior commitments about naming life insurance beneficiaries. If so, put that on the table. Be attentive to beneficiary designations on all insurance policies and retirement plans. Most companies will provide beneficiary change forms for insurance, annuities, and qualified retirement plans.

- **Decide on the issue of a prenuptial agreement well before the marriage takes place.** If you have a substantial amount of money compared with your second spouse, or vice versa, consider whether you want a prenuptial agreement. Prenuptial agreements override state laws and spell out what happens in the event of another divorce or a death. As already mentioned in this chapter, *if this type of agreement is going to be a major hurdle to your happiness, "speak now or forever hold your peace."*

- **Remember why you decided to get married in the first place.** Don't let money problems spoil your happiness. Though what your parents told you is true—"You can't live on love," you can live on a lot less money than you might have imagined if you love each other.

eight

Sensitive Issues and Bad Influences

Secret Eight:

You have the right to set the rules for the way people

live in your home.

Many sensitive family problems are swept under the rug because people simply don't know what to do about them. These are *charged* issues that we're afraid to touch, for fear of being shocked. This chapter includes sexual misdeeds as well as other forms of inappropriate behavior, particularly by children who are having a direct and detrimental impact on other children in the blended family. Gwen Bate, Ph.D., a clinical psychologist in Atlanta, has dealt extensively with the complex issues of stepfamily life. Dr. Bate cautions couples who are attempting to blend families that include teenagers, "Based on years of experience, I say, fasten your seat belts."

One of the most difficult subjects for stepfamilies to deal with is sexuality in all its various forms, from the ex-wife's new boyfriend to the ex-husband's live-in girlfriend, to the stepson's attraction to his sexy young stepmother, to the hunk that is now sharing a bathroom with his stepsister.

These are classic denial issues in many families, and they are much more prevalent than people are willing to admit. Today's teenagers—

and many preteens—have an incredible degree of awareness about sex. They are much more informed and liberated than any prior generation of teens. And the relaxed moral standards that infiltrate every aspect of our culture have created a whole new set of problems for the blended-extended family.

In biological families, the heightened sexuality of a new marriage has usually subsided by the time children have reached an age of aware-ness. In a blended family, however, the children are often exposed to a parent and stepparent who are still in the throes of romantic passion. And, though parents may not realize it, children are keenly aware of what goes on behind closed doors during this early period of the adult relationship. When a newly remarried couple is too demonstrative in their sexual attraction for each other, children—and other relatives—feel embarrassment, arousal, jealousy, or even anger.

Love and familial affection should not, however, be confused with blatant displays of sexual feeling. Stepchildren need to see expressions of love and caring between their parent and a stepparent, even if there is a risk of stirring up some competition and discomfort. It is ultimately reassuring to children to know that their parent loves and is loved.

Some studies that were done in the late 1980s suggested that there was a loosening of sexual boundaries in remarriage families, compared with the boundaries in biological families. The loosening is related to the nonbiological nature of the family, which has not had the advantage of a long developmental period to form intimate parent-child ties, as well as child-child ties. It is not surprising that people who have been perfect strangers, and who are now thrown together in the closeness of family life, might discover sexual attractions for one another. It isn't much different from the relationships that develop in coed college dor-mitories.

YOUTH WORLD

At the risk of offending parents who think their kids tell them every-thing, let me remind you there is a *youth world* out there the likes of which we've never seen before. Adults are being successfully barricaded from entry into their children's lives. These kids can talk on the telephone to two people (or more) at once with call-waiting and conference-calling, juggle another group in private chat rooms online while the TV, the CD player, and the radio blare forth the often violent and obscene lyrics of rap music. What are parents to do when even the so-called responsible media has offered nightly broadcasts about oral sex in the Oval Office? And your kids are coming to you, asking questions you never dreamed you'd have to answer.

Youth is absorbed by its own world, an aggregate force of pop culture and peer influence, with unprecedented technological advances that are both awesome for the educational aspect and frightening for the pornography it makes accessible to children. The consequence of all of these *advances* is that our kids really don't seem to know what's decent and what's indecent. Even more puzzling is the profound change in what kids will talk about. They are neither ashamed nor shy about handling subjects that would have mortified us when we were their age. So, it should come as no shock that we are seeing behavior in our homes that reflects the negative influence of our changing culture.

SLEEPING WITH MY STEPBROTHER

"Our parents married when I was fifteen and Graham was seventeen," Babs said. "I'd seen Graham around—we both went to the same high school. He's gorgeous. I mean, he was really hot. I actually had a crush on him before our parents even knew each other. My dad died suddenly from a heart attack, and then a few years later our parents met. Graham's parents divorced when his mother ran off with another man. When we first had sex, our parents were on their honeymoon. My grandmother was staying with us, but she couldn't walk up the steps, so she was sleeping in the downstairs bedroom. Graham was getting into the shower when I barged into the bathroom to get some of my things. I honestly didn't know he was in there. For a few seconds, we just stood and looked at each other. He turned on the shower and pulled me in with him. And then . . . it just happened."

At first, Babs said she felt a little guilty, but over time the guilt went away. They had full access to each other with rooms that connected. They shared a bathroom and took advantage of the situation—and made love constantly.

"There were times when I'd sit on the sofa, watching TV, and think that our folks would really freak out about it. But what were we doing that was so terrible? If he weren't my stepbrother, would it be wrong? Was it wrong? I really didn't know. Graham didn't think so. We actually fell in love. No one even suspected. I never even told any of my girl-friends. And then my younger brother popped into Graham's room one night while we were in bed together."

When Babs's mother asked her directly if she was "involved with Graham," Babs lied and said she wasn't. That's when her mother told her that her brother had mentioned finding them in Graham's bed to-gether. After repeated denials, Babs finally admitted that it was true and that she and Graham loved each other. This led to a family conference. At first, both parents were horrified, but after Graham and Babs told them that they hadn't meant for it to happen and that they were really in love, the parents cooled down, but still demanded promises that the re-lationship would stop. Both Babs and Graham agreed, but they didn't keep their word.

Graham's father was at an impasse, because Graham was due to graduate from high school within two months and would be going away to college in the fall. This was not the time to send Graham to another place to live and another high school, even if there had been that alter-native, which there wasn't. The family decided to let the matter resolve in a more natural way—allowing the geographic distance to calm the passions of these two teenagers. Graham went to stay with his aunt for part of the summer, and then went directly off to college. Ultimately, things worked out exactly as the parents hoped they would. But to this day, five years later, Babs admits she's still attracted to Graham, and would dearly love to marry him one day. Graham is presently dating someone else.

According to one psychologist who specializes in adolescent prob-lems, the parents did the right thing, considering that graduation was near and the living arrangements couldn't be changed immediately: "Was it an ideal situation? No. But you can't undo what was done. Was there a better way to handle the situation? Probably not. To have made too much more of what had already happened might have intensified the problem—made the relationship more forbidden and alluring than it already was. The parents had few alternatives."

According to Robert Klopfer, the director of Stepping Stones, a stepfamily counseling center in Ridgewood, New Jersey, strong sexual attractions are fairly commonplace in homes where step-siblings are suddenly thrown together under the same roof. "Before long, sparks fly. But once that first rush of eroticism is over," Klopfer said, "the kids figure out it's not the best idea."

Usually, it doesn't work out as smoothly as it did with Babs and Graham. One woman described how her thirteen-year-old daughter lost her virginity to her sixteen-year-old stepbrother during a summer visit. After the sexual encounter, the young girl was devastated when the stepbrother told her he didn't mean for it to happen and didn't want it to ever happen again. She admitted to her mother that she had initiated the relationship.

Kids thrown together in the same house during the years of awakening sexuality need to be watched very carefully for seductive behavior. Parents should make a concerted effort to keep these teenagers out of temptation's way, first by remaining vigilant about the possibility of sexual attractions, then by cautioning the youngsters about avoiding these intimacies.

Putting some distance between teenage step-siblings is a good place to start—not having them in bedrooms with connecting doors that don't open to a hallway. If this sounds elementary, consider how difficult it can be to create appropriate living space for a suddenly burgeoning family. Establish dress codes, such as bathrobes, to avoid awkward encounters when people are going to and from the bathroom to shower and dress. And it's best to avoid revealing clothing and sexually suggestive conversations.

The notion that new step-siblings of the opposite sex will have attractions for each other is not unlike any unrelated boy and girl having these feelings, but they should always be discouraged from acting on them while they are minors living under the roof of a blended family. Parents need to assert that they are not willing to tolerate sexual acting out. Sometimes, biologically unrelated step-siblings of the opposite sex do continue close relationships after they leave home, and later even marry each other, but the relationship should not be viewed as acceptable until they are independent adults living elsewhere.

Most people wouldn't be too alarmed if a couple of consenting adult step-siblings decided to engage in a romance. But even though biologically there's nothing wrong, there is a cultural taboo inherent in this situation. There is also the problem of always seeing each other at family functions and holidays, and having to deal with the lingering feelings that are bound to be there.

Babs said she'd never tell anyone she dates about the relationship she had with Graham, because if she and this person ever became serious, he'd meet Graham and "soon realize he was sitting across from a guy I had sex with who is a member of my family."

MORE SERIOUS TABOOS

Sexual feelings in the blended family must be understood and managed so that they won't cause guilt about *natural* feelings or cause behavior that is inappropriate. Parents and stepparents have been reticent to discuss the subject of sex for fear of appearing perverse or crazy or archaic. *It's important to realize that sexual feelings between stepchildren and stepparents occur frequently.* Reaching a level of mature acceptance of these emotions without acting on them is essential for the emotional health of a blended family.

With open, matter-of-fact communication and appropriate rules, the sexual upheaval of adolescence will pass. True tenderness should not be feared, but recognizing the difference between healthy, harmonious affection and sexual acting out is essential. What must be understood is that sexual feelings toward teenagers in one's own family are not in and of themselves pathological unless they are acted on. These feelings are normal, but must be controlled. Even one of our most moral presidents, Jimmy Carter, "lusted in his heart," but he didn't act on it. Not a one of us would care to have all our private thoughts or fantasies broadcast in neon lights. Self-discipline is vital. To ensure restraint, the family members should avoid any flirtatious behavior, and situations that are unduly provocative. A stepfather should not have to be told *not* to watch TV in bed with his teenage stepdaughter. An attractive stepmother should avoid wearing revealing clothes and should close the bedroom door when she's undressing.

DAD'S TROPHY

When Dad marries a woman young enough to be his daughter, his son might just find her as alluring as Dad did. There she is, the new stepmom, moist with suntan lotion, in a skimpy bikini, stretched out on a lounge chair beside the pool. Dad's at work. No one's there but the two of them. . . .

Roger, a handsome, successful fifty-year-old entrepreneur, had had a family—a wife and two sons in their twenties—when he decided he wanted to experience some of the pleasures and excitement he felt he had missed because of the years of striving to achieve in the business world. When Roger met twenty-nine-year-old Amy, the interior designer hired to redecorate the family vacation house, he turned into an adolescent boy who had just discovered what sex was all about. Amy was movie-star beautiful, and receptive to Roger's overtures. After a messy, costly, and acrimonious divorce, Roger married Amy. Within a year, they had a child of their own, an event that caused his grown sons to question just how much of the family estate would be available for them if their father were to die.

Soon Roger's twenty-six-year-old son, Chip, began to spend long summer weekends at the Cape Cod vacation house where his father and stepmother were living. Amy stayed the whole summer at the house to finish the decorating and landscaping. Roger came up on weekends, working in New York during the week.

It was a Monday morning when Chip made his move with his young stepmother. He and Amy spent the rest of the week in the luxurious king-size master bedroom. When Chip declared his love for Amy, she said she had no intention of leaving his father. She cautioned Chip that their relationship was dangerous, and they would have to make sure that Roger never found out. The affair between Amy and Chip went on for nearly two years, until Roger arrived home a day early to find his son and his young wife nude in the swimming pool.

Roger threw Chip out of the house, but a few days later, love-struck Chip arrived with a gun. He and his father scuffled. The gun went off, and a bullet grazed Roger's thigh, leaving him with a superficial wound that was discreetly treated in a doctor's office. To avoid adverse publicity, Roger explained that the gun just had gone off when he was cleaning it. Shortly thereafter, Roger divorced Amy. Chip and his father have not spoken to each other in years. Roger's other son married, and he maintains a close relationship with his father, but has to pretend that he has no contact with his brother, Chip. Amy married again. The sexual relationship between the stepmother and stepson, while sounding like a daytime soap opera, did cause a profound family tragedy.

LOLITA AND STEPDAD

The other side of the coin: Mom marries a man who now becomes a father figure for a teenage stepdaughter whose own father has faded from her life, and, as a consequence the girl develops a competitive relationship with her own mother. Teenage girls may send out signals that are misinterpreted, which is not to say that would be any justification for an inappropriate response. Take the case of Jill, a fourteen-year-old going on twenty-two, who thought her mother's new husband was very attractive. Jill was a budding Lolita. She and her mother, Dorothy, were not getting along for all the reasons that teenage girls often have problems with their mothers. Dorothy refused to allow Jill to wear the kind of suggestive clothing Jill preferred. She also imposed strict curfews that Jill found objectionable, and regularly screened Jill's friends to make sure her daughter wasn't "running around with the wrong crowd." Jill decided she'd show her mother who was in control by starting on a campaign of seduction with her stepfather.

Fortunately, the stepfather was not the type to succumb to Jill's seductive ploys. For several months, he tried to sidestep her flirtatious advances, but that only made Jill grow bolder. He finally decided to discuss the matter with his wife. Together they went to a family counselor, who dealt first with them and then with Jill. The counselor thought it best that Jill be treated separately, so he referred her to a clinical psychologist. By taking quick and appropriate action, the parents averted what could have been a disastrous upheaval of their marriage.

According to experts in the stepfamily field, *most inappropriate sexual incidents take place between a stepfather and stepdaughter.* While sexual feelings toward stepdaughters are not unusual, some stepdads fail to exercise wholesome restraint. Too often, stepfathers will kiss their stepdaughters too long on the lips, "accidentally" brush against their breasts, "playfully" pat their buttocks, and talk provocatively in their presence. These are signals that should not be ignored. This potentially volatile issue has to be addressed the moment it is discovered.

Although this is not incest, it *is* sexual abuse. The incidence of a stepfather's sexually molesting a stepdaughter is widespread and presents a situation that has long-term damaging effects. Even if the teenager is the seductive aggressor, it's still the fault of the stepfather, who is engaging in sexual molestation—or, even worse, statutory rape.

Although the child must always be considered the victim in such cases, the dynamics of these stepparent-child relationships can be very complicated, and ruinous to everyone.

People cannot live in a crisis atmosphere for long periods without negative consequences. Even if nothing is overt or acted upon, when a couple is forced to be on constant alert, handling one emergency while anticipating the next, their own relationship will suffer. When the family turf is a sexually charged arena, the calm blending process that needs to occur in the new family becomes increasingly difficult. *Where sexual tensions persist and triangles develop, professional help should be sought promptly.* More than family harmony is at stake. The marriage itself is at stake.

Despite the risks, there is a place for *natural* affection. Many blended families are being unnecessarily inhibited from healthy expressions of caring—a bear hug to show affection or concern or sympathy, a squeeze of the hand when a child accomplishes something wonderful, and, actually as well as metaphorically, giving the child a pat on the back or a kiss. If a stepdaughter's natural father dies, would there be anything wrong with a stepfather's putting his arm around her so that she can cry her tears of grief in the embrace of a caring adult? To any reasonable observer, the picture should be clear as to the distinction between a healthy, loving embrace and a sexually provocative one. We all know the difference.

MOM'S NEW BOYFRIEND

Lauren and Michael, ages twelve and fourteen respectively, live with their mother but regularly visit their father and his new family. For several months, Peter and his wife, Nell, noticed that Lauren and Michael didn't want to go home at the end of their weekend visits. Nell has two children from a previous marriage who are approximately the same ages as Lauren and Michael. The four children had developed a comfortable camaraderie, having similar interests in sports and music. For several weeks, the children's whispering and giggling would come to a sudden stop if either Peter or Nell went within hearing range. Peter became concerned, mainly because of his children's obvious reluctance to go home to their mother. He and Nell decided it was time for him to have a talk with his kids. Peter took Michael and Lauren to lunch.

After much coaxing by Peter, Lauren, fighting tears, broke down and said, "Mom has this guy over all the time. They're always in Mom's bedroom, not just at night but anytime he's around."

"You can hear everything they're doing," Michael said with disgust. "It's embarrassing. I hate when he's there. And I've seen him smoking pot."

Peter wasn't entirely surprised, having had problems with his ex-wife's infidelity during their marriage. To his knowledge, however, his ex-wife had never done anything in their house while he was married to her. Peter was furious at what the children had told him and at the effect it was having on them. He realized he might have to remove his children from her custody, though he knew it was going to be a hard-fought battle to establish that she was an unfit mother. Added to that issue was the serious question about Nell's willingness to take on the responsibility of raising his two children. This was something they had never actually talked about, because it had been a given that Peter's ex-wife had primary custody. And then there was the question of space—their small, three-bedroom house was tolerable for visitation, but how would it work every day?

"I'll have a talk with your mother," he told the children.

"No," Lauren said. "She'll be furious with us that we told you."

"Dad," Michael pleaded, "we want to come live with you."

"I don't know if that can be worked out."

"Dad," Michael said, "you *can't* talk to Mom and then send us back into that house. She'll take it out on us, and so will that jerk boyfriend of hers."

After talking to Nell and getting her to agree to have his children live with them, Peter petitioned the court for a change of custody, declaring that his ex-wife was an unfit mother. Before trial, the lawyers attempted to work out the problem through counseling and mediation. As of this writing, there has been no final decision, but the children are presently living with their father and stepmother.

The issue of a parent's fitness is a troublesome one for the courts. They strain to leave the children with the mother unless, as in the case above, the atmosphere is damaging to the children, and, as an alternative, the father can provide a healthy home environment for the children.

IT'S WRONG, BUT IS IT INCEST?

Incest between father and daughter is the most frequently broken of the incest taboos, but now with remarriage as prevalent as it is, the stepfather-daughter situation begs the question: is it incest when there is no biological connection between the two individuals involved? According to Margaret Mahoney's 1994 book, *Stepfamilies and the Law,* the answer is unclear and can differ from state to state.

Without any doubt, incest and sexual abuse are criminal acts. Unlike the strict ban on such situations in the past, at present most

states allow close step-relatives to marry and do not include such relationships in the legal definition of incest.

In nineteen states, step-relatives are included in laws that deal with
criminal sexual activities, while other states take into consideration the
age of the victim and the nature of his or her relationship with the
abuser. In approximately a third of the states, incest laws do not regu-
late step-relatives at all. Many states provide legal protection to minor
stepchildren against sexual abuse through laws other than those relating to incest. There is no nationwide consensus on whether laws concerning sexual relationships apply to step-relatives as long as the
remarriage exists or even after the natural parent divorces the stepparent or dies.

Some of the social, emotional, and legal issues in such relationships
were graphically illustrated in the public debate about movie director
Woody Allen's sexual relationship with Soon-Yi Previn, the adopted
teenage daughter of actress Mia Farrow, the woman he sometimes lived
with and with whom he had a child. In all manner of speaking, Allen
was the stepfather to Farrow's large brood of children. At the time of his
separation from Farrow, there was a messy court case, with Farrow's al-
leging that Allen had sexually abused her seven-year-old adopted daughter, Dylan Farrow, and that he was also having sex with her daughter
Soon-Yi. Allen was criminally charged with child molestation of the
younger daughter, but the case was dropped to spare the seven-year-old
the trauma of a trial. Allen finally separated from Farrow and married
Soon-Yi Previn, with whom he had been intimate during the same time
that he was sexually intimate with Farrow. Though Allen was never
tried and found guilty, he was also never exonerated of the molestation
charges.

With few exceptions, step-relationships are not recognized as a legal status. The absence of laws regarding stepfamilies both reflects and
maintains their status as a marginalized family structure. Blended families offer us the possibility of new definitions of "relatedness." They resemble the more traditional extended family of the past but go further
by bending the conventional notions of who qualifies as kin and who
doesn't.

The ambiguity and inconsistency of legal recognition presents a host of problems for which there are no definitive answers. *The time has come for the law to clearly define the legal responsibilities and rights of people involved in step-relationships and to establish mechanisms to enforce them.*

OTHER SENSITIVE ISSUES

Alcoholism, drug abuse, criminal activity, and mental illness are some of the sensitive issues that may confront a responsible parent who sees a child being exposed to these untenable situations in a home where he/she lives or visits.

Recall, in "Mom's New Boyfriend," the mother had primary custody of her two children. After her divorce, she became sexually involved with a younger man who was living in the house with her and the children and who was smoking marijuana in front of her children. When the children's remarried father, who had visitation rights, learned that his ex-wife was engaged in an intimate relationship with a substance abuser, he petitioned the court for a change of custody. Most courts will intervene to protect children from exposure to people suffering from the effects of substance abuse (alcohol or drugs), criminal activity, and/or mental illness.

The cases where courts have reason to change custody or visitation arrangements are those in which a parent, or *anyone* who has access to the children while under that parent's supervision, is emotionally, physically, or sexually abusing the children. Exposing a child to a home environment where there is alcoholism, drug abuse, criminal activity, or mental illness will probably be considered evidence of emotional abuse. And in the broadest sense, "anyone" includes stepparents, stepsiblings, and significant others living in the household where the child is living or visiting. If a parent or anyone else living with that parent engages in behavior that is harmful to the children, that can be sufficient reason for the court to remove the children from that environment, either by a change of custody or by termination or modification of parental rights with regard to visitation. Parents with conditions such as alcoholism, drug addiction, and/or mental illness may also be deemed unfit to raise children because they are unable to exercise the kind of judgment children need in their daily lives.

Claudia's two children were required to spend every other weekend with their father, until one Sunday, while driving the children home, he had a serious collision with another car. He was charged with driving under the influence. When Claudia questioned the children, she learned that her former husband always drank during the weekend visits, and drove the children to and from activities and back home on Sunday evening. Claudia petitioned the court for a termination of his parental rights. While the court did not terminate the father's visitation, it did modify the terms of visitation. He could see the children only under the supervision of another adult, and at no time was he allowed to drive the children anywhere.

Courts are more inclined to give the parent *supervised visitation* than to terminate all contact with the child. The individual chosen to supervise is someone acceptable to both parents, such as a grandparent, a friend, or a family counselor. That person then becomes responsible for the child's well-being.

Any parent who suffers from severe psychological or emotional disturbance, is or has been a substance abuser, or is involved in criminal behavior is a candidate for supervised visitation. Usually the arrangement is temporary, during which time the parent must attend individual or group therapy sessions or an alcohol or drug treatment program. The courts regard supervised visitation as a way of saving a parent-child relationship that might otherwise be destroyed.

How can you prepare a child who will be visiting a parent suffering from mental disturbance and/or substance abuse?

For very young children, it's best to say: "For a while the visits with Daddy (or Mommy) are going to be short, because he (she) hasn't been feeling well and isn't strong enough to take care of you for more than a couple of hours."

For an older child, the other parent might go into more detail, depending on the child's age and ability to comprehend the situation. For example, "Your father (or mother) has been under a doctor's care, because he's (she's) been sick or having a problem that he (she) is unable to handle with alcohol or drugs. He's (she's) getting help now, so you'll be seeing him (her), but with Grandma (or whoever the supervisor is) present. We hope he'll (she'll) be over it soon, and you'll be able to spend more time with him (her)."

WHEN THE ISSUE IS HOMOSEXUALITY

Though there is still ambivalence about the issue of homosexuality, today there has been a huge shift in attitude, with society's definition of "family" rapidly expanding to include gay couples with children. It is, however, a matter that is in flux and controlled by state law. For example, recently a Florida court upheld the state's ban on homosexual adoptions.

Whether homosexuality becomes a factor in deciding custody issues still depends on the laws of the individual states (and bias among the judges). The courts in some states apply the same criteria to the homosexual parent as they do to a heterosexual parent: how well the parent can meet the child's needs and what is in the best interests of the child. *If the homosexual parent measures best, then custody may be awarded to that parent.*

Other states view it differently—a parent's sexual orientation carries significant weight on judicial scales. Homosexuality is viewed as being detrimental and unhealthy and "not in the best interests of the child." Gradually, this view is being overtaken by the majority of family court decisions that do not view the sexual orientation of a parent to be automatically a detriment to the child.

If a homosexual parent is caught in a custody battle, expert witnesses— psychiatrists and psychologists—may be a source of help in the courtroom. Respected professionals can give the judge an opinion as to who will better meet the needs of the child. Often this means home evaluation and psychological evaluation of the parents' fitness, the stability of the home environment, and the child's emotional ties to each.

But what about visitation in cases where a parent finds out that the other parent's sexual orientation has changed? The presumption that a parent has the right of visitation is so strong that courts will refuse to award visitation to a gay parent *only* if the court feels the parent's sexual orientation would harm the child. Some courts modify the conditions under which gay parents may exercise their custody or visitation rights. This usually happens when "changed circumstances" occur—that is, when one parent who had no prior knowledge finds out that the other parent is gay. Courts can decide to modify custody under such circumstances and impose restrictions, such as disallowing overnight visits, requiring supervised visits, and even requiring blood tests to alleviate the fear of AIDS, but (and this is an important *but*) visitation can be restricted only when a parent's sexual orientation caused actual harm, as determined by the court. Common sense would dictate that any overt sexual activity in front of the child, whether homosexual or heterosexual, would be considered harmful to the child. The fact of the sexual orientation alone is not proof of harm. It's critical to understand that separating a child from his or her other parent, even an openly gay parent, can be the real harm to the child.

Should a child be allowed to visit a gay parent who lives with a partner? One remarried woman I interviewed had divorced her husband—whom she had known since high school—when she discovered he was gay. She said she never would have had a child with him had she known about his homosexuality. The father wanted to see his five-year-old son, but his ex-wife objected even though the father promised to be discreet when the son was visiting. The divorce agreement that included visitation rights was signed before the mother learned that her ex-husband was gay.

She acknowledged that several psychologists urged her to allow her son to see his father. They believed the father would not push his homosexuality on his son or allow his son to be molested by other men. The mother was told that her relationship with her son would also have a strong influence on his sexual preference, as would his heterosexual stepfather, who lives with the young boy. As this book goes to press, the mother has not yet petitioned the court for a modification of the father's visitation based on "changed circumstances," nor has the father sought a ruling from the court on his visitation rights.

The few studies that have been done show that children of gay parents have no greater chance of becoming gay than do the children of straight parents. In other words, the son will not become gay because the father is gay. But this begs the question: what should the mother tell her son about his father's homosexual lifestyle?

Simply put, the child should be told: "There are some people who prefer to love people of their same sex, and your father happens to be one of them. That doesn't make him a bad parent, just a parent who is different from your friends' parents. Some people have problems accepting people who are like your father, but we accept him. He loves you and has always been a good father to you, so I want you to continue to visit him, as long as you're comfortable being with him. If anything happens to change that, I want you to tell me about it."

BAD MANNERS OR BAD ACTORS?

In blended families that include children from both previous marriages, the "bad influence" frequently becomes a source of conflict. This is the stepchild who engages in antisocial behavior that has a negative effect on the stepparent's biological child. If you are that stepparent, what can be done to correct the problem without creating added friction with your spouse—the "bad influence's" biological parent? It's hard enough for biological parents in traditional households to handle such situations, but it's that much worse in a blended family. And with kids, we have to be especially careful not to label them bad or worthless. We can't give up—even a clock that's not working is right twice a day.

Recognizing the difference between harmless bad manners and serious misbehavior is a must. Although stepchildren come in all sizes, ages, and types, their behavior and their attitudes toward the stepparent and step-siblings are never quite what we imagined they would be. At first, you might find yourself noticing mannerisms that grate on your nerves. Perhaps the standards of personal grooming, cleanliness, and politeness are not of the highest order in these children who are now visiting or living under your roof.

"I wish they were more cooperative, and more upbeat," said one stepmother. "But for now, cleaner would do. I'm tired of asking them to take a shower, wash their hair, and brush their teeth. Wouldn't you think their mother would have trained them to do the basics?"

Picture this family encounter. The wife has prepared a wonderful Sunday dinner, but before she has finished putting everything on the table, her husband, a man who courted her in nice restaurants with impeccable manners, now bellows to his children, "Come and get it! Dinner."

While the wife is gaping at this man, who has never raised his voice to her, the children are at the table, shoveling food into their mouths and finishing their meals in a fraction of the time it took to prepare it. Then, without a word, her husband and his children rush into the family room to watch TV. And there she sits, with her own well-mannered children staring at each other in disbelief. She wonders what happened to the old-fashioned Sunday mealtime the whole family used to enjoy. Her children are now impatient to leave the table and join the others.

"May we please be excused?" they ask.

Their behavior highlights the difference in upbringing between her kids and her husband's. What can't be forgotten is that habits formed early, long before the stepfamily came into being, are extraordinarily difficult to change. You can aim for higher standards of civilized behavior in *your* home, but it's important to remember that we're talking about irritations and aggravations, not behavior that threatens the home or the well-being of the other children.

Lots of children are messy and impolite, but many of these children grow up to be perfectly wonderful adults who achieve in their lives and raise good families of their own. Often these children have been raised by working mothers and overindulgent divorced fathers who don't want to be disciplining the children all the time because of the limited contact they have with them. So, while standards may become too relaxed, that doesn't mean the result will be bad children.

Stepparents constantly grappling with the question of what to put up with should *learn to differentiate* between behavior that could have an indelibly damaging effect on the other children, and bad manners. If your objections to children's actions are rooted in style or a highly developed standard of politeness, the position may be very difficult to defend in dealing with the natural parent of these children—your spouse. Since you can't remake the children, you have to separate the simply annoying from the completely unacceptable. Remember—these children are a natural extension of the person you love and married.

COPYCATS OF UNACCEPTABLE BEHAVIOR

Real differences in ethical and moral values are a far more serious matter. Lillian married Spencer without having spent time getting to know her husband's thirteen-year-old son, Jamie. Jamie lived with his mother in another state, but once Lillian and Spencer were married, Jamie visited his father during holidays and for the entire summer. Lillian had full custody of two children from her previous marriage, Sandra, fifteen, and eleven-year-old Craig.

When Jamie arrived to spend his first summer with the new family, Lillian was appalled at the boy's appearance and the fact that he had recently been suspended from his junior high school for talking back to the principal. His dyed-blond hair protruded from his head in spikes. He had five gold pierced earrings in one earlobe, three in the other, and a dragon tattoo on his arm. On the sly, Jamie smoked, drank beer, and recklessly skateboarded in ways that endangered his life. Within two weeks of Jamie's arrival, Lillian could see how her son, Craig, was trying to emulate Jamie. Craig wanted to get tattoos and have his ears pierced. Lillian flatly refused. Sandra, on the other hand, ignored Jamie as much as she could, pronouncing him "a total jerk."

One day, Lillian heard a bloodcurdling scream coming from their driveway at the foot of a hill. She ran out to find her son stretched out on the concrete, bleeding, and with a bone in his leg protruding from the skin. Off to the side was a tipped-over skateboard. Jamie just stood there, shaking his head in disgust.

"I told him not to try that hill yet, but the kid wouldn't listen."

An ambulance took Craig to the emergency room of the local hospital, where the compound fracture of his left leg required orthopedic surgery that included pins, screws, and a metal plate.

Lillian was vehemently opposed to allowing Jamie to stay with them for the rest of the summer. She asked her husband to arrange for the boy to go home, but that turned out to be impossible, because Jamie's mother was traveling with a friend and was unreachable. When Craig came home from the hospital, Lillian insisted that Jamie vacate the room he had been sharing with Craig. She put her daughter, Sandra, in with Craig and gave Jamie the use of Sandra's room, but that didn't solve the problem of dealing with the influence Jamie had on Craig. She began to overhear her own son using curse words he'd never used before. Then, one night, she caught Jamie and Craig at the computer, enjoying an Internet porno Web site and watching a couple having steamy sex. Lillian was outraged, but Spencer refused to take charge of the situation, complaining that he was hardly with his son enough during the year to become a constant disciplinarian.

By the time the summer was half-over, Lillian and Spencer's relationship was suffering. Lillian begged her husband to find somewhere for Jamie to stay until his mother came home. Spencer asked his sister if she could let Jamie spend a few weeks with her, but she declined, explaining that she had to work and couldn't possibly be expected to leave Jamie alone in her apartment all day long. In desperation, Spencer finally took his son to stay with his elderly parents, but he felt so guilty—first for abandoning his son as a result of the divorce and now for forcing him to leave the house—that he became increasingly sullen with Lillian.

Despite all this uproar, no one made any serious effort to deal with the problems Jamie was having in school or with his smoking and drinking. Spencer, as his father, should have taken the lead in developing strategies to help Jamie straighten himself out. He needed to have a heart-to-heart talk with his son, expressing both his love and his concern about Jamie's totally unacceptable and dangerous behavior. If those attempts failed, Spencer should have sought professional counseling for his son. Lillian was understandably focused on the negative influence Jamie was having on eleven-year-old Craig, but she said she would have been more patient with him if her husband had even once tried to work with his obviously troubled son.

Unfortunately, Lillian had not gotten to know Spencer's child before they'd married. Jamie had been just thirteen years old, and certainly not a full-fledged delinquent. Just because the person you are planning to marry is wonderful doesn't mean his or her children are also wonderful. If your children are likely to be in close contact with your prospective stepchildren, getting to know those children should be of vital concern not only for the sake of your own children but for the sake of the forthcoming marriage. And when problems appear to be serious, there ought to be a reconsideration of marriage. Nothing is more destructive to a second marriage than problems with children who have demonstrated serious antisocial behavior and the bad influences they may bring to the new family. According to psychologist Gwen Bate, "Contact with children before marriage could help the adults set more realistic expectations. Couples need to know that issues and resolutions may change, but they do become more difficult to work through when stepchildren are older." Still, we must remember puberty can be a most difficult time, but it passes, and the kid who seemed headed for serious trouble can turn it all around once the raging hormones relax.

THE THORNY ISSUE OF DISCIPLINE

For the new couple to achieve a positive transition, the biological parent should remain in charge of decision making and limit setting when dealing with his or her children. The stepparent's role for the first year is to intentionally nurture the children in nonthreatening activities, with a goal of developing a comfortable rapport. While the biological parent remains in charge of his or her children, rules for living in the home should be negotiated. Gradually, after a year or two, when the stepparent has established a warm relationship with the children, he/she can take a more direct role in setting limits for them. Where there are some real differences of values and ethics, sometimes an objective third party, such as a family counselor, can help sort out some of the ambivalence and confusion that surrounds these issues.

Consider the situation that Anne and Gerry had to confront because Gerry's children had developed certain behaviors that she found entirely inappropriate. The couple's attempt to form a successful blended family was affected by the way their four children, all between the ages of eight and twelve, had been raised previously.

"When we were first married," said Anne, "and Gerry's kids came over to our house, my children were shocked at the way they jumped into the pool naked. But that was nothing compared to other things they did. They played with matches, and snakes, and tormented other children, including mine. And they lied about almost everything."

Anne told Gerry's children that what they were doing was not permitted in the presence of her children. They refused to listen. To make matters worse, Gerry refused to take an active part in disciplining his children when they misbehaved. Anne made it quite clear to her own children that they could not do what Gerry's kids were doing. She punished her own children for things the others were doing and getting away with. It became an intolerable situation. Two sets of rules were operating in this family. Finally, Anne told her husband that if he couldn't get his children to behave, they would no longer be welcome in the house, and he would have to have his visits with them somewhere else.

Gerry's excuse was that he saw his kids only every other weekend, so it was difficult to be disciplining them constantly, which is what had happened when he'd tried to enforce the rules. After a time, his children no longer wanted to visit their father.

"I felt that they hated me," Gerry said, "but I knew Anne was right. I couldn't stand by and let them ruin our marriage. My ex-wife wouldn't cooperate, so now I rarely see my children. I just didn't know what I was supposed to do."

Sadly, this is one of those situations that cause a father to fade out of his children's lives. The outcome for Gerry and his children has not been a good one, but professional intervention should have been tried to resolve some of the problems the family had to confront. When children destroy property, steal other people's possessions, engage in dangerous behavior, or become physically or emotionally abusive, they are committing antisocial acts that must be stopped, and that is especially true when they are having a bad influence on other children.

Not all fathers are so passive. Some who take a heavy hand to their own children may feel justified in using the same techniques with their stepchildren. While their own children may be accustomed to their father's "tough love" approach, it's usually not an appropriate measure with stepchildren. Even if the mother believes her kid needs some shaping up and the stepfather thinks it's the manly thing to do, it is not recommended. The likelihood is that strong stepfather discipline will be counterproductive. And if it reaches a point of out-of-control discipline, particularly the use of corporal punishment, professional help should be sought immediately. If that doesn't work, then it's time to reconsider the viability of the marriage.

METHODS OF DISCIPLINE

The majority of experts agree on certain key elements of discipline that will effect change in behavior and allow the family to blend into a compatible unit. For younger children, these methods are recommended:

✓ Don't compare step-siblings as a means of discipline. In other words, don't say, "Why can't you be like your stepsister?" When parents compare siblings, biological or step, they are striking a severe blow to a child's own self-image, and there is the added risk of fostering hostility toward the sibling who's being held up as a model of good behavior.

✓ All discipline strategies should address the behavior and not the person. For example, "You acted badly," rather than "You're a bad boy." In other words, avoid labels, such as "You're a liar" or "You're a cheater." Instead, say, "Lying is bad" or "Cheating is bad." Labels can become a self-fulfilling prophecy.

✓ Encourage a child's sense of guilt and remorse about his or her misbehavior, not about who he or she is. We have developed a misguided attitude about guilt. *It's not bad to feel guilty about having done something hurtful or harmful to someone else.* The capacity to feel guilt and remorse is an important part of self-discipline. To help a child develop a conscience, we have to take the time to explain why the behavior is wrong. Serial killers and hit men are the kinds of people who don't experience guilt. How many times have we heard that "the criminal showed no signs of remorse."

We have to teach values—the importance of doing unto others as we would have others do unto us, the importance of honesty and respect. *If you reason with the child, the child will grow up to be a reasonable adult.*

✓ A child needs to learn to fear the consequences of destructive behavior, rather than fear the parent who imposes the discipline. Intimidating punishments are appropriate for serious misbehavior, but the child should know the rules in advance and the consequences of breaking those rules.

✓ When a parent is ignored or the misdeed is serious, an angry scolding is appropriate, but the anger must be controlled and targeted to the behavior. Tell the child why you're angry and what he or she must do to correct what was done. Use firm tones. Don't scream, because then the child knows he or she has gotten to you—and that may be just what the child wants. This is especially true with a stepparent.

✓ Give the child some time to comply with the demand, and then, if it doesn't happen, use a sterner tone. It's a good idea to ask for an acknowledgment that the demand was heard and understood.

✓ When the parent or stepparent makes a mistake, it's best to acknowledge it. For example, if you accuse a child of doing something that they didn't do, say you're sorry for the mistake that you've made. This will earn the child's respect and also teach them to admit their own mistakes.

✓ *It's up to us to tell them what they need to know to lead a productive and happy life.* Both biological parents and stepparents must cross that barrier and talk to kids about what really matters.

✓ Set a good example. This is so elementary, but it needs to be said again. If you lie or cheat, you will have an impossible time telling your child that lying and cheating are bad.

TAKING THE HIGH ROAD

Even though stepchildren have internalized many values and behaviors from their biological family, a stepparent can still set a more positive example by demonstrating high ethical standards, honesty, and respect for others and their property, and by showing how kindness to others reaps rewards. Unfortunately, too many parents rush into inflexible positions. They fail to consider the possibility of removing their own children from the influence of the step-siblings while they work on changes with the problem child. Having children visit relatives or close friends when stepchildren are visiting is a better alternative than severing relationships. Such failures usually occur when the biological parent is unwilling to take a strong position about continuing visitation.

As I suggested in "Bad Manners or Bad Actors," there should be a tolerance for different values as long as those values are not seriously harmful. And even if there is some intolerable behavior, give it time, and try to work through it as a family. If that fails, then seek professional help, because your marriage is at stake. You may wish that your spouse never had a previous family, but that doesn't make it so. These children are your spouse's flesh and blood. The biological parent may be trying to maintain some of the children's individual traits without realizing that certain unacceptable behavior has to be addressed. Many fathers have no real understanding of how to raise children, because their wives handled that part of family life. Being patient and weighing the risks of having your spouse lose contact with his children should be carefully considered before ultimatums are issued.

DISCIPLES OF DISCIPLINE

There are better ways of handling stepchildren, especially teenagers, who are having a bad influence on siblings, step-siblings, and the marriage. And just what are the strategies? In most cases, clear expectations and accountability are not enough, especially when the teenager has gone beyond the issue of faddish dressing to underage drinking, smoking, skipping school, and shoplifting, just to name a few of the more

serious infractions. *Bribery and punishment* are potent weapons—
essential means for changing behavior. One reason people get up in the
morning when they'd rather stay in bed is that they get paid to go to
work. That's really a form of bribery. So it's worthwhile to let the difficult child know what is in it for him or her if he or she does what is expected. These expectations must be limited and straightforward, no more
than would be asked of a visiting niece or nephew. And the rewards should
be tangible and appropriate and swift.

There will be some who criticize this technique, arguing that the
child will never learn to exercise his or her own good judgment. Hog-
wash! Some might even consider bribery as ethically wrong: "They
should do it because it's the right thing to do, not because they're going
to get some special little treat." And if you think that's workable, maybe
I can sell you some Enron stock?

In his 2002 book, *The Second Family: How Adolescent Power Is
Challenging the American Family,* Ron Taffel, Ph.D., explains that this
system of bribery and punishment is distasteful not so much as a moral
issue but because "our aversion to [this approach] is rooted in the fact
that many of us are afraid of our kids. We're afraid of actually taking
anything away."

How many of us say, "If you don't eat your dinner, there'll be no
dessert," and then, an hour later, give the child who didn't eat dinner the
same dessert we said he couldn't have. We're afraid to follow through,
because we're afraid our kids will hate us for depriving them of what
they want or because we're afraid that we're not using the little time we
have with them to forge a closer relationship or both. And what will that
do to help our children be better people? It will do nothing. In fact, it adds
to further disengagement between parent and child. The kids believe
they're entitled to have all the fun and material possessions they want
without having to make any effort to earn these pleasures, nor will they
ever have to fear losing them.

Dr. Taffel maintains "incentives, in particular, serve a dual purpose
in contemporary life: by rewarding teens with or depriving them of the
things and privileges they want, we motivate them not only to learn, but
to stay connected to us." That means they need the adults in their lives
to earn what they want to have, and this connection is important when

there's so little else to tie preteens and teens to their families. This is especially critical for the parent who is now tied to another family. Anything positive to bind the child to the remarried parent is worth striving for.

Our kids feel a constant hunger for the next possession or pleasure, whether it's a new video game or going to a major sports event. They want and want, so they must learn that in order to get, they must give: "If you continue to use foul language in this house, I'm not going to buy that new tennis racket you want." "If you continue to torment your stepsister, you're not going on that ski trip with us next week." And stick to it, even if you see the kid only every other weekend. You're doing him and yourself and your relationship a big favor. You're modifying his behavior, stopping the bad influence on the step-siblings, and keeping him in the fold of the new family. I'm not naïve. I know this doesn't always work, but it is definitely worth trying for a substantial period of time before the last resort of getting professional help. If you do decide to seek professional help, you may find that the strategies proposed are very similar to those recommended here.

One important point that bears repeating: *The tone of voice for healthy parental authority should be firm, but not inflammatory—no yelling. Once you start shouting, children know they've won, because they've caused you to lose your temper—that is, control of the situation. And kids will take control as soon as they think they can.*

Sometimes the natural parent of the incorrigible child may believe that your expectations are unfair. You can hope to convince your spouse that certain behavior is unfit, but you cannot expect to greatly alter values that were formed by the parents' way of bringing up their children. Even quite young children are perfectly capable of understanding that there is one set of rules at one parent's house and another set of rules when they visit the other parent. Maybe the issue is the use of foul language. You don't use that language, nor have your children ever used or even heard those words in their home. You have a perfect right to forbid the use of certain words in the presence of you and your children. It's your house. You set the rules, with one caveat: let your spouse enforce those rules with his own children.

Helpful Guidelines

- **Blended families should be aware of the increased risk of sexual attractions between step-relations.** By being vigilant and making certain that the members of the stepfamily are not in such intimate contact with one another, the couple can discourage the kind of sexual acting out that can destroy their new family.

- **Avoid sexually provocative interplay.** Wholesome displays of affection, tenderness, and caring are good. Typically, kids are not cheerleaders for the relationship between one of their biological parents and the new spouse. Too much lovey-dovey stuff can provoke hostility toward the stepparent because of jealousy and resentment, and the feeling that the other biological parent is being replaced.

- **Appropriate dress should be an absolute.** No see-through nighties or prancing about in underwear, except for very young children. Bathrobes should be required of everyone over the age of six.

- **Prepare your child to recognize sexual abuse.** Kids are having sex earlier and earlier. It's not "a good thing," but it's a fact of life. Children need information to protect themselves from all dangers of sex. A child must understand that the wrong kind of touching by another person—for example, a stepfather—must be reported to the mother immediately.

- **Get to know your prospective stepchildren.** Prior to marriage, spend enough time with the children of the person you intend to marry so that you will be fully prepared to live with these children as a part of your own family. An engagement is important, because it allows time for the couple to get to know each other. When there are children from a previous marriage, an engagement is even more important, because now there are more people to get to know well—your betrothed and his or her children. If you see *serious* behavior problems in these children, remember they could be very damaging to your own children. You might even want to reconsider the prospect of marriage.

- **Rules of the house should be negotiated between husband and wife.** After rules are decided, they should be discussed with the children in a family setting. Children's views should be taken into consideration. Where there are real ethical and value differences, the couple should seek the help of an objective third person, such as a family counselor.

- **The biological parent should be the primary disciplinarian of his or her own children.** Children are naturally resistant to taking orders from someone they may consider an intruder into their family. Even when that is not the case, the stepparent establishes good rapport by being nurturing and nonthreatening. After a good relationship is in place, the stepparent can gradually begin to assert some authority, especially when the biological parent is away from the house.

- **Separate the kids before causing a child to lose contact with the noncustodial parent.** If there is a strong reason to prevent the stepsibling's bad influence on another child, allow visitation to occur elsewhere, or, when possible, send the children who permanently reside in the house to visit other relatives during visitation until the problem can be worked out.

A Death in the (Blended) Family

S e c r e t   N i n e :
A child who loses a parent needs special attention
and understanding.

Prior to the twentieth century, most stepfamilies were created not by divorce but by second marriages after the death of a spouse. In fact, the term "stepfamily" derives from *steop,* an Old English word meaning "bereaved" or "orphaned."

Death in a stepfamily poses a variety of problems, particularly when a child loses a biological parent (whether the death occurs before or during the remarriage). Think of all those scenes from movies that show a small child standing in a cemetery next to an open grave as a coffin that contains the child's deceased parent is lowered into that freshly dug hole. And who can ever forget watching the televised funeral procession of President John F. Kennedy and seeing John Junior raise his small hand to salute his father?

While it is true children are more resilient than adults, their adjustment depends on how well they are helped through this tragic time. For the parent and stepparent to be of real help to their child, they must recognize and understand the child's feelings and what motivates his or her behavior.

When the surviving parent marries after the death of the other parent, the children enter the new stepfamily with a recent history of profound loss and change beyond their control. Some wonder if they are "unlovable" and somehow to blame for all that has happened. Most children feel helpless and angry because of the turbulence that the death of a parent imposes on their lives. They are living within a new set of relationships because of the surviving parent's choices, not their own. Both the timing of the death (before or after the remarriage) and the role of the parent who died (custodial versus noncustodial) are important factors to consider in dealing with the grieving child. A stepfamily formed *after* a parent's death can present a different set of issues from a stepfamily formed subsequent to divorce but *before* the parent's death. And if it is the custodial parent who has died, the dependent child's sense of loss is likely to be even more profound.

A RANGE OF EMOTIONS

Too often the adults in a family, who are locked in their own emotions, are not thinking of the traumatic impact the death of a parent has on a child. Unlike the grief that is felt by the child or by the surviving parent in an intact family, a divorced parent may experience emotions ranging from "good riddance" to guilt, to renewed regrets. And the child's grief may be compounded by loss of power and control, guilt, loyalty conflicts, anger, fear, and uncertainty about the future. It's important to understand that behavior that might otherwise be viewed as dysfunctional could very well be normal for the circumstances. By the same token, when behavior does go over the line, that, too, must be recognized.

Loss of Power and Control

Powerlessness interferes with a child's confidence and sense of security. That feeling of powerlessness can be magnified when the child is required to do certain things occasioned by the death, such as attend the funeral, perhaps view the open casket, or wear clothes he or she might not want to wear.

Guilt and Loyalty Conflicts

Many children assume they were in some way responsible for the loss of a parent. They believe their "bad" behavior was the reason the parent got sick and died. These feelings of unworthiness can manifest in many different ways, but one of the most painful is withdrawing from friends and family.

Guilt can also consume a child if they feel disloyal to the memory of the deceased parent because they enjoy the company of a stepparent. This can even cause the child to push that stepparent away.

Anger and Confusion

If a parent dies when the children are quite young, he or she is often remembered in an idealized way, a saintlike figure to be revered. If the parent dies when the children are adolescents, many conflicts, anxieties, and competitions that are normal between adolescents and parents may never be resolved. The child is left with a huge chasm in his or her life, and the normal process of becoming independent may be disrupted because the formation of an adult relationship with that parent has been abruptly foreclosed. Sometimes the death of a parent causes such serious problems for a child that the entire family is affected by the anger the child feels. This is particularly true of adolescent children who lose a mother.

Fear and Uncertainty

Children believe their families will always be the one constant in their lives. When death destroys their traditional family unit, their trust in adults, even in the remaining parent, is shattered. Children may be afraid that all relationships will end in failure or, worse yet, that their other parent may also die. This fear may make it difficult for children to form a bond with their new family members. And when the surviving parent shows love and commitment to the new stepfamily members, fear of abandonment can become overwhelming to children.

At this crucial time, it is especially important for the surviving parent and the stepparent to assure children of their love and to show that they care. Extra attention and expressions of love are necessary. It takes time for children to understand how they actually fit into the new family, to feel secure, and to realize there is enough love to go around.

The Need to Belong

Children have a strong desire to belong. Their security depends on a feeling of acceptance by the other family members. From infancy, a child works to establish his or her place in the home. The death of a parent and a second marriage by the surviving parent disrupts that security. Children form attitudes, opinions, and behaviors that reflect their family's outlook. They absorb the values and convictions of that family. When a stepfamily is formed, many of the old values and rules are cast aside in favor of new ones. It's a tough thing for a child to wipe away the years of personal development, and immediately become a part of a new family with a whole new set of rules and principles.

Children in stepfamilies may even be experiencing a shift in the birth order. The oldest child has a special role that may change because a step-sibling is now the oldest. This can be terribly confusing for a child who is dealing not only with grief but also with an entirely different position in a new family.

Adults who understand the changes and confusion children face will be better able to ease the transition into the stepfamily so that it can become a truly blended family. A willingness to give it time and to compromise will be critical in reaching success. Each child must be given a chance to be special and significant within the new family.

Understanding Is Key

Adjusting to the death of a parent requires a reasonable period of grief. Children cannot be expected to enjoy the new family until they have had a chance to feel hurt and sad and angry about the losses and changes they have experienced. Children of any age are confused if it is not clear to them what is going on around them. Of course, a child's misbehavior must be confronted and corrected. However, parents and stepparents need to understand that "acting out" is not always the result of hostility, resentment, or personal differences. It may be caused by confusion over a situation the child cannot handle.

Adults need to let children know they understand how upsetting it is to have to deal with so many changes. They need to acknowledge and accept the child's feelings and be conscious of the fact that the child who has just suffered an enormous loss must now accept a significantly different lifestyle. It's best to talk to the child about the changes that have taken place and those that may still occur. When troublesome signs of withdrawal are evident, adults should take the initiative for this talk even if the child isn't opening up. Children can adjust to changes if they understand what is happening and what they can count on. Understanding the child may be *the* essential ingredient for building a strong relationship.

HAUNTED BY THE DECEASED SPOUSE

When a parent remarries shortly after the death of his or her spouse, the new stepparent faces particular challenges.

Melanie married Alex, a widower with a teenage daughter, Rosalie. Soon after the marriage, Melanie realized her stepdaughter was not only suffering from normal shock and grieving over her mother's death, but also carrying the heavy weight of unresolved feelings about her mother.

Melanie, who had been through a difficult divorce and lived alone with her two children, four-year-old Timmy and eight-year-old Jessica, met Alex a year after his wife, Lola, was killed in a car accident. Melanie was by nature an optimistic, gregarious person who tended to see the glass as half-full. Alex and his daughter, Rosalie, were more introspective, quiet, and reserved. They were people who did not show their feelings.

Although Melanie was receptive to anything they might want to tell her about their relationship with Lola, she couldn't get through the cloak of silence about their past life as a family. Melanie construed that to mean the grieving process was ongoing. She decided to help by encouraging them to talk openly about their grief. She had no intention of trying to replace Lola, either as Alex's wife or as Rosalie's mother. She just wanted to offer solace and a path toward the future. Despite all her efforts, neither her husband nor her stepdaughter would open up to her about their loss. The more she tried, the more Rosalie pushed her away.

When Melanie and Alex married, she and her two children moved into Alex's house, which was larger than hers. Still, there were only three bedrooms, so eight-year-old Jessica and fourteen-year-old Rosalie had to share a bedroom. This arrangement proved to be fraught with problems. Rosalie resented Jessica's presence in what she considered her space—her bedroom. Since Jessica went to sleep earlier than Rosalie, Rosalie had to tiptoe around in the dark and wasn't allowed to keep a light on to read. Melanie and Alex hired an architect to draw plans for an addition to the house. Rosalie was impatient with everyone, but she began to take out her frustrations on Jessica, teasing her about her looks. When she wasn't tormenting Jessica, Rosalie was morose at home and at school. There were days when she didn't come home from school until dinner and offered no explanation for her whereabouts.

Any attempt to encourage Rosalie to talk about her feelings continued to meet with sullen silence. Melanie felt her own energy waning as she watched her children in this unhappy situation. Melanie began to question her husband about Lola, but his answers were evasive. Living in the house where Lola and Alex had lived gave Melanie access to their friends and neighbors. And that's when some truths emerged. Melanie learned that Alex and Lola had not been happy together and that he had poured himself into his work as an escape from the marital problems. And at the same time, Lola and Rosalie were having the kind of conflicts teenage girls often have with their mothers. Lola's sudden death had left both Alex and Rosalie grief stricken and guilt ridden.

Melanie began to see that she was shortchanging her own children in her efforts to help her husband and his daughter. She became angry with her stepfamily and with herself for having allowed the situation to deteriorate to the detriment of her children. She was weary of always being the upbeat cheerleader and getting nowhere. She lost patience with Rosalie's grief, her self-centered ways, and her cruelty to Jessica.

Melanie said, "I was expected to make allowances for Rosalie because of her mother's death. My aunt, who was my mother's sister, died when my cousin, Ginny, was in her teens. Ginny is now in her forties, and still misses her. My mother raised Ginny. She encouraged her to grieve, cope, and move on with her life. She told her, 'Life sometimes plays dirty tricks on us. Your mother would not want you to make her death a reason for an unhappy life. She would want you to always cherish her memory, but get on with your life and fulfill your dreams. And we, who love you as our own daughter, are going to provide a good, safe home for you so that you can have all the things she wanted for you.' "

One day, Melanie sat Rosalie down and told her that she cared deeply for her and would help her any way she could, but that she could no longer allow mistreatment of Jessica and it had to stop.

Melanie also made some promises to herself—to spend more time with her children away from Rosalie and to pay more attention to helping Alex find enjoyment in their marriage. By concentrating on the positive things she was able to do with her life, she set an example that was favorable for the family.

This was an improvement, but no panacea—the past continued to mar the present, but with less and less of an impact as time went by. By shifting her focus to the present and the future, Melanie saw a positive change in Alex and in her children. Eventually, Rosalie went off to college and created a happier life for herself.

Rosalie was angry not only about her mother's death but also because she had no control over her life and her father's decision to remarry. When Rosalie had finally accepted her mother's death, and began to have her father all to herself, she suddenly had to share him with a new wife and children.

Rosalie needed help in dealing with her feelings of regret, betrayal, guilt, and rage. The little child in Rosalie could not admit her anger toward her mother for having so suddenly—and permanently—left her. Her stepmother and stepsister were convenient scapegoats. Anger at a deceased mother is as common as anger toward a deceased spouse; often, the deeper the love, the greater the anger at being abandoned. This may not be a rational feeling, but it is a common one and has to be resolved in order for healing to take place. Making excuses for a child's bad behavior because of the loss of a parent is not the way to equip that child for life, and not dealing with anger, and all the other conflicting emotions, can leave permanent scars.

THE STEPMOTHER'S ROLE

Dealing with grief-stricken stepchildren, as well as the ghost of the departed spouse, can seem overwhelming, especially if the recently deceased parent was having conflicts with her child or is being remembered in an idealized way. Whatever the conflict or the view, idealized or realistic, the loss can dwell within children for the rest of their lives, and that is particularly true when a child is not mature enough to separate fact from fiction and has had no preparation for the sudden loss.

A woman who marries a recent widower has a special role as stepmother. For a child, the death of the mother is one of the most traumatic experiences. Expressions of grief can vary enormously with each person. Sometimes they take forms not easily recognizable. Some widowers may seek solace in sixteen-hour workdays, leaving the care of the child to the stepmother. A child could suddenly become a discipline problem, or the child's grades could drop.

Grief and depression can't be allowed to become the primary focus of the stepfamily indefinitely. If grieving persists for longer than a year, professional help is needed.

Stepfathers also have a role to play in consoling grieving children, but the challenge to the stepmother is far more profound. Stepfathers usually don't do the day-to-day nurturing. A stepfather may not expect—or be expected—to take the role of a deceased father. But it's all too easy for a potential stepmother, who is deeply in love with a man with children, to believe that she can save the stepfamily from their sorrow.

Beware of this rescue mentality; it can backfire all too easily. Stepchildren who have just lost a natural parent *don't want to be saved by the new stepparent.* Though adolescents have difficulty losing a parent, therapists believe the most troublesome time for a child to lose a mother is from ages five to eleven. At these ages children are likely to suppress their feelings and act out in other ways. Stepsons may appear to be coping more easily than stepdaughters, but stepsons are merely trying to be masculine and not show their emotions. It doesn't mean they don't suffer them as much as young girls.

Hope Edelman, author of *Motherless Daughters,* has recommended that couples delay their wedding for at least one year after the death of a mother so the children can experience each of the holiday seasons *without* her before a stepmother enters their life.

A NEW HOME

A postscript to Melanie and Alex's story: Melanie and Alex chose to live in his house, the same one he had shared with Lola, because it had more room to accommodate the blended family and provided less disruption for the grieving teenager. But whenever possible, it's best to avoid that situation, so that the new family can start afresh without having to confront ghosts from the past.

From the first wife's good china to the family photos to sleeping in the same four-poster bed as the first wife, second wives in all circumstances have to muster real diplomacy and control about redecorating, especially when there are children who continue to live in the family home with the new stepmother. In the case of a parent's death, it's especially important to restrain your desire to erase all evidence of your predecessor, because the familiar surroundings are usually comforting to children who are still grieving. Yes, every woman has the right to decorate her own home, but the issue of timing is critical. Wait a few months before parading movers into and out of the house. Start with the place that is uniquely the couple's domain—the master bedroom. Even if you have to experience the silent horror of purple walls in the living room, work gradually. And don't redecorate a child's bedroom until you can safely say he or she has overcome a deep sense of loss and wants new wallpaper. If the child wants to leave it the way it was, just close the door if you can't stand the sight of it. A day will arrive when change will be accepted and not set off evacuation alarms.

MOVING THROUGH GRIEF

Studies have shown that after the death of a loved one, a person moves from initial shock and sadness to anger and a sense of betrayal, and finally toward acceptance.

There are basic steps that help us work through the grieving process whenever there is a death of a loved one: accepting the reality of the loss, experiencing the emotions associated with the loss, adjusting to the environment in which the loved one is no longer there or change has occurred, and reinvesting the energy used in dealing with the loss in new relationships and life events.

It is not unusual for people to become stuck during this grieving process and remain angry or immersed in sadness. When that happens, an outside force is needed to help them move forward with their lives. Sometimes, by default, a stepmother has to fill that role. She, after all, represents the future for a family who has lost a mother.

Another typical reaction to the death of a parent or a spouse results in constant thoughts about "what might have been." This can cause a deep sense of remorse, because the thought of what might have been is quickly followed by the realization that it is too late. Even harder to deal with is the fact that memory can play tricks on us when we remember a lost parent with whom we had conflict. No matter how much we try to remain balanced in our thinking, we remember only either the good things, making us feel even more abandoned, or the bad things, leaving us with continuing anger, combined with a longing for what might have been.

Usually, children receive little or no warning of the impending death of a parent. The child is better prepared for a tonsillectomy than for the extraordinary trauma of death. In the upheaval that follows, the child's emotional trauma often gets short shrift from adults. Sometimes it's only after stepfamily life has begun that the child's struggle with grief can be addressed. Experts agree that it's good to talk about feelings of loss while looking for distractions from the sadness.

When a child who has just experienced the death of the custodial mother has to move into the home of the father and stepmother, conflicts are almost sure to arise. Bringing the conflict into the open is usually the best course of action. A stepmother can initiate a conversation along these lines: "I know how hard it is for you to get used to me, and to see another woman married to your father. If you want to talk about it, I'm happy to listen. But please understand that your mother's death was not my fault, and it's not fair to take your feelings out on me. I have no wish to take your mother's place, but I love your father, and I honor your mother's memory. And I'm here to stay."

By saying this, the stepmother acknowledges her feelings and shows a willingness to talk about the death; most important, she conveys the message that the door is open for a future relationship.

While grieving, and sometimes rebellion, is going on, the stepmother should not allow herself to grow bitter, because people change and attitudes evolve. Unhappiness over losing a parent is understandable and acceptable, but it's not acceptable for a stepchild to blame the stepparent for that unhappiness. Yet because of the turmoil of emotions, the child may not even realize what he or she is doing. Pointing it out in a kind and sensitive way can work wonders toward eliminating the problem.

Grief counselors recommend that adults help children reengage with life. Adults can guide a child to join a sports team to raise their feelings of self-worth, and to have a healthy outlet to blow off steam. Pursuing a love of music or art or other hobbies should be encouraged. Ideally, the new stepfamily provides the children with an opportunity to have their faith in adults and family life reaffirmed.

Unfortunately, many children hold back from participation in a new stepfamily, because they have lost trust in the certainty of the adult world. They fear another painful loss and instinctively protect themselves, sometimes in ways that are self-destructive and also harmful to the other members of the family.

DEATH OF A NONCUSTODIAL PARENT

When a noncustodial parent dies a child's day-to-day life may not be ruptured as traumatically as if the custodial parent died, but the sadness, grief, and feeling of loss may be just as intense. Even if the ex-spouse had been a difficult person to deal with, that person was still a parent to the children, and for the sake of the children, any hostility that still exists should be concealed. There's no point to an ongoing vendetta with a dead person when all it can do is damage the children. To give the child support and comfort, the divorced parent (and even the stepparent, if that is what the child wants) should attend the funeral services. Memorials and funeral services are for the living, not the dead.

When Barry was seven years old, his father died accidentally at a construction site. At the time of death, his parents had been divorced for three years, and his mother, Clarice, had been remarried for almost a year. She didn't want to go to the funeral, because of the hateful relationship she still had with her former in-laws. They blamed Clarice for the divorce, and wanted nothing more to do with her once she remarried.

During the years immediately before the death, Barry had a close relationship with his father, whom he loved very much. They saw each other every other weekend and for a month in the summer. The boy was heartbroken when his dad died. Then his mother told him she didn't want to attend the funeral. Barry cried bitterly and said he didn't want to go alone. Luckily Clarice's husband, Greg, stepped in to handle the problem. Greg persuaded Clarice to take Barry to the funeral, to remain unobtrusive, but to stay close to her son throughout the services. Predictably, everyone behaved with civility, and the child had the comfort and closeness of his mother during the entire day. Their relationship is all the better for it.

A child needs to understand in detailed terms what will happen during mourning. Experts advise that children should attend funeral services if they want to, and as long as they are prepared for what will take place. If the child doesn't want to participate, that choice should be respected. If the child chooses to attend, the surviving parent should stay in close proximity to the child throughout the services and the burial. If the child's relationship with the stepparent is a good one, then both the surviving parent and the stepparent should be there to give support.

It's helpful to assist the bereaved child in preserving the memory of the deceased parent. This can be done by allowing the child to keep framed photographs of their dead mother or father, by visiting the grave and leaving flowers or a drawing, and by telling the child some heartfelt stories about the gone-but-not-forgotten parent. It's best, however, not to do these things more than occasionally, for obvious reasons. Women who want to forget they ever had an ex-husband may find it difficult to have to see his picture perched on a desk in their child's room, but that difficulty needs to be put in perspective. If the deceased father is erased from the child's life, the mother runs the risk of having her child feel his/her love for the dead parent is taboo.

One woman who lost her mother at the age of six, and a stepmother at age twenty-six, was deeply grateful to her father's third wife, who put together a "family wall" showing the children with all their "mothers."

EXPLAINING DEATH TO A CHILD

Death can be very scary and confusing to children, and they need help to understand and express their grief. Today it's generally acknowledged that it's better to tell children the truth about death. No matter how hard society tries, it's futile to hide death from children. Typically, the child doesn't experience death the same way an adult does, nor are children usually brought in at the moment of death, but unless the death is sudden, a child is usually aware of the parent's illness and will see the physical decline at close range. When adults *avoid* the subject of death, children become confused by a loss of contact with a loved one. While it is impossible to protect children from the aftermath of death—grief and mourning—it is possible for the adults to create a comforting atmosphere in which the child can express feelings and ask questions.

When adults try to protect children from the tragedy of death, it often backfires, and then the child feels uneasy about a loss he or she doesn't understand. It's best that the child not feel deceived by a story that isn't factual. Give children credit for their resilience. The stepparent's task is to provide a nonthreatening, secure environment where children can talk about their feelings when they feel ready. Children of different ages conceptualize death and grief in various ways, depending on their level of maturity and their ability to perceive the world around them. For example, most children under the age of six think that death is reversible. They will miss the parent that died but will also be waiting for him or her to return. This can be very traumatic for other family members, because the child may ask over and over again, "When is Mommy/Daddy coming back?" As painful as it may be, it's best to let the child know that Mommy/Daddy is not coming back.

According to psychoanalyst-pediatrician D. W. Winnicott, M.D., "Fear of loss of the mother is the earliest terror we know. Separation anxiety derives from the literal truth that without a caretaking presence we die."

Sometimes young children act as if they have not heard anything that's been said. It may take many talks of sad clarity for the reality of the loss to sink in. During this long process, the child continues to re-experience the loss. The child may develop profound empathetic concerns for others experiencing loss, including storybook characters like Cinderella. Or seeing a dead animal on the road may revive the child's sense of loss. Some might want to say the parent (or other loved one) has "gone to heaven," if that fits into the family's religious convictions.

Elementary school children may understand that the death is final, but they may perceive death as a punishment for misdeeds or as something caused only by specific illnesses or accidents. These children may not view death as universal or inevitable, and they often do not accept the fact that they, too, will die sometime in the distant future. This may be the time to explain the inevitability of death, and that it usually occurs when someone is old, but not always.

There are many teachable moments to explain death to children. For example, a good opportunity may occur during a television show where a character dies. And then there is the death of a pet, which can present a perfect opening for a discussion about death. A word of caution: *Don't describe death as sleep.* Likewise, don't talk about a pet's being "put to sleep," because a young child may then fear going to sleep. Death is death; it's not sleep.

Experts recommend that children be told that death is final and a natural part of the life cycle.

Some grief counselors believe it's also important to explain how the death occurred. This can be very hard for parents to do, as they may not want to impart such painful information. Here are a few examples of how to honestly explain certain forms of death to young children:

- If the death occurred by car accident, an adult might say, "A very sad thing happened. Your mother was driving, and somehow another car went out of control and hit her car. Her body was badly hurt. The doctors and nurses tried to fix it, but her body stopped working anyway. Usually accidents can be avoided by being safe, but sometimes they just happen for reasons we don't understand."

- If the death occurred due to a terminal illness, the parent might say, "Mom was very sick. Her disease couldn't be stopped, and her body got tired of fighting it and wore out."

- If the death occurred by suicide, the parent might say, "Mom was very sad about some things in her life and decided that she didn't want to live anymore. Some people don't realize when they are unhappy that things can always get better and that there are always people around who want to help you. Nothing is ever so bad that it is worth killing yourself."

EXPERT INTERVENTION

Adults in the family should understand that they are not always able to provide their children with all that they need. Seeking outside support is not a reflection of their incompetence. Some behaviors that children may display are good indicators of a need for expert intervention:

- Persistent anxieties about their own death

- More than one destructive outburst where there is physical harm to themselves, others, or their surroundings

- Euphoria—as if the child is in complete denial about the death of a loved one

- Unwillingness to speak about the deceased loved one

- Inability or unwillingness to form new relationships

- Lack of interest in school and decline in academic performance

- School phobia

- Stealing

LAST RIGHTS

When a custodial parent dies, courts are bound by laws that require the child to be relocated to the home of the surviving biological parent, providing the person is a fit parent. This means the courts are not given much latitude to consider unique circumstances in the child's life. It is almost impossible for stepparents to be granted custody after the death of the biological parent, even if the consequences of removing the child from the only home the child knows is damaging to both the family and the child.

Mattie's mother was pregnant with her when she divorced Thomas, who spent the next eleven years working as an engineer in Saudi Arabia. During those years, there was very little contact between Thomas and his daughter. They saw each other three times and spoke on the telephone once or twice a year, and Thomas sent birthday and Christmas presents a few times. When Mattie was one year old, her mother married Arthur, a man who had never been married before. The following year they had a daughter, Antoinette. Mattie and her half sister were only two years apart in age. Growing up, they were very close, and Mattie called Arthur "Daddy," just as Antoinette did. When Mattie was twelve years old and Antoinette was ten, their mother died in a plane crash. Mattie's natural father was granted custody (on his demand) and brought Mattie to live with him in Saudi Arabia. Arthur lost his lawsuit to keep Mattie, a child he was very attached to and considered his very own daughter. He, Antoinette, and Mattie testified in court, each expressing the wish to remain together as a family, but the court denied their request. In Saudi Arabia, living with a Palestinian housekeeper, Mattie became depressed. Her grades suffered, and she became socially withdrawn. Despite the protests of her biological father, Mattie, on reaching her eighteenth birthday, flew back to the United States to live with Arthur and her half sister, Antoinette.

Mattie's case vividly illustrates how powerful the right of the natural parent is even in the face of possible emotional and psychological harm to the child. When the custodial parent dies, the child is forced to suffer the additional loss of contact with the only close family the child knows. And if the other natural parent is not available or is not a fit person to take the child, then the child goes to other blood kin—grandparents, aunts, or uncles. The stepparent has no legal rights to the child, nor is the relationship between the half siblings a significant factor.

Very recently, a circuit court judge in South Dakota gave a thirteen-year-old boy the chance to decide where he wanted to live—with his biological father or with his late mother's male partner. The decision was part of a settlement in a case that had dragged on for several years. The judge, Max Gors, said of the boy, "He came to me and said: 'I want to get this case settled. I'm tired of being in court and I'm tired of being on TV. I just want to be a kid.' "

Timmie, whose mother died in a car accident when he was ten, had been living with her former boyfriend, Chuck Novotny, a farmer, for several years. After Timmie's mother died, his biological father filed for custody. Though for most of his life the boy had not lived with his father, the father had kept in touch with his son. What was particularly unusual about this case was the fact that the mother and Novotny had ended their relationship three years prior to her death, but Timmie had continued to live with Novotny, and the two developed a close father-son relationship. Though the court ordered that Timmie now had to go to live with his biological father, Novotny appealed, and during the years of appeal, Timmie remained in Novotny's home. After appeal, the case was remanded for a new trial. In 2001, Judge Gors ruled that Timmie should live with his father in Illinois during the school year and in South Dakota with Novotny for the summer. But Novotny appealed again, and in the meantime, the state of South Dakota revised its laws regarding child custody, adding another wrinkle to the already protracted and complicated case.

Up until that point, according to the state law, the only way a person could obtain custody of a nonbiological child was to prove that the parent was unfit or had abandoned the child. But South Dakota changed the law to say that if there are "extraordinary circumstances," the court should make a ruling based on whatever was best for the child. The South Dakota Supreme Court ruled that Timmie's case included extraordinary circumstances. As of this writing, Timmie is still splitting his time between his biological father and Novotny. This is a most unusual outcome, and some legal scholars believe this decision puts too much pressure on a child in a custody battle.

There is no doubt that the South Dakota case will be cited by stepparents who have raised stepchildren, only to lose them to the non-custodial biological parent when the custodial parent (spouse of the stepparent) has died. But this case is still an anomaly and not likely to produce similar results in other states.

The separation, due to the death of a parent, of living loved ones, presents a crisis for the blended family and a serious problem for the legal community. However, there is one remedy worth trying to bridge this stepparent and child separation occasioned by death. A biological parent who has remarried can include in his or her last will and testament a stipulation that the stepparent be given visitation. This should be considered when the stepparent and the child have had a close and long-term relationship. Though the stipulation is not automatically enforceable, it is worth taking the chance that a court may honor the wishes of the deceased parent. There is a greater likelihood that the court will enforce such a provision if the other biological parent either is not fit or is deceased.

A STEP FORWARD

When Allison married Miles, he was sharing custody of his nine-year-old daughter, Laurie, with his ex-wife, Cheryl, who taught school. They lived a few blocks away from each other, so Laurie grew comfortable enough to pop in to her father's house after school on a fairly regular basis, especially since she liked Allison and since her mother couldn't always get home in time for Laurie after school. Allison, a freelance writer, worked at home. Over time, and at Cheryl's invitation, Laurie began to call her stepmother "Aunt Allison." Cheryl came to rely on Allison, not only to provide a place for Laurie to go after school but also to take Laurie to some after-school activities, including her weekly piano lesson.

Allison had never been married before, nor was she able to have children. She began to view Laurie as her daughter, too. When Laurie was sixteen, her father died of a sudden heart attack. Everyone was heartsick, even Miles's ex-wife, who spent many hours consoling both her daughter and Allison. Though Laurie no longer needed after-school supervision, she continued to visit with her stepmother on a regular basis. For the next several years, Miles's widow, his ex-wife, and his twenty-one-year-old daughter developed a real family relationship, even spending holidays together.

As Laurie said, "Though I never called my stepmother 'Mom,' she is my second mother, and I not only have Allison to thank for always being there for me, but I have my own mother to thank, who was good enough and smart enough to share me with Allison. They are both great women. My father would be proud of all of us."

Helpful Guidelines

- **Allow the child time to grieve.** A parent should not marry immediately after the loss of a spouse, because that doesn't give the child time for a normal grieving process. The presence of a new stepmother or stepfather requires its own adjustment for the child, and that adjustment shouldn't be taking place during the period of grief. A year of living through holidays without a stepfamily is recommended by experts.

- **Recognize that a child's grief may take many forms.** With children, anger, aggressiveness, feigned indifference, obsessive-compulsive behavior, sleeplessness, a desire for isolation, listlessness, and phobias can be normal and natural parts of the healing process during recovery from the death of a parent. (If this behavior goes on for two to three months, however, get professional help.)

- **Create a receptive atmosphere, and offer special attention.** That means talking about feelings and offering an affectionate embrace. The adults who are in close contact with a child who has lost a parent are the ones who must offer every form of reassurance that they will be there to love and protect the child. Holding and hugging a child can often be more comforting than words.

- **After a reasonable time, redirect the child's attention.** A child will wilt from prolonged morbid sadness, so the child should be encouraged to reinvest his or her energy into new activities—sports, artistic pursuits, and so on. The family should arrange some pleasure trips.

- **Be aware of the risk of separation anxiety.** A young child who suddenly loses contact with a parent can be permanently damaged. To prevent such damage, the child must have the reassurance of another family member, and that can come from the loving presence of the other parent, a grandparent, or an aunt. Introducing a new person to the child at this time is not helpful.

- **In the kindest terms, tell children the truth about death.** To avoid the danger of having a child maintain false hopes that the parent will come back, it's best to explain that death is permanent and a part of life. Avoiding the subject will confuse a child. To help a child through the grieving process, offer enormous doses of patience, love, and understanding.

- **Let the child decide whether to attend the funeral.** Allow the child to attend the parent's funeral if the child wishes to do so. If the child doesn't want to attend, that should be respected, and under no circumstances should the child be made to feel any guilt about *not* attending.

- **The surviving parent should attend the funeral as support for the young child.** Unless there are special circumstances, such as visible contempt toward the parent from the widow or widower of the deceased, it is appropriate to attend the funeral service, but that does not necessarily mean sitting with the family—unless invited to do so. As soon as the service is over, the surviving parent should make himself or herself completely accessible to the child, who needs reassurance and a warm embrace. If there is open hostility, have another close relative accompany the child—a grandparent or a favorite aunt.

- **Don't allow a grieving child to take out their hostility on the stepparent.** Being kind and understanding doesn't mean the stepparent should be a scapegoat for the child's anger, fear, or resentment that may occur because of the parent's death. The surviving parent should spend more time with the child, and during that time he or she should lovingly but firmly discourage outbursts against the stepparent.

- **Recognize when the child needs counseling.** Behaviors that seem odd and troublesome probably are, and should not be tolerated. We all know when a child is acting destructive or self-destructive. For the sake of the child and for the sake of the other family members, get help.

t e n

Can We Talk?

S e c r e t   T e n :

Make civility, respect, and compassion the touchstones

of your communication.

If people were randomly stopped on the street and asked what they want out of life, most would answer, "I want to be happy." If asked, "What do you think would make you happy?" the answers might range from finding one's soul mate to good health, to wealth, to an exciting career. But after years of research and countless interviews, I've concluded that what almost everyone wants more than anything else is to have a close and loving family.

The previous chapters have explored long-term differences over children, money, ex-spouses, former in-laws, current in-laws, holidays, and manners and values. What means do we have at hand for resolving these conflicts and creating confidence in the strength of the new family? Is there really a way to get along with so many different people coming together and trying to form a new family, some eagerly and some unwillingly? *Communication is the vehicle that has the best chance of taking you where you want to go.*

As humans, we have the unique ability to speak, which allows us to make our thoughts known, to share our feelings, to give information, and to form intimate and lasting connections with other human beings. Simply put, to be happy, we need to get what we want, and conveying our needs through language allows us to do that.

Unfortunately, language can also deter us from getting what we want. It can even destroy the good relationships we have. Many of us have trouble opening ourselves to others, because at a subliminal level we're afraid to speak our minds, to speak at all. What causes this fear of speaking out? Maybe we think we'll sound stupid, or we're afraid that the words will be taken the wrong way or that we'll be disliked and rejected. Maybe this was true in our childhood—or in our first marriage. But this is a pattern that can be changed.

The ability to say the right thing at the right time for the right reason isn't a God-given talent. It takes work to learn communication skills. Sadly, most of us don't know how much we need to improve these skills. We're so eager to have our say, especially when we are in the heat of battle, that we fail to listen to the other person, and the other person is doing the same thing. Both people talk past each other, and nothing gets resolved. And yet skillful talk—as in good diplomacy—can triumph over war. On a smaller scale, good communication can make the difference between family blending and family dissolution.

A smile and a nod won't do the job. Body language has its limitations, because it can convey only the here and now. Language, however, can communicate in limitless ways. Memories can be shared, plans for the future can be shared, worry and ways of solving problems can be shared, joy and grief can be shared, loneliness can be averted, and information can be exchanged.

But too frequently we hear cries for help: "We just can't communicate" or "I can't talk to my kids" or "I can't talk to my parents" or "I can't talk to my in-laws" or "My husband never talks to me" or "My wife really doesn't know me." Many stepparents say, "If my ex or my spouse's ex could just talk, we could work out so many problems with the kids." "Just talk" means getting the point across to a receptive listener; choosing words that are constructive, clear, and thoughtful; and using tones that are soothing rather than inflammatory, whining, sarcastic, or demanding.

It may sound simple, but it is probably one of the most difficult tasks to accomplish. "Talk is cheap," they say. Don't believe it. Of course, what they mean is that if you don't follow through, the talk was meaningless. But saying what you want in the right way is the first step toward getting someone to follow through.

DEFUSING CONTROL ISSUES

Remarried couples are often in situations that pit one set of controls against another. Control is troublesome in relationships when those involved struggle over who's holding the reins. And how many of us have ever seen or been involved in a relationship where control isn't a presence to a greater or lesser degree? When it is to a greater degree, it has within it the seeds of destruction.

When couples have a mutual problem to solve, they mistakenly take it to the wall with an air of superiority and control, instead of pressing for a solution that is acceptable to each of them.

To bring about change, talk cannot be a war of words.

"I'm right, you're wrong."

"No, I'm right, and you're wrong."

When one person tries to force a change of action or opinion by barking orders and hurling accusations and labels, the other person naturally resists—unless that person is a wimp, which presents a whole new set of problems. The content of the message is lost as both parties channel their efforts into a destructive battle of wills.

If one says, "I can't talk to you about anything concerning your kids. You never listen to what I have to say."

The other retorts, "If you had anything to say that wasn't an accusation, maybe I'd listen."

Or "Your kids never pick up after themselves."

The response may be "And your kids are no better." Or "Why are you always picking on my kids?"

That kind of repartee is all too common in blended families.

What about another approach?

"I'm not happy when rooms are messy; besides, our house is really cramped when we're all in it. I think we need to work together to get the kids to be more cooperative. If you can get them to put their dirty clothes in the hamper, I'll try to get them to help clear the table after dinner. Just that alone would be a big help."

Because these are not arm-twisting or accusatory words, they have a better chance of avoiding argument and getting a good reception, and reaching the desired goal.

The likely response would be "Okay, I'll try that."

It's the difference between accusatory communication and constructive problem solving. Speaking to each other in a manner that is designed to resolve conflicts, rather than inflame them, is one of the most important skills couples need to acquire if their marriage is to endure.

A BETTER WAY

William had two sons, and Marie had one daughter when they married. Marie was constantly angry, because William gave her no support with his children. He undermined her authority by negating her efforts to enforce discipline.

Every time they discussed the problem, William would say, "I don't know what you want from me." Harold Bloomfield, Ph.D., a family therapist, advocates a different approach—that the couple have a talk in which the person confronted with the problem must not refute everything, but ask for further explanation. Something on this order:

MARIE: I get so angry with you, because you don't support me when I discipline the children.

WILLIAM: Explain what you want me to do.

MARIE: Well, we talked about laying down some rules for chores, homework, and bedtime.

WILLIAM: Could you be more specific on what I should do?

MARIE: If we have a particular time to go to bed and I tell the kids, "It's bedtime," instead of letting them stay up, as you do, I want you to support me. When you don't, they know that they don't have to listen to me. I love you, and I want this marriage to work, but it won't work if you undermine me with the kids.

WILLIAM: I love you, too. We both want the same thing, but you expect the kids to go to bed too early.

MARIE: Okay, would you rather make it a half hour later? Will that work?

WILLIAM: Yes, and I'll try my best to enforce it. It may take a few nights.

MARIE: That's all I ask.

Marie and William examined a conflict, and through conciliatory conversation they explored the causes of the conflict, including the role of attitudes and behavior in fueling the conflict. Alternative ways of responding to the conflict were considered. For example, they modified the assumption that a particular bedtime hour was absolute. Both husband and wife gave a little bit in order to move off dead center. But now it's up to William to enforce the new rules. If he accomplishes that, the conflict is eliminated. But if he fails to act immediately, a gentle reminder of what he promised to do is advisable.

TELLING IT LIKE IT IS

Because relationship issues tend to be sensitive, couples often talk around them or cloak them in a more general topic. For example, a couple might argue repeatedly about spending money, when in fact the heart of the matter may be their distrust of each other's motives about spending for children from a previous marriage versus spending on the children of the remarriage. As hotly as they may argue, it is less disturbing to focus on money and extravagance than to confront the more sensitive issue of resentment over spending on the former family. To resolve an issue, the couple has to confront the personal and relationship aspects lurking beneath the topic issue.

Hardly anybody lives happily ever after. As Cinderella rode off with Prince Charming, they were probably arguing about where they would spend their honeymoon. She wanted to go to Saint Barts, and he wanted to head back to the castle. Who knows—maybe they never even got to the altar!

Only when issues escalate into problems do we feel backed against the wall with no way out, and this happens when:

- An issue is never identified.

- An issue is recognized but ignored; therefore, it continues to fester.

- An issue is confronted but never effectively settled, because a solution is arbitrarily imposed rather than mutually worked out.

When the issue seems to be an insurmountable problem, we hear comments like "There's nothing to talk about here" or "This is beyond the talking stage." Feeling angry with your spouse about something he or she said is normal. It becomes a problem if the person continues to feel angry and doesn't express it.

LEARNING TO SPEAK UP

According to Deborah Tannen, a leading expert in the field of communication skills, men see confrontation as an effective means of communication, whereas women generally shirk from it. Often this reticence is due to the woman's fear that she will not be able to express herself clearly and constructively or that she may make the situation worse. This places women at a real disadvantage, because women who are incapable of occasional angry outbursts are incapable of wielding power. Tannen says that women's "avoidance of confrontation opens them up to exploitation. In a word, they don't stand up for themselves."

A source of frustration for Elaine was spending every Christmas with her husband's family. Tony came from a big, robust, close-knit Italian family. At Christmas the relatives who lived far away traveled to the big family compound, where several brothers and sisters lived with their individual families side by side with the aging parents.

By contrast, Elaine came from a Midwestern Scandinavian family where less was more. Conversation was sparse and unemotional. Any subject likely to produce a difference of opinion was avoided, and the food was wholesome but not particularly interesting. Even Christmas decorations were understated—one tree and a wreath on the door, instead of lights strung all over the property.

Tony was always quick to schedule the Christmas get-together with his family. He just assumed that was where they would spend the holiday. Elaine found comfort in the quiet simplicity of her family's celebration, and she missed seeing them, because they lived several hundred miles away.

She and Tony had begun to have problems in their relationship over more than the issue of where to spend holidays. So when the subject came up once again, Elaine finally spoke up. She told Tony she resented that she always had to spend Christmas with his family and that she wanted to be with her family that year. She also told him that if he didn't want to come, he could do what he wanted to, but she was taking the kids and visiting her folks. To her amazement, Tony said he would go with her. When she explained how angry she had been over this matter, Tony said all she had to do was *let him know* how strongly she felt about it. He was puzzled as to why she had never taken a definitive stand before.

To Tony, a low-key approach signaled that it didn't really mean much to Elaine. He was used to women who asserted themselves, often vociferously. In fact, in his family, as is true in many Italian families, the women are very much in charge of the home and family celebrations. He knew that his mother and sisters would have had no hesitation letting him know what they expected.

When styles differ, trying harder by doing more of the same will not solve problems. For Tony, becoming even more aggressive to get his point across would be as self-defeating as Elaine's becoming even more reserved and soft-spoken to make her point. Elaine needs to speak up, and Tony needs to listen when she does.

COMMUNICATION TIPS

For the Speaker

- Don't be afraid to say what you feel.

- Don't give mixed messages.

- Don't use closed questions to appear flexible when your mind is sealed.

- Don't presume to read the other person's mind.

- Use conciliatory tones.

- Don't become accusatory, don't berate, and don't play "gotcha."

- Put the focus on one issue at a time.

- Acknowledge your own weaknesses in solving the problem.

- Show that you value the person you're speaking to.

For the Listener

- Be attentive and calm.

- Don't interrupt.

- Don't belittle.

- Don't be arrogant or defiant.

- Show that you value the person you're listening to.

- Ask for clarification if you need it.

- Be willing to compromise for the sake of the relationship.

I LOVE YOU, BUT...

Noreen is a stepmother to Forrest's children, Alfie and Carla, ages fourteen and twelve respectively. They also have a two-year-old son of their own. After three years of marriage, Noreen became frustrated and anxious about her inability to forge a good relationship with her two stepchildren, who visited every other weekend and one night a week.

"I've tried my very best to be good to your children and to love them," Noreen remembers telling Forrest, "but they just won't accept me. They hate me, and I don't know why. And now we have our son, and this tension isn't good for him or for any of us."

Forrest explained to Noreen that he felt she was asking him to choose between his children from a previous marriage and their child together. He reminded Noreen that she knew when she married him that he had a family, and that he would always remain close to all his children. Then he added, "I didn't want another child, but to make you happy, we had one. So, try to get along with my children and stop badgering me about them."

Those last comments were "fighting words," and, predictably, a full-fledged battle erupted.

Had Forrest begun by acknowledging the problem and accepting Noreen's efforts to get close to his children, he would have found a basis to unite with her in working toward a solution. Instead, he drew a line in the sand.

He might have said, "I know how hard you've tried and how difficult it's been to get much response from my kids, but I'm going to work on it with you. I think it's going to take more time. Having the baby has been tiring on you especially, but also on me. You know how much I love you and the baby. I think my kids are a little jealous of the new baby. Let's give the relationship between you and my children more time to grow. And you don't have to love them. Just be kind to them, and I'll make sure they treat you with respect."

By learning to check defensive responses and to accept your spouse's feelings, marital relationships are strengthened and problems get solved.

Implicit in Forrest's actual response was a not-so-subtle form of coercion. "I love you, *but* if you keep badgering me about my children, then I may stop loving you." It's easy to fall into this verbal trap, because the words masquerade as acceptance. But they are really a denial and an ultimatum—I won't love you *unless* you do as I say.

A better way: "I love you *and* wish you'd allow the relationship with my children to develop more gradually." This is a statement of unconditional love, plus a noncritical, constructive suggestion for handling the problem.

Then there are the words that are aimed at coercion through guilt: "If you really loved me, you would . . ."

And more charged statements—accusations that presume a whole history of wrongdoing:

"You never . . ."

"You always . . ."

Any one of these verbal traps provokes further conflict and forces the discussion into the past. The aim is to stay in the present and to move forward to a peaceful resolution.

COMMUNICATION KILLERS— AND HOW TO AVOID THEM

I love you but . . .

Bad. I love you, but we don't have the same values when it comes to raising all these kids.

Good. I know our values sometimes differ when it comes to raising all these kids, but I love you, and we can work it out together.

Bad. I love you, but my first obligation is to my children. They didn't ask to be put in this situation.

Good. My children are having a tough time. Of course, you understand that right now I have to give some priority to them, but I love you and know you'll help me work it out. We'll do it together.

Bad. I love you, but I resent all the money you throw away on your children over and above all the alimony and child support you have to pay.

Good. I've always appreciated the financial obligations you have, but we really need to conserve so that we can meet those obligations. I believe that spending more time with the kids, instead of spending more money, would make them happier, and it would help our financial situation. Let's try it.

If you really loved me . . .

Bad. If you really loved me, you would stop harassing me about my kids.

Good. I'm having a hard time getting my kids to adjust. So, I'm counting on you to be patient until we can get this worked out.

Bad. If you really loved me, you'd stop bugging me about my ex.

Good. I'm just as bothered by my ex as you are. I'm trying to distance myself from her/him. Did you know that your love is what gives me the strength to work this out?

Bad. If you really loved me, you wouldn't ruin our holidays with your kids, who don't want to be with us.

Good. I'm so sorry your children resent spending holidays with us. I know that hurts you, but that's how most kids are. They're into their friends and their lives. Let's ask them if there are other times of the year when they would rather visit, or you could take some time to be with them alone. Let's do what will make everyone happy.

You never . . . and you always . . .

Bad. You never listen to me.

Good. Sometimes I feel as if I can't get your attention. I know you're busy and preoccupied, but there are times when I really need your undivided attention, and this is one of them.

Bad. You never give me any support with your parents, who expect us to travel there every year, and we just can't afford it.

Good. Sometimes it's really hard for me to get your parents to understand that it's easier for them to come here for a visit than for us to spend so much airfare to travel with all the kids. They'd be more receptive if *you* explained it to them. That would be the best support you could give me.

Bad. You always take up for your own kids.

Good. I don't think you realize how often you take the side of your kids. I know it's a natural thing to do, but I think it gives the wrong impression to the rest of us. If you could sometimes take my side, I would feel so much better, and it would be easier for all of us.

DON'T BOARD THE RUNAWAY TRAIN

Messages and meanings in family talk can act like "stealth weapons," according to Deborah Tannen. They cause family fights to escalate toward an impasse rather than a resolution. We need to recognize what they are in order to avoid them.

Personal Attacks

For example: "It figures you would say something like that about my daughter, coming from your low-class background" or "No one else cares enough about you to tell you this" or "If you had any feelings, you wouldn't even *think* what you just said."

Personal attacks are particularly destructive because not only do they hurt for the moment, but they are not easily forgotten. They escalate the argument at hand, and they can cause harm for years to come.

People who engage in this type of warfare are not content to win a fight based on the merits of their perspective. They want to smear each other's character and destroy each other's credibility.

It's worth remembering that in a biological family, where there is a history of nurturing and loving over a long period of time, angry words may be more easily forgotten and forgiven, particularly if they are not ongoing attacks. When people are joined together who have no common history, they are not yet "family" in the emotional sense of the word. Consequently, their responses may be much more defensive and long lasting, even if the insulting words are said only occasionally. Personal attacks are going to be indelibly imprinted on their memories, leading to further conflict and unhappiness.

Piling On the Issues

"This is just like the last time. You said you wouldn't give her any more money. Are you married to her or to me? And one more thing—I'm furious that you let her sit with us at our wedding."

Couples may be tempted to bring in past issues to make their positions stronger, but it deflects attention from the problem at hand, plus it makes the other person angry to have to deal with something that's already happened and can't be changed.

Bringing In Testimonials

"I'm sick of being a maid to your kids. Neither you nor your kids ever lift a finger to help. I shouldn't be surprised. Everyone knows what a pigsty you used to live in. And just the other day, I heard someone say that you were always lazy."

When someone says, "Everyone knows what a louse you really are" or "Everyone says the same thing about you," the person is trying to add weight to what might be a weak position. And it works by making a person respond even more defensively. It escalates the personal threat of an attack by bringing in the alleged support of others to bolster one's position. What it doesn't do is allow a fair discussion of the issue at hand, and it therefore lessens any chance of resolution.

What Else Is Inflammatory and Self-Defeating?

- Using closed questions to appear flexible when the mind is actually sealed shut: "Don't you think you could just accept the way my family celebrates the holidays?"

- Sending messages that say yes when they mean no, and vice versa.

  MARY *(sarcastically):* I can't think of a single thing I'd rather do this weekend than drive two hours to get your kids.
  JOHN: You don't have to go if you don't want to.
  MARY: I said I'd go, didn't I?

- Any statement in which someone claims X-ray vision to read your mind: "I can tell you don't like my children."

If you can simply *avoid* all of the above inflammatory and self-defeating phrases, you will have a much better chance of resolving problems successfully.

THE POSITIVE POWER OF WORDS

Andrew was an angry fourteen-year-old who was having out-of-control shouting matches with his stepmother, Jackie, and stepbrother, Josh. Marcus, Andrew's father, was desperately unhappy, because he feared losing the relationship with the son he loved very much. They had always been close, until Marcus's remarriage to Jackie. Marcus described how he resolved his relationship with his son and his new family. He saw that his son had become volatile, a trait that had not been apparent before his parents' divorce and father's remarriage. Hoping to find out what was bothering the boy, Marcus decided to take him away for a fishing weekend.

After a day of fly-fishing, Marcus and Andrew cooked dinner together. During that time, Marcus told Andrew that while his divorce from Andrew's mother was a painful but necessary end to a difficult marriage, he had deep feelings of regret about the day-to-day separation from Andrew. He told him that an absence of Andrew in his life would be intolerable.

Andrew opened up. He told his father that he felt he wasn't wanted anymore.

"It seems no one cares about me," he said. "When I visit, I have to sleep on the floor on an air mattress in Josh's room. I don't even have one drawer to put my clothes in. I live out of a suitcase. I just don't feel that I belong there. And I have to compete with Jackie and Josh to get your attention in the little time we have together. They have you all the time."

Marcus was surprised. In all his angry outbursts, Andrew had never mentioned these issues. Marcus thought a minute before replying.

"I'll always love you, Andrew. Wherever I am, you belong, and don't ever forget that. They don't regard you as an intruder. Jackie understands how difficult this is for you, and wants to express her feelings, but she's shy and has a hard time showing them. I want all of us to take more time to work this out. How would you like for us to have a weekend to ourselves every couple of months?"

Andrew smiled and nodded through tears of gratitude. He and Marcus hugged each other.

Marcus knew that wasn't the end of the problem, because he had to work on Andrew's relationships with Jackie and with her twelve-year-old son, Josh.

"And how about if we take Josh, and all three of us go to a ball game together?"

"Sure," Andrew said.

"I'm going to get bunk beds for Josh's room, and you can have a chest for yourself in the study. His room is too small for any more furniture. Is there anything Jackie could do to make you feel more welcome, or maybe we should just work on the things we've talked about?"

Andrew nodded.

Marcus did all the right things, and they worked: He took his son on a weekend trip away from the new family so that he and Andrew could talk freely. Andrew could feel more comfortable on neutral territory. Marcus also opened the talk by expressing how much he loved Andrew, and how important it was to him that they have a close relationship. He offered solutions to the immediate problems that would be easy to fulfill, and then asked Andrew to allow some time for everyone to get better acquainted.

Wisely, Marcus talked to his son in private. Had he discussed these issues in the presence of Jackie and Josh, Andrew would have felt outnumbered and probably would not have opened up to his father.

Adults in blended families should let the children, all of them, know that they are always available for a heart-to-heart talk. They should also make certain to spend one-on-one time with each child, and let their own child know that their love for and commitment to that child is unshakable.

INFORMATION, PLEASE

Children need to know what's happening in their lives. It's important to explain what's going on—divorce, death, remarriage, change of custody, moving to another house, to name just a few of the big ones.

Some children will pepper you with questions, but even the child who does *not* ask deserves an explanation. Of course, you need to take into account the level of a child's intellectual and emotional maturity. Don't tell too much. The fact that you may feel lonely or frightened about the divorce is not what the kids need to hear. Parents should not turn to children for emotional solace. And remember that love and information are still not enough. Children also need a structured environment that gives them a sense of predictability and security. The points listed below may sound elementary, but too many parents make the mistake of thinking their children already know what's happening, and fail to tell them what they need to hear.

Fundamental Talking Points for Divorce

1. Tell the child that there is going to be a divorce,

2. That it is not *in any way* the child's fault,

3. That the child does not have to choose between his/her parents,

4.   That the child is loved by both parents, and

5.   That the child will be living with mother/father but will continue to see both parents.

6.   Give the child an opportunity to ask questions, and try your best to answer them, because the content of the questions will probably reveal the child's insecurities, which need to be addressed.

Fundamental Talking Points for Remarriage

1.   Tell the child you're planning to get married to Jane or Joe, a person they should have had reasonable contact with before this announcement,

2.   That you love your child and that your forthcoming marriage will in no way diminish that love,

3.   That there will always be a place at your new home for your child to visit (assuming the other parent has custody), or that your child will be living with you and Jane or Joe, and any of the other family members who will be there, too.

4.   Reassure your child that he/she can always come and talk to you about any problems that arise while living in the new blended family.

5.   Let the child know that he/she will continue to have contact with the other parent and the other parent's family.

6.   Give the child the opportunity to ask questions. . . .

GETTING BACK ON TRACK

Not all heart-to-heart talks produce good results. For a variety of reasons, people often try to avoid what they consider to be a confrontational subject, or in certain situations they may even want to keep the pot boiling. Many stepchildren who have loyalties to the biological parent are afraid of the vulnerability associated with allowing themselves to become close, so they argue or create difficulties in order to keep a stepparent at a safe distance. The same situation can arise when a couple tries to resolve a problem in their new family. How should a person respond to a manipulative, argumentative, or derailing statement and get the discussion back on track?

- **Postponing the discussion:** "I would prefer to talk about this later."
  Response: "I realize that's what you prefer. I think we need to deal with it right now."

- **Refusing to acknowledge the conflict:** "I don't think we have a disagreement, so there's nothing to talk about."
  Response: "I realize you don't think there's a problem, but I do. Please let's continue this discussion."

- **Going on the offensive:** "I can't believe you even brought this up."
  Response: "I know this is unpleasant for you. Ignoring the problem won't make it go away. We really need to talk."

- **Piling on the issues:** "It's not just this one incident. You also . . ."
  Response: "Can we take the issues one at a time? We'll get nowhere if we try to deal with too many at once."

- **Rewriting history:** "I never said that. You must've misunderstood me."
  Response: "Perhaps there was miscommunication on both our parts. So let's promise to be clearer about what we're saying."

- **Appealing to the crowd:** "Lots of other people agree with me, and think you're . . ."
  Response: "I wish we could let others speak for themselves so that we could get back to the problem."

Each of these manipulative ploys was countered by a more direct response in order to continue the discussion toward a resolution. The responses are firm, but not inflammatory. They let the other person know that you understand what's going on, that you wish to move beyond blame and want to deal openly with the issues.

KNOW THE PLAYING FIELD

There are limits to what you can change in your relationships with other family members. You may even come to realize that the person you married (or the relative of the person you married), who lives in your home and is now in your family, may be someone without scruples or may be so desperate that he or she will do anything to get his or her way. While these people may seem like agents of the devil sent to wreak havoc in your life, they are only trying to deal with their own pain. They may be so afraid of intimacy, so mistrustful of others' intentions, perhaps so damaged or hurt inside, that they seek to make others' lives as miserable as their own.

If you find yourself locked in a futile struggle, it may be time to redefine what it is you want. Any person's original intentions can get lost in the irrational desire to win an argument. It's important to back off enough to assess whether the result is achievable or whether the discussion has become so counterproductive that it isn't worth pursuing, at least for the present.

Until you develop certain specific skills to avoid making the situation worse, expressing yourself fully and forcefully comes with certain risks.

Sometimes there is no easy solution. When the question of where to spend this Christmas comes up, you can't be in two places at once, so one person wins and the other loses. In a situation where one person gets what he or she wants and the other person does not, conflict and resentment are part of the consequences. The person might say, "I know I'm getting what I want, and you're not, but you're very important to me, so next year we'll go where you want to go."

The risk of ignoring serious problems in the stepfamily is greater than the risk of confronting them, provided the discussion to resolve conflict is done in a spirit of conciliation. Remember: good things don't usually come easily. Labor brings forth babies, pain straightens teeth, and good communication makes a happily blended family.

Helpful Guidelines

- **Define and confront the issue that's causing the problem.** Particularly when you're talking to a spouse, try not to camouflage the real problem, even if it's painful or embarrassing to reveal. The relationship will be stronger, more intimate, and more enduring when the couple can communicate in an honest but loving manner.

- **Be ready to compromise.** When you see that the other person is receptive and wants to resolve the problem, be flexible and consider alternative solutions to the conflict. The relationship is worth it. But be prepared to let the other person have a say, because no one wants to have a solution arbitrarily imposed on them.

- **Discuss the problem in private.** To reach a level of comfort for open communication and to avoid embarrassing the other person, find a mutually convenient time and place to discuss the problem in private.

- **Keep the tone conciliatory, and don't shout.** Words are important, but so is the tone of voice that delivers the message. Try saying the words "We need to talk" in a friendly voice, and then say those same words in an angry voice. Immediately, you will realize that what our mothers told us was true—you can get more with honey than with vinegar.

- **Men and women have different sensitivities.** Typically, a man who fears losing freedom pulls away at the first sign he interprets as an attempt to control him, but his pulling away is just the signal that sets off alarms for the woman who fears losing intimacy.

Understanding each other's style, and the motives behind it, is a first move in breaking this destructive cycle.

• **Remember to convey love or fondness for the family member.** Just starting with words that show love and kindness paves the way for a better discussion and for a greater chance of reaching a consensus.

APPENDIX

STEPFAMILY LAW

Lawmakers continue to be slow in recognizing nontraditional family structures, particularly those created between residential stepparents and their stepchildren.

Most of the important legal issues that affect stepfamily members center on questions of support, custody and visitation, and inheritance, as well as other matters of civil law. All of these areas are regulated at the state level, so it is essential to check with a lawyer in the state in which the family resides, or with the particular court that has jurisdiction (the right to render a decision) in that state.

In the context of stepfamily law, the basic premise is that stepparents and their stepchildren are *legal strangers* to each other. The current "law of stepfamilies" consists of a series of limited exceptions to this principle. There is no uniform treatment of the stepparent-child relationship from one state to another, as there is in regard to enforcement of biological child support obligations, known as the Uniform Reciprocal Support Act. The lack of a law that applies to all the states means that there is no comprehensive legal definition of the stepfamily or blended family in American law.

In 1987, the Family Law Section of the American Bar Association began work on the Model Act Establishing Rights and Duties of Stepparents. The act defines a stepparent as "a person who is married to the person . . . who has custody of a minor child." The act addresses three key issues relating to stepparent rights and duties: the right to discipline, support duties, and custody and visitation rights.[1]

At times of crisis or transition in the family, people seek the protection of the law. This protection is typically invoked by stepfamily members who have relationships of economic and emotional interdependence. Failure of the law to recognize and protect the stepparent-child relationship in these circumstances often results in hardship for individual family members.

A typical and most unfortunate example is when a remarried custodial parent dies and the nurturing stepparent with whom the child lives and has a close attachment is not legally recognized even though the child's other biological parent is deceased or otherwise absent from the child's life.

In one situation a stepchild endured economic hardship when his mother's request for child support from a stepfather was denied even though the child had become dependent upon his stepfather over an extended number of years.

In another case, the stepfather encouraged the mother to terminate the biological father's relationship with the child, promising to adopt the child as his own. The stepfather never got around to the adoption, so when the couple divorced after seven years, the child received no support from the stepfather, nor did the court impose a support obligation on him.[2]

In situations involving inappropriate sex, the law fails once again to protect the interests of stepchildren by excluding the stepfamilies from the definition of criminal incest. For example, a stepfather who had engaged in sexual activity with his stepdaughter was acquitted of this criminal charge because the relevant statutory definition of incest was restricted to biological families. A handful of states have now included stepparents in the definition, and others rely on laws regarding statutory rape or child molestation where incest laws do not apply.

In recent years, scholars of the family have criticized this gap

[1] Joel D. Tenenbaum, "Legislation for Stepfamilies—The Family Law Section Standing Committee Report," *25 Fam. L. Q.* 137 (1991).

[2] *Ulrich v. Cornell,* 484 N.W.2d 545 (Wis. 1992).

between current legal norms and the actual family experiences of many individuals in our society. An additional cost associated with this narrow definition of family is the absence of clear and positive roles for stepfamily members. It is easy to criticize the current status of the law regulating stepfamilies, but it is much more difficult to affirmatively define a legal stepparent-child status that would recognize and protect stepfamily members while preserving a family law system that is fair, certain and predictable.

In considering law reform, two important questions must be answered. First, what constitutes a legally significant stepparent-child relationship? Second, what rights and responsibilities should be associated with stepfamily membership?

The simplest answer to the first question appears in the Census Bureau's definition of stepfamily: the relationship formed whenever an individual marries the custodial parent of a minor child and thereafter resides with the child. This basic definition is used in a number of existing state laws that recognize stepfamilies for specific purposes. For example, the Missouri stepparent support statute provides, in a straightforward manner, that "a stepparent shall support his or her stepchild to the same extent that a natural or adoptive parent is required to support his or her child as long as the stepchild is living in the same home as the stepparent." Oregon, Washington, Utah, and South Dakota have similar laws.

When deciding stepfamily-child issues, judges in some states may employ a doctrine referred to as *in loco parentis,* which in Latin means "in the place of a parent." This is usually not used in matters of inheritance or in awarding damages for the wrongful death of a parent by a third party, but it may, for instance, be used in matters concerning the child's right to financial compensation when a stepparent is injured in a workers' compensation case.

Some states are recognizing stepfamilies for a specific purpose when the stepparent and the child are tied together by more than the stepparent's marriage to the child's parent. For example, the New Jersey inheritance statute establishes preferential rates and exemptions for bequests made to "any child to whom the decedent... stood in the acknowledged relation of a parent, provided such relationship began at or before the child's fifteenth birthday and was continuous for ten years thereafter." Many states use this common-law *in loco parentis* approach by requiring some form of responsibility by the stepparent before legal rights and duties apply. In most states, stepparents who stand *in loco parentis* to their stepchildren are entitled to discipline them and are subject to the same limitations on the use of force as biological parents.

On the other hand, in many states stepparents have no enforceable obligation whatsoever to support their stepchildren. But even in the eighteen states where lawmakers have imposed a statutory stepchild support duty, it is much less significant than the duty of biological or adoptive parents.

With the growing number of stepfamilies, numerous legal questions have arisen about the relationship between the residential stepparent and the minor child with whom he or she resides following marriage to the custodial parent. The courts and the legislatures in many states have been asked to address issues such as the stepparent's authority to consent to medical treatment for the stepchild and the stepchild's right to sue a wrongdoer in the event of the stepparent's wrongful death. The most prevalent legal matters involve the rights and liabilities of the stepparent at the time of a divorce from the custodial parent.

THE RIGHTS AND DUTIES OF STEPPARENTS AT THE TIME OF DIVORCE

In the case of divorce or the death of a custodial parent, a stepparent may seek to continue a visiting relationship or quite possibly a custodial relationship with a child who has been close to him or her for a period of years. So, too, may a custodial parent seek child support from a stepparent in circumstances where the custodial parent, stepparent, and child cease to live together in a shared household.

The Stepparent Who Has Adopted the Stepchild

In some stepfamilies, the spouses decide that stepparent adoption would best serve the interests of the family. For that to happen, the spouses must both give their consent, the court must find that this important change serves the child's best interests, and the parental rights of the noncustodial parent must be terminated either by death, by consent, or involuntarily by order of the court. This has the effect of changing the legal relationship to that of a biological parent with all the rights and duties that a parent has toward the child. In the event of divorce, the adoptive stepparent would be obliged to pay child support and would have options for custody and visitation in the same way as a biological parent.

Stepparent Support Obligations

Historically, the child support laws of every state imposed support responsibility for a minor child exclusively on the child's two legal parents and no responsibility on the residential stepparent. Although a number of states have created certain limited exceptions to this important principle of economic responsibility, these developments usually apply where there is an ongoing marriage between the stepparent and the custodial parent, and rarely result in a postdivorce support duty for stepparents.

A minority of state statutes currently establish stepparent support obligations for minor children, but these laws are limited to the period when the stepparent is married to the child's custodial parent. These time-limited responsibilities are generally enforceable only by third parties, such as the state public assistance agency, and are not directly enforceable by the custodial parent or the stepchild due to a common-law doctrine which bars lawsuits between ongoing family members. Unfortunately, these court-imposed obligations do not extend beyond the termination of the stepparent's marriage to the custodial parent, so there is no legal basis for a child support claim at the time of divorce.

Written Contractual Obligation

If, at the time of the marriage or even thereafter, a custodial parent and a stepparent enter into a contract that includes a promise to pay stepchild support following divorce, the contract may be a successful basis for collecting stepchild support.

Oral or Implied Promises

It is worth noting that custodial parents have had little success in asserting oral or implied contractual responsibility. For example, the stepparent's statement during marriage that "I will always care for your child" (or the stepparent's behavior of paying for support of the child during the marriage) usually will not establish an enforceable postdivorce duty. The general rule is that the courts will not impose legal support obligations on a stepparent after that stepparent is divorced from the custodial parent unless it is in a written agreement.

A Legal Doctrine That May Cause a Court to Impose Duties of Support

One exception that a court may use to get around the usual rule of relieving stepparents of support obligations relies on a doctrine called equitable estoppel. What it means is that a person may be estopped (prevented) from denying a child support obligation if the stepparent acted in a way that would cause a great inequity. A case like this would occur where the custodial parent relies to his or her detriment and to the detriment of the child on the express or implied representations of the stepparent. What would constitute detrimental reliance? One instance would be a custodial parent ceasing to collect child support payments from the noncustodial parent during the period of the marriage. But detriment would have to be shown, and this would be hard to prove if in fact the stepparent's contribution during the marriage was a benefit rather than a detriment. If the stepparent's support caused the child's other parent (who normally would have support obligations) to squander a child's inheritance, this might be argued as detrimental reliance. There are a few cases where the doctrine was successful, but usually that occurred when circumstances were extraordinary.

Stepparent Visitation and Custody Rights

The legal system has been more willing to create enforceable visitation rights for stepparents than to impose support obligations following divorce. In the context of visitation, stepparent rights have been viewed by courts in the same way as they have viewed visitation rights of other third parties, such as grandparents. In each of these situations, the stepparent's or grandparent's interests must be balanced with the competing and clearly superior interests of the custodial parent to have autonomy and control over his or her child. Above all, the welfare of the minor child takes priority.

Generally, these third parties (grandparents and stepparents) have sought and received limited recognition and rights of access, but the law is still in a state of flux on the issue of enforceable stepparent access with regard to minor children. In this context, access means visitation between the child and a nonresident person. There are no uniform rules nationwide to inform stepparents about the likelihood of succeeding with a contested request for postdivorce visitation. In every state, however, the parent's rights are favored over those of the stepparent. Still, there is a growing awareness that a devoted stepparent of many years may be granted visitation rights, particularly if the court deems it to be in the best interests of the child to have an ongoing relationship with another loving adult. Courts may even allow a child to express a preference on the matter of having visits with a stepparent who has played a major nurturing role in the child's life. As a general rule, a majority of courts in stepparent visitation cases apply the standard of the best interests of the child and ask whether enforceable ongoing visitation by stepparents will likely enhance the future well-being of the stepchild.

Conclusion

In both philosophical and legal terms, the obligation of stepparents does not survive the termination of the marriage that created the stepfamily as it does in the biological family. It's simple to require immutable rights and responsibilities with the biological family but complicated, confusing, and uncertain to apply these within a step-family. Each case has its own set of circumstances, so lawmakers are reluctant to impose statutory mandates. The traditional system of family law is predicated on the important assumption that the bio-logical mother and father have exclusive relationships with their children. Stepfamily members seeking a broader legal definition of the family have frequently encountered stiff resistance, because their position is viewed as a threat to traditional values. There is embed-ded reluctance to complicate the system by moving away from a preference for nuclear families, and that continues even though the demographics have changed so dramatically—to the point where the blended family structure now is more common than the nuclear family structure.

For lawmakers, the task of translating these social realities into a responsive system of family laws in the future is a challenging one, but the laws in this area are continuing to evolve as more and more state courts and legislatures are addressing these issues. Only when this challenge has been met will the basic goals of the family law system be realized for the families of the twenty-first century.

This area of law widely varies from state to state, so specific factual questions should be directed to an attorney in the concerned jurisdic-tion. It may be necessary to consult an attorney just to determine what the correct jurisdiction is to file a petition.

STATES WITH STATUTES RELATING TO STEPPARENT RIGHTS AND OBLIGATIONS

There are four general categories of statutory provisions on the issues concerning stepparent laws. First, it is important to note that there are ten states with no laws at all covering the subject of stepparent rights and obligations. Then there are the four categories: custody, access (visitation), support, and the adoption of a uniform set of laws known as the Uniform Marital and Divorce Act (UMDA). The breakdown of the various states with regard to these categories is as follows.

States with No Statutes on This Area of the Law

Alabama, Arkansas, Florida, Idaho, Indiana, Maryland, New Jersey, Rhode Island, South Dakota, and Wyoming.

States with Statutes on Custody by a Third Party

Alaska, Arizona, California, Colorado, Connecticut, Georgia, Hawaii, Illinois, Kentucky, Louisiana, Maine, Massachusetts, Michigan, Minnesota, Mississippi, Missouri, Montana, Nebraska, Nevada, New Mexico, New York, North Dakota, Ohio, Oklahoma, Oregon, Pennsylvania, South Carolina, Tennessee, Texas, Virginia, and Washington.

States with Statutes on Access (Visitation)

Alaska, California, Connecticut, Hawaii, Illinois, Kansas, Louisiana, Maine, Michigan, Minnesota, Mississippi, Nebraska, New Hampshire, New York, Ohio, Oklahoma, Oregon, Tennessee, Texas, Virginia, Washington, West Virginia, and Wisconsin.

States with Statutes on Support Obligation During the Marriage

Delaware, Hawaii, Iowa, Kentucky, Maine, Missouri, Montana, Nebraska, Nevada, New Hampshire, New York, North Carolina, North Dakota, Oklahoma, Oregon, Utah, Vermont, and Washington.

States That Have Adopted the Uniform Marriage and Divorce Act* (UMDA)

Arizona, Colorado, Illinois, Kentucky, Minnesota, Missouri, Montana, and Washington.

FIVE COMMON TAX TRAPS FOR BLENDED FAMILIES

As if coordinating visitation and sharing expenses weren't complicated enough, blended families also face a confusing array of tax rules, and as of the writing of this section, we are confronted with an administration that is eager to overhaul the entire federal income tax code. For now, the discussion assumes the federal tax code has not been radically changed.

1. *Who claims the dependency exemption?*

Generally, for divorced parents, the parent who has custody of a child for the greater part of the year is entitled to claim the child as a dependent. However, the custodial parent may allow the noncustodial parent to claim the exemption by completing IRS Form 8332, "Release of Claim to Exemption for Child of Divorced or Separated Parents," which the noncustodial parent must attach to his or her return. If the custodial parent has little or no taxable income, it may make sense to allow the noncustodial parent the benefit of the exemption. A custodial parent should think long and hard before signing away the exemption for future years. Form 8332 can be filled out to apply to the current year only, and this would be the wisest course of action, because circumstances may change and the custodial parent may regret forfeiting the exemption.

---

* As to custody, most courts have taken the position that in a divorce proceeding between a biological/adopted parent and a stepparent, the court does not have the authority to award custody of a stepchild to a stepparent, because the divorce court may only make orders concerning "children of the marriage." One exception exists in those states that have adopted the Uniform Marriage and Divorce Act, which provides in Section 401(d)(2) that a person other than a parent may commence a custody action if the child is not in the custody of one of his or her parents.

If parents entered into an agreement or had a divorce decree entered after 1984 that states the noncustodial parent can claim the exemption without regard to any condition (such as payment of child support), the noncustodial parent may claim the child as a dependent. The noncustodial parent should attach a copy of the agreement or decree to his or her return.

For parents who never married, the general rules relating to dependency exemptions apply, and only the parent who provides more than half of the child's support is entitled to claim the dependency exemption. It is not necessary that the child live with the parent claiming the exemption.

2. *Who claims the child tax credit?*

Only a parent who rightfully claims a child as a dependent can take the child tax credit for that child.

3. *Who can claim the child and the child care credit?*

Unlike the child tax credit, the custodial parent may still claim a credit for child and dependent care expenses even if the custodial parent does not claim the child as a dependent. A noncustodial parent may not treat the child as a qualifying child for purposes of the child and dependent care credit even if the child is claimed as a dependent on the noncustodial parent's return.

4. *Can the IRS seize a joint tax refund to satisfy one spouse's child support or other obligations?*

The IRS can seize the entire federal tax refund on a joint return to satisfy child support, spousal support, student loan, or state tax liabilities. Fortunately, however, if one spouse is not legally responsible for the payments and has income reported on the return, that spouse is entitled to a prorated refund. The nonobligated spouse should file Form 8370, "Injured Spouse Claim and Allocation," with the joint return and write "Injured Spouse" in the upper left corner of the return.

If a return has already been filed, the taxpayer should complete and send Form 8370 with copies of all W-2 and 1099 forms to the same service center where the return was filed.

In community property states (Arizona, California, Idaho, Louisiana, Nevada, New Mexico, Texas, Washington, and Wisconsin), part of each spouse's income may be treated as legally belonging to the other spouse. In that case, an injured spouse who does not work may still be entitled to obtain a partial refund of overpaid taxes.

5. *Can the IRS force a taxpayer to pay an assessment resulting from a former spouse falsifying a return?*

Generally, both parties to a joint return can be held liable for the taxes, interest, and penalties assessed. However, if a taxpayer files a joint tax return and later discovers that the former spouse falsified the return, the taxpayer may qualify for "innocent spouse" relief. And under certain circumstances, the innocent spouse may be relieved of the liability. If the taxpayer signed the return without knowing of the falsity, usually an understatement, and had no way of knowing, and if given the facts and circumstances it would be unfair to the innocent spouse, that spouse can apply for relief by filing Form 8857.

AUTHOR'S NOTE

Because of my background as a lawyer and a judge, I recognize that many of the problems I have discussed are not the fault of the members of a blended family, but rather a failure on the part of our society and the legal system within it. Stepfamilies are not given the same respect and rights as those given to nuclear families. This is true in our communities, churches, and schools, and above all our courtrooms. The legal system does not provide a structure for the enforcement of stepparents' and stepchildren's rights. *It is failing the very people who are reading this book.* What's more, through cynical attitudes, prejudices, and often benign neglect, our churches and schools ignore or disrespect those stepparents and stepchildren who are in great need of understanding, support, and legal rights. Blended families should not feel powerless when it comes to their status as a family, and they deserve nothing less than what is afforded nuclear-family members.

By way of illustration of the law's inadequacy to deal with this problem, here's what happened to a close personal friend of mine, one I've known for over thirty years. Alicia was in her mid-twenties when she married Sam, a widower with two very young children. Alicia loved Sam and the kids, and she was willing to give up a budding career in the publishing industry to become a full-time stepmom to two-year-old Ellen and four-year-old Mike. Sam did not want any more children, and Alicia grew to love Ellen and Mike as if they were her own offspring.

Eight years into the marriage, when Ellen was ten and Mike was twelve, Sam and Alicia began having irreconcilable differences that ultimately led to a divorce. Although Alicia wanted to work harder to save the marriage, for Sam it was over. And so, divorce proceedings began. It was then that Alicia's lawyer told her the devastating news: she had absolutely no rights with regard to the children. She asked Sam if she could at least have visitation. He refused, saying, "It's best that we have a clean break."

The case went to trial. Alicia received a small amount of monthly alimony, but what she really wanted was to not lose contact with the children she had raised. Tragically, and it is tragic, she had no legal right to even visit them, because the biological parent chose not to allow her that visitation—this despite the fact that it was the children's express wish to live with Alicia and have their father be the one to visit!

Twenty years have gone by since that court decision was rendered, and not very much has changed. The law has not kept pace with the enormous shifts that have occurred in our society. Alicia's case would probably have the same outcome today in most states as it did two decades ago.

Stepparents—and I'm focusing on those who are or were legally married to the child's custodial parent—exist in a kind of legal and social limbo and are rarely considered "real" fathers and mothers, even though they are functioning on a daily basis as parents.

While the act of marriage creates legal rights and obligations between stepparents and their spouses, stepparents are for the most part without legal obligations or entitlements regarding their stepchildren. As the law stands now, a stepparent generally has fewer rights than does a legal guardian or a foster parent. Even when it comes to approving emergency medical treatment for a minor child, without express written permission from the biological parent, the stepparent has no authority to give that approval. A stepparent can't even sign a permission slip for a child to attend a field trip to the local museum or a historical site. These situations, and many more, come up every day in the lives of stepparents and stepchildren who live together. Having to search for the noncustodial parent to obtain consent when the stepparent is available is an absurd outcome and omission in the law.

As in my friend's case, if the marriage ends, in almost all states the stepparent has no right to custody and, in a large number of states, no right of visitation. Some small comfort: now the visitation laws do vary from state to state, and a stepparent through counsel can *seek* visitation rights. Custody is another matter. It is almost never granted to a stepparent if the biological parent seeks custody. Be mindful of the fact that even in the states that give stepparents the right to request custody or visitation, there are no presumptions working in their favor.

There is an overriding rationale to the present state of the law—divorce courts can make decisions concerning only "children of the marriage," and on that premise the courts maintain they have no authority to award custody to a stepparent.

One exception exists in the Uniform Marriage and Divorce Act, ("Act") which is in effect in eight states—Arizona, Colorado, Illinois, Kentucky, Minnesota, Missouri, Montana, and Washington. This "Act" provides that a person other than a parent may try to gain custody if the child *is not* in the custody of one of his or her biological parents. This has an extremely limited application and doesn't begin to accommodate the already huge and growing population of people living in blended families. The reason is simple: the issue of visitation normally comes up when the biological parent and the stepparent are divorcing. The "Act" does not serve the interests of the stepparent, because the child *is* already in the custody of his or her biological parent.

Twenty-three states have become more lenient when it comes to the right of the stepparent to *request visitation* with a stepchild—Alaska, California, Connecticut, Delaware, Georgia, Hawaii, Illinois, Kansas, Louisiana, Maine, Michigan, Minnesota, Nebraska, New Hampshire, New York, Ohio, Oregon, Tennessee, Texas, Virginia, Washington, West Virginia, and Wisconsin. In six other states—Arizona, Idaho, Indiana, Kentucky, Maryland, and Utah—even though there is no particular statute allowing stepparent visitation, court decisions have occasionally allowed the stepparent to request visitation. But if you are in Alabama, Florida, Iowa, or South Dakota, you're out of luck—these states expressly *prohibit* the stepparent from even requesting visitation. These archaic and egregiously unfair laws need to change.

I strongly believe that a stepparent who is living with the custodial parent and the child, and who is assuming the parental role for the child, should be considered a "de facto parent." Simply put, the "de facto parent" is *a parent not by law but by the facts of the situation.*

I also believe that when the marriage ends through divorce or the death of the biological parent, but the relationship between the child and the "de facto parent" has lasted for many years (and both the children and the stepparent want to continue the relationship), visitation rights should survive the end of the marriage.

Establishing a "de facto parent" category for stepparents should not invalidate or even diminish the existing rights and obligations of both custodial and noncustodial biological parents. Rather, this category would simply empower a stepparent to act as an *additional parent* in the absence of the biological parents and to have the right to seek visitation if the marriage should end by either divorce or the death of the parent who is the biological parent. The stepparents who would normally seek custody or visitation are those who have a close and loving relationship with a stepchild. After all, when is a child ever harmed by an abundance of love and nurturing?

If conflicts regarding children were to arise between any of the biological parents or stepparents, they could be resolved by mediation or in court based on two criteria: (1) the length of the stepparent's de facto parenthood, and (2) the best interests of the child. In short, this would work the same way as conflict resolution between biological parents who divorce.

For example, if the child lives with a custodial parent and a stepparent, the stepparent as a de facto parent should have the right to decide if the child needs medical attention, particularly if the custodial parent is not immediately available.

There are some experts in the area of family law who go beyond just visitation rights, and call for a corresponding obligation of financial support for a stepchild in those instances where a stepparent, usually the stepfather, has been supporting a stepchild for most of that child's minority. It's doubtful courts would want to expand their jurisdiction into the area of stepparent support obligations, nor would there be a strong constituency advocating these obligations. Currently, few courts have ruled in favor of stepparent support payments after divorce, and each of these cases has been decided on an individual basis. Only Missouri has a law that continues stepparent support obligations after divorce, apportioning child support between the noncustodial parent and the stepparent.

Until there is legal recognition of the stepparent as a de facto parent, the spouse who is the biological parent of a child can sign a power of attorney authorizing the stepparent to act on behalf of a minor stepchild in his or her care, particularly in cases of emergency.

I have chosen to emphasize the issue of visitation because it is so important in protecting the needs of minor children and in maintaining the nurturing and loving relationship many of these children have with good stepparents.

And so, to you the readers, this is a call to action. There are many stepfamily support groups in your cities, towns, and communities that can be enlisted to help in getting legislation drafted to promote visitation rights for stepparents in states that do not have such provisions. You, the adult members of the blended family, will have to contact your state legislators and ask them to introduce and support appropriate legislation to protect stepparent-stepchildren relationships. Blended families are here to stay; it's time the law acknowledged, respected, and protected their status in our society.

Let's all become proactive in this very worthwhile cause.

BIBLIOGRAPHY

Arendell, Terry. *Fathers and Divorce.* Thousand Oaks, Calif. Sage Publications, 1995.

Baram, M., and E. Gest. "Celebs Who Sign on the Dotted Line." *Cosmopolitan* 231, no. 5 (2001): 54.

Barnes, G. G., P. Thompson, G. Dal, and N. Burchardt. *Growing Up in Step-families.* Oxford: Clarendon Press, 1998.

Beal, Edward, and Gail Hochman. *Adult Children of Divorce.* New York: Delacorte, 1991.

Begley, M. "Prenuptial Agreements Make Good Business Sense." *Business West* 16, no. 7 (1999): 57.

Berger, Roni. *Stepfamilies: A Multi-Dimensional Perspective.* New York: The Haworth Press, 1998.

Bernstein, Anne. *Yours, Mine, and Ours: How Families Change When Remarried Parents Have a Child Together.* New York: Macmillan, 1989.

Bray, J. H., and S. Berger. "Noncustodial Parent and Grandparent Relationships in Stepfamilies." *Family Relations* 39 (1990): 414–19.

Bray, J. H., and E. M. Hetherington. "Families in Transition: Introduction and Overview." *Journal of Family Psychology* 7 (1993): 3–8.

Bray, J. H., and J. Kelly. *Stepfamilies: Love, Marriage, and Parenting in the First Decade.* New York: Broadway Books, 1998.

Cohen, Miriam Galper. *Long-Distance Parenting: A Guide for Divorced Parents.* New York: New American Library, 1989.

Coleman, M., and L. Ganong. "Remarriage and Stepfamily Research in the 1980's: Increased Interest in an Old Family Form." *Journal of Marriage and the Family* 52 (1990): 925–40.

Crytser, Ann. *The Wife-in-Law Trap.* New York: Pocket Books, 1990.

Duncan, Greg, and Saul Hoffman. *Economic Consequences of Marital Instability.* Chicago: University of Chicago Press, 1985.

Eckler, J. D. *Step-by-Stepparenting: A Guide to Successful Living with a Blended Family.* Virginia: Betterway Publications, 1988.

Edelman, Hope. *Motherless Daughters.* Reading, Mass.: Addison-Wesley, 1994.

Engel, M. "Expensive Steps: The Effect of Divorce Financial Decisions on Stepfamilies." *Stepfamilies* 12, no. 4 (1992): 7–10.

Engel, Margorie. *Weddings, a Family Affair: The New Etiquette for Second Marriages and Couples with Divorced Parents.* Carpenteria, Ca.: Wilshire Publications, 1998.

Etzioni, Amitai. *The Monochrome Society.* Princeton, N.J.: Princeton University Press, 2001.

Furstenberg Jr., Frank F., and Andrew J. Cherlin. *Divided Families: What Happens to Children When Parents Part.* Cambridge, Mass.: Harvard University Press, 1991.

Furstenberg Jr., Frank F., and Graham B. Spanier. *Recycling the Family: Remarriage after Divorce.* Beverly Hills, Calif.: Sage Publications, 1984.

Ganong, L. H., and M. Coleman. "The Effects of Remarriage on Children: A Review of the Empirical Literature." *Family Relations* 33 (1984): 389–406.

Gardner, R. *The Parents Book about Divorce.* New York: Bantam Dell, 1980.

Grinwald, S. "Communication-Family Characteristics: A Comparison between Stepfamilies (Formed after Death or Divorce) and Biological Families." *Journal of Divorce and Remarriage* 24 (1995): 183–196.

Hayes, R. L., and B. A. Hayes. "Remarriage Families: Counseling Parents, Stepparents, and Their Children." *Counseling and Human Development* 18 (1986): 1–8.

Hetherington, E. Mavis. "An Overview of the Virginia Longitudinal Study of Divorce and Remarriage." *Journal of Family Psychology* 7 (1993).

Hetherington, E. Mavis, and J. Kelly. *For Better or for Worse: Divorce Reconsidered.* New York: W. W. Norton & Company, 2002.

Karbo, Karon. *Generation Ex.* New York: Bloomsbury, 2001.

Keshet, Jamie K. *Love and Power in the Stepfamily: A Practical Guide.* New York: McGraw-Hill, 1987.

Lauer, R., and J. Lauer. "The Long-Term Relational Consequences of Problematic Family Backgrounds." *Family Relations* 43, (1991): 286–91.

Mahoney, Margaret. *Stepfamilies and the Law.* Ann Arbor: University of Michigan Press, 1994.

McDonald, M. "My So-Called Life as a Stepmom." *Redbook,* November 2001, 72.

Meckler, Laura. "Census Issues Report on U.S. Families." Associated Press Online, April 13, 2001.

Moreau, D., and K. Young. "Yours, Mine and Ours." *Kiplinger's Personal Finance Magazine* 47, no. 8 (1993): 70–76.

Naisbitt, John. *Megatrends.* New York: Avon, 1991.

Pasley, Kay. "Views of Stepfamily Life from the Older Generation." *Stepfamilies* 18, no. 5 (1999): 5–6.

———. "What Stepparents Do to Get a Stepchild to Like Them." *Stepfamilies* 18, no. 6 (1999): 6–7.

Pogrebin, Letty Cottin. *Family Politics: Love and Power on an Intimate Frontier.* New York: McGraw-Hill, 1983.

Quick, D., B. Newman, and P. McHenry. "Influences on the Quality of the Stepmother-Adolescent Relationship." *Journal of Divorce and Remarriage* 24 (1995): 51–72.

Rabkin, Jay. "Dear Dad's Dollars." *American Spectator* 33, no. 5 (2000): 50–51.

Rosenberg, J. "Your Money." *Los Angeles Times,* November 4, 2001.

Savage, Karen, and Patricia Adams. *The Good Step-Mother: A Practical Guide.* New York: Crown Publishers, 1988.

Shimberg, Elaine. *Blending Families.* New York: Berkley Trade Paperback Edition, 1999.

Strother, J., and E. Jacobs. "Adolescent Stress as It Relates to Stepfamily Living: Implications for School Counselors." *The School Counselor* 32 (1984): 97–103.

Taffel, Ron. *The Second Family: How Adolescent Power Is Challenging the American Family.* New York: St. Martin's Press, 2002.

Tannen, Deborah. *You Just Don't Understand Me.* New York: Ballantine Books, 1990.

Turkat, Ira Daniel. "Divorce-Related Malicious Parent Syndrome." *Journal of Family Violence* 14, no. 1 (1999): 95–97.

Wallerstein, Judith S. "Children of Divorce: A Ten-Year Study." In *The Impact of Divorce, Single-Parenting and Step-Parenting on Children,* edited by E. Mavis Hetherington and Josephine D. Arasteh, 198–214. Hillsdale, N.J.: Lawrence Erlbaum, 1988.

Wallerstein, Judith, and Sandra Blakeslee. *Second Chances: Men, Women and Children a Decade after Divorce.* New York: Ticknor & Fields, 1989.

Wallerstein, Judith, and Joan B. Kelly. *Surviving the Breakup: How Children and Parents Cope with Divorce.* New York: Basic Books, 1980.

Warshak, Richard A. *Divorce Poison.* New York: HarperCollins, 2001.

Woodham, Martha. *Wedding Etiquette for Divorced Families.* New York: McGraw-Hill, 2001.

Wray, Herbert, and Suzi Parker. "When Strangers Become Family." *U.S. News & World Report* 127, no. 21 (November 29, 1999): 58–66.

Resources

❖

Stepfamily Association of America, Inc.
650 J. Street, Suite 205
Lincoln, Nebraska 68508
Tel. 800-735-0329
www.saafamilies.org/programs/chapters/htm
SAA provides support or links to support groups in the various 50 states.

Grandparents United for Children's Rights
137 Larken Street
Madison, Wisconsin 53705
Tel. 608-238-8751

Children's Rights Council
3001 I Street NE, Suite 401
Washington, DC 20002
www.gocrc.com
CRC works to assure children contact with both parents and extended family.

Alliance for Non-Custodial Parents Rights
www.ancpr.org
ANCPR provides help with issues of child support, custody, and visitation.

The National Fathers' Resource Center
www.fathers4kids.org
This organization is a resource for helping divorced fathers with issues of child support, custody, and visitation.

About the Author

BARBARA LEBEY is a lawyer, a former judge, and a wife, mother, and grandmother in a blended, extended family. Her first book, *Family Estrangements,* was featured in *People* magazine, as well as on *Good Morning America* and *The Today Show.* She lives with her husband in Atlanta, Georgia. To learn more about the author, you can check her website at www.barbaralebey.com.